# Beyond Cotabato

## Curran L. Spottswood

FLEMING H. REVELL COMPANY

Library of Congress Catalog Card Number: 61-5927

*Printed in the United States of America*

1.1

Grateful acknowledgment is made to *The Presbyterian Outlook* for permission to use portions of the hymn "Rise Up, O Men of God!"

Acknowledgment is also made for permission to use material from *Songs From the Slums* by Toyohiko Kagawa, copyright 1935 by Whitmore & Smith. By permission of Abingdon Press.

Acknowledgment is also gratefully expressed to Miriam Teichner for permission to use the poem "Awareness."

25506

*This book is dedicated
to the person
whose courage in the face of danger
whose patience in dealing with six boys
and whose steadfast love
inspires me to keep trying:
to my wife Mariam
without whom
the chapters that follow
would have been impossible*

# For Reference

*Abaca.* Plantation.
*Agong.* Heavy metal drum, Philippine status symbol.
*Apo.* Sir or Lord.
*Baen.* Lunch bag.
*Banca.* Dug-out canoe.
*Balot.* An egg almost ready to hatch, considered a delicacy.
*Barrio.* Village.
*Boyka.* Wooden clog.
*Bolo.* Large machete-like knife.
*Buyo.* Betel nut with possibly medicinal properties.
*Carabao.* Water buffalo, used as a work animal.
*Cargadore.* Guide.
*Cimiento.* Cement.
*Cogon.* Tall grass used for thatching.
*Cotabato.* City meaning "Stone fort."
*Datu.* Tribal chief.
*Kris.* Large curved knife.
*Nipa.* A low palm whose leaves are useful for thatching or mats.
*Padi.* Tithe or tenth handful of rice.
*Pandesal.* Biscuit.
*Partrera.* Midwife.
*Patati.* Woven sleeping mat.
*Rakem.* Tithe or tenth handful of rice.
*Tienda.* Sidewalk store.

# Contents

# 1

## Throttle Wide Open

THE PLANE WAS shiny new—at least on the outside. The fresh coat of fire-chief-red paint glistened in the Manila sun. I opened the door. "Look at all those instruments! She's ready to go!"

Then I remembered the first time I had seen her, at Clark Field, among the 101 other surplus planes. Her fabric had been torn and flapping in the breeze. Now she was clean, re-covered, freshly painted. She was a lady! I turned to the mechanic and asked, "Is she completely checked?" "Yes." "Did you drain the right wing tank and flush it out?" "Yes, I did." Satisfied, I crawled in, grinning all over, started the engine, and taxied out to the runway.

Ah-h-h, the throaty roar of the 185-horsepower engine was music to my ears! After flying a 65 h.p. Cub for four years, I looked on the L-5 ambulance plane as if it were a junior-sized Super Fortress! I had loaded the plane with foot lockers, three suitcases, a typewriter, a duffel bag, and an assortment of tricycles and other Christmas presents. Mariam and the three boys were flying to Tuguegarao by Philippine Air Lines, and would arrive at 1 P.M. It was Christmas Eve! As "Santa Claus," I just *had* to make it there, for I had with me in the plane all the Christmas gifts for the next day, our first day in our new home in Tuguegarao, 10,000 miles away from Florida and our families we had left behind.

I pulled out a faded pre-war road map, the only map I could find, and began to check the route. "Let's see. It's 300 miles, more or less. Now, where is Tugueg. . . . What's that name? Oh yes, Tuguegarao. Why, that's practically at the tip-top of the island of Luzon." As I talked on to myself, I succeeded in finding it on the map, and noted that it was located on the large Cagayan River, and that there was a road running parallel to the river. "That should be a cinch to find," I thought, in the enthusiastic confidence of youth. Lindbergh could not have felt more excitement heading out over the Atlantic than I did heading out for the Cagayan Valley.

The plane climbed smoothly as I crossed over Manila, capital city of the Philippines, with its more than 2,000,000 population. On my left I could see Bataan, Corregidor, scenes of some of the bitterest fighting of World War II, and I remembered the heroism of the valiant Filipinos and Americans who died there. Underneath me lay the University of the Philippines, already re-opened and carrying on, in spite of bombed buildings, and burned ruins, a monument of the determination of the Filipino people to rise above the destruction of war and take their place of leadership in the Far East. To my right I could see the majestic beauty of the Sierra Madre mountains, with the bright green rice paddies spread out in orderly lines at the foothills. Forty-five minutes later I had passed the city of Cabanatuan, and was nearing the Cordillera Central Mountain Range, dividing the fertile plains of Central Luzon from the mighty Cagayan Valley to the north. I began looking for one of my check-points, Bongabong, a little town known to be the headquarters of the Communist-led "Huks." Yes, there it was. It looked peaceful enough by day, though I knew that by night there were often raids. No trucks or buses dared travel the road at night. Along the highway there were military roadblocks every five or ten miles, with dugouts hiding mounted machine guns.

As the plane hummed along, I was enjoying the beauty of

the "emerald islands," and thinking pleasant thoughts of the exciting prospects that lay ahead of me as a young missionary just assigned to the vast, challenging Cagayan Valley, covering most of Northeast Luzon. Suddenly, I was jolted out of my pleasant reverie by an evil sight which every pilot fears—a solid, seemingly endless white cloud mass that began just below me, and stretched out as far as my eye could see. Pulling on carburetor heat, I began to climb, and to pray for holes in the clouds. I could remember clearly those Civil Aeronautics Administration rules against flying over a solid overcast. They were good rules, too, for it was mighty easy to get lost over that blanket of snowy white, lose sight of land, and maybe run out of gas. But other thoughts kept crowding into my mind. "This is Christmas Eve. I've *got* to make it. My wife and boys are away from home for their first Christmas, in a strange town where they don't know a soul. 'Santa Claus' just must arrive!" I flew on.

The altimeter read 10,000, and unwound slowly toward 11,000. The air was cold, but the coldness of my arms and shoulders was nothing compared to the ice in the pit of my stomach. Thirty minutes ticked slowly, oh so slowly by. The cold fear in the pit of my stomach grew larger. I could tell from the road map that I should be over Bayombong in the Solano Valley. I searched frantically for some break in the clouds, and then suddenly, there was a hole! Hope sprang full-grown in my breast. I rolled the ship over on a wing tip and started down, praying for a green valley with gentle slopes and a landing strip. Horrors! What I saw were giant mountains, gaunt peaks, and no houses or roads of any kind. Then I noticed that the plane was drifting toward the west. "Ah, I know. The wind has blown me off course." Whipping the plane around, I set a compass east-north-east, to compensate for the hard wind. I glanced at the gas gauges. Both tanks were down to the halfway mark.

Ten, and then fifteen, minutes crept by on icy feet. It began

9

to rain slowly. I was already past the "point of no return." I had to go ahead. While I was still determined to make it, I was beginning to have some second thoughts about my great adventure. "Huh! You think you're such a fine pilot. What are you doing out here in the middle of nowhere, in the middle of a drizzle, with no land in sight? What made you think you could fly over strange territory, in the worst season of the year?" I knew that I would have to go down soon. I would be out of gas in a matter of minutes. The ice in the pit of my stomach seemed like 100 pounds. Would I make it safely down somewhere? Or would I crack up on one of those bleak mountain peaks? I began to sing hymns to keep down my panic. Or rather, I began to shout hymns, as I methodically switched the carburetor heat off and on, and searched the white blanket below me for a break. Never had one young man prayed so fervently!

"If I ever get . . . *there's* a hole! . . . There's another!" Oh joy, Oh bliss, Oh rapture divine! I could see land again. I pushed down the nose of the L-5, pulled on full flaps, and dove as steeply as I dared. There was the river! I had reached the Cagayan Valley! Just as I was beginning to unwind a little, and to breathe a great sigh of relief, the engine sputtered, spit— and quit! I froze. I hurriedly glanced at the left gas tank. It stood at EMPTY. There was a moment of complete, deadening silence. Then I recovered enough to turn the tank selector to RIGHT TANK. The engine coughed, caught on, and began to purr again. My own heart "caught" and began to beat again.

I knew I had in the right tank only fifteen or twenty minutes' worth of gas left. "Hurry, man. Hurry!" I headed toward the river, to try to find *that* highway, the one and only road going up into the Cagayan Valley. I knew that if I followed the road on up the Valley, I would sooner or later find Tuguegarao, and the one and only landing field shown on the map for a distance of over one hundred miles. I had just *one* landing field, and I had to find it in a drizzling rain—and I had only a few minutes more to fly. Brother! What a spot to be in! Ten minutes dragged by. I could feel the dryness of my throat nearly choking me. I had to find a place to land quickly. Yet, all I could see below me were small rice paddies, green with young rice shoots, and to the east the purple, foreboding eastern mountains.

Then time really ran out. The engine sputtered, and I knew I had less than one minute to land. I dove for the road. Luckily, it was straight, though narrow as a ribbon. There were no cars or jeeps or buses in the way. I turned into the wind, pulled on half flaps, and steadied the needle at 70 m.p.h. I strained forward to see through the rain-streaked windshield, but the plexiglass was just a foggy blur. I leaned my head out of the window to peer through the drizzling rain, to find the outline of the roadside ahead.

Full flaps. . . . 65 m.p.h. . . . then 60. . . . Wrump. . . . Srump. . . . The two front wheels hit. The plane slowed to 50 m.p.h. The tail came down, and I braked slowly to a stop. The propeller came to attention in front of me. Suddenly, I was weak all over. The strain of nearly three hours of skirting the edge of destruction hit me all at once. I slumped down exhausted in my seat. "Thank God. Thank God." I muttered these words over and over.

"Hey, Mac, what's the trouble?" was the next thing I heard. I was in no mood for this "Hey, Mac" business. I crawled out of the plane. I saw just in front of the plane a red Chevrolet bus, marked "Red Line Transportation Company." It was overflowing with grinning, excited passengers, packed in among the pigs and chickens, baskets of vegetables, boxes, cartons, spare tires. Heads crowded through the windows, and a steady stream of bodies came pouring out of the door of the bus, to see what was happening. The same raucous voice repeated, "What's the trouble?"

I answered in a casual, if weak, voice. "Oh, nothing much, just out of gas. Say, where is Tuguegarao?"

11

The friendly Filipino driver smiled reassuringly. "You just passed Tuguegarao about ten miles back." Then I remembered a cluster of low clouds "down on the deck" about five or six minutes back.

"Could you let me have five gallons of gas?" I inquired.

"Easy," he replied, and in a few minutes he was helping me pour it into the tank. As we worked, I asked him where he had learned to speak such excellent English. I learned he had been in the American Army under MacArthur. We finished gassing up, and then I walked around to the front of the plane. I really noticed that road for the first time. It was a bare twelve feet wide. There was just a foot and a half to spare on each side of the wheels. The wings of the plane were thirty-six feet wide. That I, an amateur pilot, had landed one ton of airplane on this little stretch of road, at 60 m.p.h., in the rain, was hard to believe. God *was* my co-pilot.

I climbed back into the cockpit for the take-off. Amid the waves and cheers of the many passengers on the bus, I tried to appear as cool and nonchalant as possible. But my knees were shaking, because I *knew* now the the size of that road! The motor roared to life. I checked the magnetos at 1500 r.p.m., and then gave the engine a full-throttle check. The tachometer needle quivered near the 2000 r.p.m. mark. The brakes released. The heavily loaded little plane hit one pothole after another in the rocky road, as it slowly gathered speed. It hit a large hole, bounced, hit, bounced again, and then—I was air-borne! As I circled for altitude, I flew over the Red Line bus. The passengers waved eagerly. Cocky, and confident with the knowledge that I had 1000 feet of altitude, I had gas in the tank, and I was only five minutes away from a genuine landing field, I waved grandly back, thinking to myself, "Spottswood, you are a real pilot!" I headed south down the road.

Just as I finished congratulating myself, the engine spit, sputtered, coughed, and quit. Again! There was no place to go but down. "Thank heavens, I'm over the road. No time to turn into the wind. Land straight ahead. Hope I can make it." I put down the flaps. The plane was going 65 m.p.h., and then 60. Full flaps . . . and then the road rushed up toward me. The wheels hit. "I can't see in this rain!" The tail was down—40 m.p.h. . . . and then a huge chuck-hole on the right swerved the plane sharply, and it dove into a ditch. Then a sea of mud covered everything. I sat slumped over in the cockpit, severely shaken up by the blow of my head against the instrument panel as the plane jolted to a stop. The propeller and the nose of the plane were now out of sight, buried in the mud and water of the hole, which turned out to be a carabao, or water buffalo, wallow. The tail of the plane stuck up at a sharp 30° angle. I sat rubbing the big bump on my forehead, too tired and discouraged to move. "Scratched up my new airplane," I moaned to myself, "and it's not even paid for."

About that time I heard a familiar, friendly voice say, "Hey, Mac! What's the trouble now?" Here was my buddy of the bus, who had helped me not five minutes before.

"I wonder if you'll help me pull this plane out of the ditch, and set it over there in the vacant field."

Almost before the words were out of my mouth, twenty or thirty Filipinos had left their warm, dry places in the Red Line bus and jumped out into the rain and helped me pull the plane out of the ditch. The drizzling rain had turned into a harder downpour now. It took a minute or two to clear the barbed wire from around the propeller. We pushed the plane onto a level spot in the vacant field, and began unloading the suitcases, typewriter, bag, and most important of all, Santa's precious cargo. It was now 5 P.M. on Christmas Eve. My friend, the driver, finished his inspection of the underside of the plane, crawled out, shook the propeller as hard as he could, and then marveled, "Hey, Mac! This plane isn't even damaged!"

For the first time since landing I really looked at the plane.

13

By now the rain had washed off much of the mud. I could see there was hardly a scratch on the plane. Its red paint glistened in the rain. "Glory be to God," I thought. He had wrought another miracle. How could I have gone into that 10- by 20-foot carabao wallow at 35 m.p.h. or more and not seriously wrecked the plane? I did not know. All I know for sure is that it was not the work of the pilot. God was there!

Santa Claus needed to get going! It was impossible to fly the plane any more that day, in the rain and deepening dusk of the late afternoon. I would have to get home some other way, for a lovely wife and three small boys were anxiously waiting for me at Tuguegarao, our northernmost mission station on the island of Luzon. I could see the bus was already overloaded, and could not possibly squeeze me and all my baggage into its crowded interior. I was wondering what to do—and eyeing the foot locker of Christmas gifts, wondering if I could possibly carry it on my back—when a kindly Philippine Army officer stopped in his small army jeep, and offered to take me and all my load on in to Tuguegarao. Just at 6 P.M., through the help of many kind Filipinos, and the incredible love and mercy of God, I reached my destination.

My feelings were mixed as we drove up to the mission house, our first home in the Philippines. What a house! In the wet and gloom of that rainy night, its cement walls, pock-marked with bullet holes from the recent war, dark, unpainted, looked more like a prison than a home. The house had been built in 1912, bombed and burned during the war, and then partially restored. It still had a bare, unlived-in, boxlike appearance. Fifty yards from the front door I could see a bomb crater some thirty feet wide, and almost as deep. The small kerosene lamps which provided the only illumination indoors cast weird shadows across the windows. I was wondering if I had really come to the right house, when I heard a baby's demanding cry piercing the gloom. A knock on the door brought scurrying feet. Cautiously, the door was opened. I saw a face in the light, and then a loud *"Spotty"* punctuated the night air. Then—I knew I was home!

I thanked the army officer, who had gone to so much trouble and gotten wet on my behalf. Then, with great joy, I went inside to see the kids. Here was my family, seated around the table eating supper. The room was stark, empty of any furniture except the big table and chairs. Curran, our oldest son, four years old, was waving a soup spoon at me. "Hello, Daddy. How did you get that mud all over you? Mother will be mad!" David, three years old, a sober, solemn individual, with luminous dark eyes and a lovely complexion, said simply, "Hi, Daddy," and went back to work on his plate. Stephen, the baby, a chubby, blonde one-year-old, and half-hidden under a layer of food, merely grunted.

Mariam, the queen of the family, smiled her warm, welcoming smile, and her "eyes of blue" shone with joy and relief at having Daddy safely home. Formerly Mariam Harrold, this attractive young woman, a trim five-foot-two of Southern charm, had come from Gainesville, Florida. As I looked at her, sitting so serenely at the head of the table, I remembered again with amazement the trip she had made to join me. I had been rushed out to the Philippines in June, 1946, to help in the reopening of Union Theological Seminary in Manila. It was not until seven months later that Mariam and the three boys could come out, for Manila was heavily bombed during the war and no housing was available for families. When the "Go Ahead" was finally given for her to come, this brave young woman set out alone, with three small babies, and traveled 2700 miles across the continent of America by train. Still without anyone to help her, she boarded an old wartime troopship at San Francisco, and went two decks down into the hold to travel third class for the one-month trip to the Orient. Taking care of three small babies, eating greasy food, breathing hot, piped-in air way down in the steaming hold of the ship, feeling seasick most of the way, Mariam lost fourteen pounds between San Francisco and Manila. By the time she arrived, she had "earned her colors" as a missionary wife.

Little did I realize, as I sat down gratefully to our Christmas Eve supper, what a tower of strength Mariam would prove to be in the years ahead in the work of Christ in the Cagayan Valley. Trained at Florida State College for Women, and later at Yale Divinity School, Mariam had a quick mind and a flair for languages which were to prove greatly helpful in the years ahead. I did not know *how much*, as we talked into the wee hours of the morning about our new assignment to the Cagayan Valley, and wondered what lay ahead for us. But—as we filled little stockings and prepared for the coming of Christmas morning in our new home—we were both deeply grateful for each other. We were grateful for the coming of Jesus Christ into the world, and for the thrilling adventure to which He had called us, in seeking to witness for Him in the Philippines. We were glad to be alive! And we were thankful for the challenge of being a missionary for Him!

It would be Christmas in a few hours. Christ was born! We were His!

# 2

## Yale

THE WEEK OF Christmas brought us many opportunities to get acquainted with the warm, friendly people of Tuguegarao, which was to be our home for the next twelve years. Tuguegarao is a large town of about 5000 people, situated on the banks of the Cagayan and Pinacanaywan Rivers. It is in the heart of the province and was a prosperous town before the war. However, it was heavily bombed and burned by the Japanese as they marched down from the northern coast of Luzon. Then the Americans bombed it level. As soon as the war was over and houses began to go up again, it was struck by a terrible typhoon. Then a fire finished the destruction. Three times was enough!

Curran and David were enchanted with the stories our church members told us of the "Japanese times." Almost every family in the church could tell gruesome but true stories of husbands bayoneted, fathers or brothers tortured. In fact, the mission house—our home—had been Japanese Army officer headquarters at one time, and prisoners were tortured in *our* bedroom. There were even rumors of buried silver coins under the banana trees in our side yard! Curran and David, and the little puppy dog somebody gave us, could all get happily dirty digging for money, morning or afternoon.

But the war was over now! The Filipino people, with a marvelous resiliency, were busily rebuilding their lives. Tuguegarao was a hustling, thriving community, with old, half-bombed houses side by side with hundreds of grass-roofed huts, shanties put together from old scraps of army canvas, rusting sheets of G.I. roofing, and scrap lumber. It was an interesting place to live, and yet it was a far cry from anything I had known at home. Soon after we arrived, it began to rain. It rained steadily for a solid week. In the dreary dampness of our old cement house, ugly, pock-marked, and dark, I began to fret. I began to feel restless and discouraged. Doubts came creeping into my mind about my ministry. "What in the world am I doing here, 10,000 miles from home, in this farthest-north Philippines mission station?"

My mind flashed back to my junior college days. I remembered the thrill of the baseball team's victories. Then, on to Mississippi State I went again, in my daydreams, playing on the tennis team. I remembered one especially exciting game against the University of Alabama. We won! I spent two thrilling years fighting on the State's great boxing team, when she had tied for Southeast Conference title. I was one of those going to the finals of the Southeastern Conference championship. I began reveling in other school memories. . . . Bloated with pride and egotism, wallowing in boyish self-esteem, I wondered silently, "How did I ever get from the boxing ring into the ministry?"

I remembered the day I had been offered a scholarship to Yale Divinity School. I was vaguely interested in God, and in doing good. I was even more interested in the adventure of going to a big, famous school in a big city in the distant East! So I accepted the offer and went to Yale. It was breath-taking—409 Prospect Street looked like the pot of gold at the end of the rainbow. To a small-town boy from Mississippi, New Haven, Connecticut, seemed tremendous. I was awed. To an athlete, Payne Whitney Gymnasium was a dream, with its twelve floors of swimming pool, boxing rings, courts of all kinds. The Yale Library was even better—so big and beautiful I could hardly

18

catch my breath when I saw it. I began my studies in a rosy cloud of enthusiasm, taking a little of everything.

Hard times set in, though. The scholarship didn't pay all of my expenses. I needed money for clothes, shoes, transportation, and incidentals. And there was none! Then, walking home from school one day, I noticed a big sign advertising a fight at the New Haven arena. "Reckon I could?" I wondered. I mulled over the possibility of earning some money in the fight ring—and then abruptly answered myself, "Of course not!" However, the next day I entered a smoke-filled room up on the second floor of a back street. I asked around and found the talkative manager, Harry. Cigar in mouth, he said, "Whatta ya want, kid?" in best movie tough-guy style.

"I need to earn some money," I admitted.

"O.K., kid. Take off your shirt." The glint in his eyes said, "Sucker meat," to me. As I peeled off the shirt, I noticed a crowd gathering around the ring in the center of the room. Harry said, "Kick off your shoes, kid, and slip these on."

I was caught. Too late now. "Am I going to get clobbered! What an idiot I was to come in here."

My throat was dry as the gloves were tied on. The other boy came out smoothly, jabbed, and feinted, trying me out. But fear put lightning in my feet, and after a couple of minutes of sparring, jabbing, and grunting, Harry came over and said, "O.K., kid. Come around tomorrow at 3 P.M. Maybe you can earn a few bucks."

I was in. I trained carefully for several weeks. Then came my first professional fight, at Bridgeport, Connecticut—the lowest level of preliminary fight. I won, probably because the other fellow was more scared than I. After the fight, I received seven dollars for nine minutes of work. Harry picked my succeeding opponents carefully, choosing young men who were nearly all of the same type—strong, tough, with hard rights, but not too fast. Easy to fight, if I didn't get "nailed." But those lethal rights

19

worried me. I couldn't always be lucky. Still, I kept on fighting. I needed dollars. Six fights went by. I won them all, three by knockouts. The old ego was expanding. Occasionally the newspapers were mentioning "Yale's Fighting Parson."

Back to school for classes, bull sessions, a little work. I was happy at Yale. My fellow students were some of the finest men I had ever met anywhere. Yet, I was vaguely dissatisfied. I didn't know what it was, but something was lacking. I was only a very ordinary student, and I often wandered around in a fog, intellectually as well as spiritually. The New Testament course was a "lulu." Our professor was personally warm and friendly; but his approach in the classroom was strictly scientific. It wasn't long before the faith I had had when I arrived had gone out of the window, and I was completely disoriented. I hardly knew whether I was coming or going. I read books, wrote reports, and then read more books—books, books, and more books, most of which did not speak to my need.

Slowly, almost imperceptibly, I began to realize what was missing on the campus. In my simple, naïve way I had come to the divinity school expecting to meet some real experts in Christian living—like Peter, the Bold and Courageous, like Paul, the Flaming Apostle. The early apostles who strode in and out of the New Testament were men who marched up and down the length and breadth of the Roman Empire, daring their all for their Living Lord. The professors at Yale were tops—but they were professors. They had Ph.D.s, they taught brilliantly, they wrote books. But somehow, I was still wistfully hoping for just one professor who was a "Doctor of Glowing Faith," or a "Doctor of Radiant Prayer." One of the incisive minds of the campus, Dr. Halford Luccock, understood, and like a flash of lightning on a summer night, he growled, "What this campus needs is one real Christian around here, so we can see what one looks like."

After two years of living in luxury in the beautiful men's dormitories up on "Holy Hill" I became more and more dissatisfied. I could not get Peter out of my mind, that brave man who had spoken to the High Priest after Pentecost as if he owned the Temple, that courageous man who spoke boldly the name of Christ wherever he went. Peter was a *Man of Action*. I knew that if Peter had been at Yale—if Peter had felt vaguely dissatisfied, if Peter knew that his Christian experience was missing something—he would *act*.

In the library one day I was reading the life of Kagawa. I was arrested by his poem "Shinkawa," written during his life in the slums of Kobe in Japan. It touched me to the quick.

> One month in the slums
> And I am sad,
> So sad,
> I seem devil-possessed
> Or mad.

> Sweet heaven sends
> No miracle
> To ease
> This hell;
> The careless earth
> Rings no
> Alarum bell.

But here there are slippery streets which are never dry:
   They are lined with open sewers, where rats come out to die.
Tattered paper doors stand wide to winds that beat;
   The houses are all of a reddish black, like the hue of stale whale meat.
Filth on the flimsy ceiling, dirt in the misty air;
   Elbowed out of their crowded rooms, people are everywhere.
All night long they crouch in the cold, huddled on broken benches—
   Where there's never a moment's lifting of the heavy offal stenches.

> The painted idiot girl,
>   Upon whose back
> Vile pictures were tatooed in red
>   Will never lure men to her den again.
> She is dead. . . .

These words ran like quicksilver through my veins. Finally, I knew what I had to do. After a week of searching, I found a room down on Grand Avenue, in the slums of New Haven. The room was 6 by 10 feet, but half of it was filled with the family's junk. I bought a secondhand cot, borrowed an apple-crate for a dresser, and I had my new home. It was located on the fourth floor of an old tenement firetrap. There was almost no heat of any kind. After the steam-heated comfort of my three-room suite on "Holy Hill," with hot and cold running water, I found the change to my cold, damp room quite a jar. I found that the biting nearly-zero temperature of an early morning really speeded me up, however. I could get out of bed, dress completely with shoes, socks, and sweater, and be out in two minutes!

I was now a part of the family. Bill, the father, was an alcoholic, who worked for the W.P.A. to feed his five growing children—when he was sober, that is. Bill had a warm smile and possessed the "gift of gab," so that he could put the "touch" on a statue. He was good-looking, easygoing—and completely irresponsible. His wife, Rose, was a tall, strong, rawboned woman, with a ready smile and a heart as big as the house. There was a young twelve-year-old daughter, two boys ten and eight, another girl, and a baby—all dirty, scraggly-looking, thin and sickly. The apartment in which they lived was a typical "sleeping-car" tenement flat, four rooms one after another, with only a window at each end. The two middle rooms had no windows, and were very dark. My first visit to the fourth floor had nearly floored me. The strong stench of accumulated filth, stale coffee, cabbage and other food odors, and tightly-packed human bodies had nearly made me sick. It was a combination of smells I was to encounter daily from then on.

My little "closet" room was just off the living room, at the end of the line. It was small and dark. But the rest of the apartment was even darker, and dirty, and full of the noise of children crying, Bill's shouting, Rose's crying. My little room was my retreat—and I did a lot of thinking when I was in it. What should a Christian do in such a place? How could I help to relieve the human misery of which I was now a part? How could I help this family?

I did not know all the answers, but I did know I had to make a start. So, I began hauling out all the accumulated junk that had been pushed back in my corner, and I began to scrub that little room until I had it shining. Then, I begged a board here, borrowed a hammer there, bought a can of paint, until finally I had two little benches across the tiny corner of my room, painted bright blue, a picture of Jesus tacked up on the wall, and a little corner table with a vase of flowers to serve as a worship center. I had the world's smallest chapel, perhaps—but it was a little spot of beauty in all this filth, a little "Family Altar." The children came in eagerly when I invited them, and I taught them some songs about Jesus. Bill and Rose were skeptical, but they came in anyway. I read a few verses of Scripture, and we sang and prayed. We talked it over and decided that once a day we would all come together in my little room for a few minutes of worship.

We were a long way from the Kingdom of God. There was little understanding of what this was all about. But I think we all appreciated the few moments of relative peace and quiet. I taught the children how to read different verses in the Bible. We even had typed programs for our little "services" once a week. I did not have any vain ideas of how much good I was doing. Bill was still an alcoholic. Rose was still overwhelmed by the problems of poverty, sicknesses, seeming hopelessness.

And yet, we were planting seeds in the minds of the kids. We might be bringing in the light of God's love—and *hope*. At least, there was *peace* in my own soul now. I was at last a part of the human race. I was down in the midst of human need.

With my new "family" to think about, I needed money more than ever. That meant I had to fight. One day after my twelfth fight was over, and I had won by a K.O. in the second round, Harry surprised me with, "Hey, kid, whadda ya say let's try one in the big city, huh?" Nobody knew better than I that I was just an average fighter, with fear in his feet, but I was thrilled that Harry even thought I could fight anybody down in the "big time," and so I blurted out, "O.K. by me." After two weeks of feverish training, we got on the train and headed for New York City! I was weighed in, examined by a doctor, and then we went out to celebrate by buying a new pair of fighting trunks.

The big night came. I donned my new, deluxe trunks, had my hands wrapped, and we went out into the arena. When the first preliminary fight was over, I crawled through the ropes with about as much enthusiasm as a soldier would face a firing squad. The bell rang. "Fight fair. . . . Go to your corners in case of a knock-down. . . . Touch gloves and come out fighting," the referee intoned. I came out of my corner with my left hand high, my chin tucked in, moving cautiously. A little sparring and I could see my opponent was no ball of fire. I relaxed a little, smiled and breathed for the first time. I danced away, and then came in, tried a left which he caught, and then cockily moved out of his range and started in again. . . . Wham! The piano caught me just above the left ear. The lights went out. When they came on again, I was on the floor, and the referee was counting out, "Six . . . seven . . . eight . . . nine." I got up unsteadily. Suddenly the arena was filled with stars and planets, and I went down again. At the count of nine I was groggily getting up, when the referee stepped up to me and opened my mouth. "O.K., kid. You're hurt. Better get that mouth sewed up." With my tongue I traced a cut that divided my lower lip. That ended my fight in the big city. Harry and I rode back to New Haven without a word.

The next day I had two black eyes, and my lower lip was so swollen and sore from three stitches that I couldn't eat. I had received $25 for that fight, but I figured out that after paying for our round-trip tickets to New York, buying lunch, getting the new trunks, and paying the doctor for the stitches in my lip, I had a net gain of $2.50, just $2.50 for the worst licking of my life. Enough was enough! I determined then and there to quit fighting. But not on a defeat. I had to win my next one. Luckily, my last fight was in the New Haven area. A lot of the guys from "Holy Hill" came down to see the fight. I think they were sorry for me, for the shellacking I had taken, rather than deeply interested in the fine art of boxing itself. Anyway, the fight was over by the second round and I had won.

So ended my career as a fighter in the ring. Now I had to continue fighting, but against a more wily, slippery foe—whiskey! Bill was now out of work. He had come home drunk one Saturday night. Then, because Rose bawled him out, he went out Sunday to stay out of her way and got "soused" again. Monday he was too groggy to get up. Tuesday he finally went to work, but he was several hours late—and lost his job. Here it was January, the coldest month of the year, the rent was unpaid, the electric company had already turned off the lights because of unpaid back bills, there was no food in the house—and Bill was out of work! Bill was a painter, but nobody wanted any painting done when the snow was two feet deep on the ground. There were seven hungry mouths to be fed and so I loaned the family money, with the agreement that Bill would get off his bed and go out and find work—any kind of work. By haunting the city employment office, Bill finally found a day and a half's work, and had earned $3.50 by the time he came in Saturday afternoon. He walked into the cold, dark apartment—found the lights off, the baby crying and sick, the other children cross and complaining, his wife loudly demanding the rent money. He stayed home five minutes, took a good look around—and then took the whole $3.50 and went out and got staggering drunk again. Such became the pattern of our life in those cold, dreary days.

I could remember back from my fraternity days the casual attitudes of most of my fraternity brothers: "Ah, a little drink won't hurt you. It just relaxes you, peps you up, helps you have a good time." Well, I knew better now! A lot better! I had learned more from Bill about the curse of alcohol and the dangers of social drinking than I had learned from ten books on sociology!

One Friday night I went to the show, trying to get Bill and the kids and the problems off my mind. The picture was a "shoot 'em up," and in the course of the evening we got rid of two horse thieves and true love triumphed. I came out of the theatre relaxed and happy. As I came out on the sidewalk, I noticed a group of three or four panhandlers, working the crowd. One man pushed up to me and said in a pitiful voice, "Brother, I need a cup of coffee mighty bad. Could you spare a dime?" I brushed roughly on by the fellow, ignoring his outstretched hand. However, when I got home my conscience began to hurt. Suppose the old man was really hungry? He *really* looked it. I didn't sleep well that night. Several times during the night I saw an old man, with an outstretched hand, looking me in the eye.

The next morning during my prayer time I felt led by the Holy Spirit to really investigate the situation. What help would a down-and-out man be able to get in a big, impersonal city like New Haven? If a man were really in need, where would he go? If *I* were the one hungry, what chance would I have? Such questions pressed in upon me. I decided to find out. I let my beard grow for three or four days, borrowed some old clothes of Bill's, and began my firsthand experiment in living the life of a "bum" on the streets of New Haven.

"Brother, can you spare a dime?" The first fellow I approached brushed past me without so much as a glance. "Fellow, can you spare a dime for a cup of coffee? I'm so cold." Again I got the brush-off. The third time I tried a new technique. I stepped almost in front of the next couple and repeated my "Brother, can you spare a dime," and threw in a silly grin for good measure. My prospects threw me a nickel and grunted something I could not understand, and then pushed on past.

This experiment in sharing and caring took place about 11 P.M. in front of the largest theatre in New Haven. The temperature stood at 16°, and there was a stiff, biting wind that seemed to peel the skin off my cheeks. It snatched at my old, battered coat, tugged at my trousers. My old tennis sneakers were scant protection against the ice and snow of the street. Pulling my sweat shirt up to my chin, I tried again. I stepped in front of an attractive young couple—and this time I got a cigarette! "Can't eat this," I thought. So it went for another hour. It was midnight, and I had had no supper. I was hungry, and cold through and through. I had "touched" eighteen people, but still had a take of only fifteen cents and two cigarettes. Though my statistics were low, my stomach was rapidly reaching a conclusion. Fifteen cents would buy a cup of coffee and a doughnut. I headed for the nearest all-night diner.

I repeated the experiment the following four nights, to get some real basis for judgment. The responses were about the same. The largest amount I received for a whole night's begging was fifty cents. The general picture seemed to be that most people felt that anyone asking help on the streets was a "bum." If a fellow happened to be really in need, really hungry, it was just too bad. He'd starve. I had only one heart-warming experience, one night. When I went into my "Brother, can you spare a dime?" routine with one young man, he replied, "Come on

27

with me. I'm hungry, too." And we had a good supper. One Christian response out of more than fifty tries! I realized that I myself, a Christian minister, had earlier come in the 98 per cent category of those who "passed by on the other side."

I now knew the general public's response, and so I decided to investigate further and see what response I could get from the police. About midnight the next night I approached a policeman walking his beat, head bent downward against the cold, earmuffs on, hands buried in his big blue coat. I approached him respectfully. "Sir, I am a stranger in this city, with nothing to eat and no place to sleep. I don't have any money, and I don't know anybody. I wonder if you could help me?" With a frown he said, "Go down to the corner of Church Street and ask the sergeant to let you sleep in the jail." This was better—no food, but at least a place to sleep. On the way down to the jail, I strapped my small 35 mm. camera to my thigh, just in case the sergeant decided to frisk me. I walked on into the precinct station and found four other cold, shivering men who had had the same idea. The recession was really on, and there were many unemployed in the city at that time. We were quickly searched, and then led down to a cell block. Each man was locked in a separate cell. Mine was an oversized closet, about 6 by 8 feet, furnished with cast-iron toilet, a dripping faucet, and a double-decker bed with wooden mattress. What a layout! I unstrapped my camera and took pictures of the interior of the jail. Then I lay down and tried to sleep in the bitter cold, on that hard bed, without any pillow or blanket. I was terribly hungry, but at least I had been taken in off the street.

The third stage of my experiments in being a "down-and-outer" was to investigate the help such a person would receive from institutions for welfare and relief work. I decided to try the Yale Hope Mission, knowing that with its big budget and staff, they were well equipped to render excellent help. I figured the Hope Mission should be able to do a much better job with the poor and the outcast than some of the other social agencies. I went there about four in the afternoon, and told my "hard-luck story." I was given a card which entitled me to a bed in a clean dormitory. The place was clean and neat, but the approach was purely mechanical. Supper consisted of cold, unpalatable food, though served in nice dishes. Afterwards, we were herded in to the chapel for a service led by some Yale undergraduates. The service, I am sure, was a fine training ground for the students, but it was rough on the listeners. There was no genuine ring of truth to help the needy, near-desperate men who were my dormitory mates. I ranked the Yale Hope Mission "A" for buildings and equipment, but much lower down for personal relationships or real helpfulness.

The next night I tried out another institution, the Salvation Army. Here the food was slightly better, although the dormitory was much worse. However, here in the services the leaders really tried to reach us, speak to our needs, and give us something to hold to. The religious program was run by converted drunks who knew what it was like to be cold and hungry, out of a job, and really discouraged and desperate. This program I rated in my little book, "much better."

To make my study cover a wider field, I next decided to go down to New York City and spend a few days. I decided to try the city's unemployed and transient men's dormitory. It was a huge ten-story building, which had been converted into a dormitory during the height of the recession. It was a bitter cold night. I was dressed, as usual, in dirty blue dungarees, sweat shirt, and an old jacket. I got to the building quite late, and was thinking to myself, "Here's where I walk the streets tonight." To my surprise, just as soon as I approached this cold, impersonal building, one of the men on duty opened the front door for me and ushered me in, saying, "Come on in, mate. Ten minutes late or so ain't gonna make no difference. It's cold outside." And it was. I went in, and was given a card which entitled me to eat, spend the night, have breakfast, and then move on.

The huge cafeteria was already closing up when I got there,

but with scarcely a grumble the man on duty served up another plate for me. Such a spirit of concern and understanding in this, the world's largest city, I could not understand, until I later learned that the staff was made up, not of city employees, but of volunteers taken from the ranks of the unemployed, the destitute, the needy. They were kind in a gruff way because they had been on the other side of the fence. They had experienced walking city streets in hunger and despair. While their kindness was covered with roughness and profanity, it wasn't mechanical. The dormitory was row after row after row of steel cots, laid head to toe, nearly a thousand in all, each provided with a clean sheet and a blanket. I had difficulty sleeping because of the noisy "elevated" that roared by just thirty feet away from our window. Then at about 11 P.M. a drunk was brought in and put to bed just next to me. He reeked of alcohol. Thirty minutes later he was sick, and vomited all over the floor, bed, and blankets—and was too sick to care. I tried to move to another cot, but there were no vacant beds. Finally, by reversing my position in bed, putting my head at the foot of the bed, I was able to sleep, although not quite as well as if I had been in my old suite at Yale.

After six weeks of experimenting I decided to bring my informal, personal survey to a close. I had reached some pretty definite conclusions, some of them not very comforting. I had learned, through actually trying my own luck, that a really poor, starving, honest man would practically die of starvation. I had found that most people were cold and suspicious of the man on the street, brushing off the one asking help as a "bum," or worse. I had discovered that institutions, founded with the best of motives, were apt to give cold charity, or worse. The tragic thing was that the Christian institutions did not do much better than the municipal agencies. In this so-called Christian land of ours we had "large professions and little deeds." These results stirred me deeply, for I was to be a Christian minister.

After these weeks of wandering the streets at night, I had to return to my books for some serious study of the theories of Christian ethics, Christian education, philosophy, and the like. It was with a fierce determination to hit those books—to "lick" those books—that I went back to the apartment on Grand Avenue my first night back from New York. But, alas, there was no studying to be done that night. Bill had found a job again, and at long last the lights were back on in our dingy fourth-floor apartment. Big-hearted Rose was celebrating by giving a party. She had ordered a big bag of doughnuts, and a huge pot of coffee was bubbling on the back of the stove. As I mingled among this boisterous crowd—Rose had invited all the tenants of the second and third floors of the tenement—I marveled again at the amazing strength of this woman. Rose was determinedly cheerful, warmhearted, optimistic. How in the world could she keep going in the eternal "rat-race" of trying to feed seven mouths daily, keeping the landlord from ejecting them, and enduring the day-in and day-out crying of that sickly baby? I didn't know. I just marveled.

There was a catch in my throat as I looked at Mary, the oldest daughter, and imagined the future that probably lay ahead of her. Budding adolescence—a street-corner romance—quitting school—an early marriage—and a tenement flat again, with her own crying, undernourished, pitiful brood. It did not take too much imagination to see her as the Rose of the next generation. However, tonight she was all smiles. She was right in the thick of the party. Of course, she could not go to bed until the party was over anyway, as she slept on the sofa in the living room. Going to bed for her meant kicking off her shoes, pulling up a blanket, and lying down.

Billy, Jr. was one of the cutest ten-year-olds I had ever seen, with medium brown hair, dark, merry eyes, an easy, friendly smile that made you think of a bull pup. He was my pal . . . and also my problem. Soon after I arrived at my new Grand Avenue "home," I had asked Rose, "Do you have a bathroom?"

She had answered, "Of course," and then took me to a little door opening off the kitchen. I found a tiny room 4 by 4 feet. On one side was a tiny half-sized metal tub, filled to the brim with the latest load of coal. On the other side was a one-piece cast-iron toilet, the odor of which sent me staggering back into the kitchen. In the weeks that followed, as I became friends with the family, I had been able to persuade Rose to let me move the coal out of the bathtub into a box, and clean out the bathroom. Even though it was still dark and airless, at least I could enter it without a clothespin on my nose. I was proud of my handiwork. But the second part of my campaign—to get the tub *used*—proved to be more difficult. That first Saturday night I had heated a big can of water, poured it steaming into the tub, and called out to my pal, Billy, "Want to be first?"

His startled and completely unbelieving response, as if he was sure he must have heard me wrong, was, "Me, take a bath? *Now?* Why, it's snowing outside!" I unsuccessfully approached each one of the children, but an hour later I gave up, a much sadder and wiser man. Not one child had taken a bath. I too went to bed without a bath, for the water was cold by this time, and there was no more kerosene in the house for the stove.

During the following weeks I gingerly approached the problem from a different angle, using the "dangling carrot" technique. I told the boys, Billy and his eight-year-old brother, Bobby, that each week that they took *one* bath, complete with a tubful of water and *soap*, I'd take them out for a treat—to the movies, to the zoo, or to the downtown gymnasium. They shook on the deal, though they let me know they thought they were getting the rough end of it, and that if it weren't for our friendship they'd never consider it. I'm sure no proud father ever felt any greater sense of achievement than I did, on a fine Saturday afternoon, when I would set out with those two clean boys in tow, all scrubbed pink and shining.

# YALE

A knock at the front door of our house in Tuguegarao brought me back with a jolt to the present. The rain was still falling outside the window in the flooded yard. It was still a dark and dreary day. And yet, reliving these old Yale days with all their tender memories had given me a fresh outlook for the work that lay ahead. Summing up all these accumulated thoughts, as I got up and started to the front door, I said to myself, "Well, maybe Yale succeeded, after all. My years there upset me, disturbed me, made me dissatisfied enough to move to Grand Avenue to really *try* to come to grips with human need. I am sure my efforts seemed mighty weak and puny, but at least I made a beginning. Yale forced me to read and study—and Grand Avenue taught me to *pray*."

Never again would I have a complacent, small-town idea of Christianity as just going to church, and "being good." I left Yale with a new prayer on my lips:

> God—let me be aware.
> Let me not stumble blindly down the ways,
> Just getting somehow safely through the days,
> Not even groping for another hand,
> Not even wondering why it all was planned,
> Eyes to the ground unseeking for the light,
> Soul never aching for a wild-winged flight,
> Please, keep me eager just to do my share.
> God—let me be aware!
>
> God—let me be aware.
> Stab my soul fiercely with others' pain,
> Let me walk seeing horror and stain.
> Let my hands, groping, find other hands.
> Give me the heart that divines, understands.
> Give me the courage, wounded, to fight.
> Flood me with knowledge, drench me in light.
> Please—keep me eager just to do my share.
> God—let me be aware.
> —"Awareness," by Miriam Teichner

# 3

## Unexplored

WHEN THE RAINY season in Luzon was finally over, the three district superintendents of the Cagayan Valley—the Reverend Benito Tovera, the Reverend Ciriaco Inis, and the Reverend Mariano Gines—took me in hand to acquaint me with this great valley. These were the men who had pioneered the work in the early days, and each of them had given more than forty years of service. They told me tales of traveling many miles upstream by small "bancas" (dug-out canoes), day after day, in the days before any roads had been built in the valley. They told me of standing on street corners and preaching in places where there was not even one evangelical Christian. They told me stories of the heroism of early Christian converts who secretly read their Bibles at night by candlelight, and then hid them up under the rafters of their bamboo huts to keep from being caught and imprisoned by the friars, who forbade the owning or reading of Bibles. These men were the early "Circuit Riders" of the Philippines, riding horseback, going by boat, and most of all hiking, into all the far corners of the vast Cagayan Valley.

As I looked with them at the map, I could see that only about half of this big area of 125 miles by 100 miles was settled. Other parts of the map had no settlements at all, and were marked "Unexplored." There were still some frontiers where new pioneers were needed. As I studied my road map, I was particularly struck by the long stretch along the Pacific coastline of North-east Luzon, where for a distance of 250 miles there were only two small towns marked on the map. This whole great area between the giant Sierra Madre mountains and the sea was blank on the map, also "Unexplored." Figuring the width of this un-explored territory as varying from thirty to fifty miles, and the length to be nearly 250 miles, I could see that here was an area of approximately 10,000 square miles that was largely untouched.

The foothills of the mountains came down to within five or six miles of our front porch, arousing all sorts of taunting questions in my mind. What kind of people lived over those towering mountains? Were there tribes who wandered through those endless hills? That word "Unexplored" challenged me. It dared me!

For several weeks as I traveled up and down the Cagayan Val-ley with the superintendents, I asked questions, trying to find even one person who had hiked through the Sierra Madre range to reach the east coast. Finally I met a lumberman who had log-ging operations up in the mountains. He told me that most of the people in the interior of the mountains were pygmies, called Negritos, ranging in height from four and a half to sometimes five feet tall. He also told us of Palanan, a good-sized town on the coast, where there were not only Negritos but also Tagalogs and other Malay groups. I wanted to go and investigate. Pastor Inis, the energetic superintendent of Isabela Province, wanted to go too. He was sixty-two years "young," straight of limb, lean, and wiry. He had been wanting to make that trip for years, to see about the possibility of our opening up work over on that vast untouched east coast of Luzon with only the one town— Palanan. What a challenge these people presented to us as Christian workers, representatives of Him who said, "I am the light of the world"! For here was 10,000 square miles of dark-ness. We found another young man, Pastor Valdez, who was interested in investigating this great area, and so we began to round up equipment, blankets, first-aid equipment, food, and made definite plans for an exploratory trip to Palanan, Isabela.

We made plans to go immediately. We knew that even though our rainy season was just over in the valley, on the other side of the Sierra Madre mountains the seasons were different. If we did not go at once, we would run into the time of their storms and heavy monsoons. But on the very day that we were scheduled to start our trip, I got sick. I had diarrhea, and could not eat. We were in Jones, Isabela, the remote little town where Pastor Valdez had been making arrangements for Negrito guides, and there was, of course, no doctor within miles and miles of us. After resting a few hours, I got up and tried to "wear it off" by hiking, sweating, and just not eating. We returned to the house of Pastor Inis, where I took some castor oil and hoped for the best. Though unable to eat Saturday and Sunday, I still insisted that we begin our hike on Monday morning. This was our most important "out-reach" plan, and I did not want to postpone it until after the rainy season. To get there and back in time, we would have to start at once. I think I secretly thought, "Even though I'm a little sick, I'm sure I can keep up with Pastor Inis." How much my respect for that "young" gentleman was going to increase in the days immediately ahead!

In our borrowed army knapsacks and back-packs we loaded canned sardines, mosquito lotion, and all the other paraphernalia we needed, plus almost a sack of rice. We were ready to go! We took a jeep to San Mariano, at the end of the road, and by early afternoon we were on the trail, hiking. How heavy those forty-pound back-packs became! Every step up the mountain trail they grew heavier and heavier. I quickly realized how weak I was from not eating. And I learned with agonizing clarity the appropriateness of the word "tenderfoot" for the first rung in Scouting. In the course of the afternoon we had to ford five streams which, while only one to four feet deep, were quite wide and swift, real mountain streams. This meant taking off shoes, socks, rolling up pants, and wading across. The streams, though never deep, were covered on the bottom with large rocks, grown over with green algae that made them as slick as glass. Never in my life had I had such painful experiences. My tiny number elevens had led such a sheltered life since boyhood in shoes that they were really tender. My Filipino companions roared with laughter to watch the big "Americano" take one step, wince with pain, rest, step on a sharp rock, let out a yell, or fall down and get wet all over. It was no joke to me, however, for by nightfall I had a gash in each foot that became sorer with each step. Our first night we were fortunate in coming to a clearing on the mountainside where there were about twenty small huts. The hospitable "mayor" turned his bamboo house over to us, and we slept the sleep of a tenderfoot.

On Tuesday at breakfast I could scarcely eat, but we started on anyway. By eleven I was too weak to struggle any further. We stopped in a tiny village of Kalingas on a hillside near a rushing river. As we walked into the clearing between the bamboo huts covered with grass, there stood a group of five Kalinga warriors in G-strings. They were tall, muscular, strong and poised. One held a seven-foot spear, another bow and arrows, the rest bolos or machetes. They stood quietly, silently, their piercing eyes fastened on my face. The tallest Kalinga with the spear began to balance it in his hand. The hair on the back of my neck was standing straight out. Finally our "old man," Pastor Inis, asked the Kalingas who their "Apo" was . . . and soon the two "old men" were deep in conversation. When they finished, the old chief of the village by gestures and grunts led me to his house. I had a high fever by this time, and I was having chills. As soon as I slipped off my pack and lay down, I fell fast asleep.

When I woke up, the sun was sinking in the west. The sleep had cleared my head, and I remembered the malaria medicine I had in my first-aid kit. After taking a double dose and some hot Hemo I carried for such times as these, I felt better. Looking around, I became conscious of poverty and filth such as I had never seen before, even in the slums of Shanghai in China. At least four men or women had a skin disease that just ate the skin off their bodies in large rings. They looked as if somebody had carefully sandpapered the skin right off most of them. Three women had large thyroid tumors. They were all so dirty it was nauseating to be near them. Yet I kept reminding myself, "Here are the homeless, the hungry, the naked for whom Christ died." During our discussion on what we should do, we all agreed that it was mandatory that someone pioneer the work and open up this area.

We were still far from Palanan. At first we decided that the two pastors should go on without me, and that I would try to make it back to the jeep. However, after another two hours of rest I felt better. Encouraged, we decided to get two more cargadores to carry my pack and the large sack of rice that was too heavy for one man, and see how we got along. I took some sulfaguanidine. Though I didn't know for sure what was the matter with me, I figured that by taking quinine for malaria and sulfa for stomach trouble, I was bound to hit one of the problems. Being free of the army pack worked wonders, and I hiked through the afternoon much more easily, though still quite weak. I took more sulfa at suppertime. Then I saw a serious problem arising. We had brought food for three or at most four men for five days. We were now six men at the end of our second day, and those guides ate like wolves!

Wednesday was the toughest day of the trip. During the night it had started to rain. Six of us were squeezed under three raincoats under three trees, trying vainly to keep out the rain, which had started out gradually, but deepened into a real downpour. Small rivers of cold water pushed in under the raincoats and ran down our backs. We were miserable. The rain stopped at 4:30, and we all slept like dead men for about an hour. Then the cold and dampness forced us awake, and we were on the trail again before daylight. We were in the very highest part of the mountain range now. By 9:30 A.M. we were starting over the highest mountains of the trip, after going up one mountain and down another for endless hours. The mountain peaks, between 6000 and 7000 feet high, were in the clouds most of the time, and we were at an altitude of close to 3000 feet in the pass. Here the trees reared up to a height of 150 feet, making a solid canopy of jungle green that effectively cut out all sunlight. Here in this dank, lush rain-forest the grasses and ferns grew ankle-deep to sometimes waist-high, and our legs and arms were whipped and cut by their razor-sharp edges. The deep, gloomy, tropical jungle was at its worst as we wearily edged ourselves forward in the half gloom. Eerie shadows whetted our imagination as "shapes" armed with spears would appear ahead of us and then slip off in the distant trail ahead. Weird insect cries and unfamiliar bird calls punctuated the jungle stillness, and I often felt the hair rising on the back of my neck at some unexpected shrill cry. There was one jungle "varmint" that made a noise like an old electric razor. First, it seemed to turn slowly, sort of sputtering along, but then the "motor" would get into high gear with a raucous, high-pitched whine that set our nerves on edge. Brother Inis finally caught one, and said it looked much like an ordinary, large cricket.

We fought a losing, rear-guard action against the blood-sucking leeches. They are tiny, wormlike creatures that abound in the dark, damp jungles. They fastened themselves on our legs and dug into the flesh. After the first mosquitolike bite, they could not be felt. They got under our pants, down in our socks, under the edges of our shoes. When they have enough blood so that they are puffed up like tiny balloons, they drop off the body, leaving the legs and feet still wet and sticky with blood. In one hour, after a rain, we would pick as many as fifteen or twenty off our legs.

39

Occasionally, as we neared the top, the gloom fell away, and we could see the blue of the sky, and white clouds scudding by. Due to the additional cargadores, we had had to cut our meat ration to two sardines per meal. This transition to a diet of rice and fish three times a day meant a real adjustment for my stomach. I tired much more easily. After three hours on the trail I found my stamina was gone. Every step upward required strenuous effort. Brother Inis was tough as a hickory nut. Though he often had to rest, he kept going. I hope I can do as well at sixty-two!

It rained hard on the trail all the next day as we walked along the top of the high ridges. We had spent the night at an altitude of over 5000 feet. It was very cold and damp. During the day we made rapid progress, chiefly due to the inspiration of dozens of piles of Japanese bones we saw along the trail. It seems that in the last war between 2000 and 3000 Japanese retreated to Palanan to escape the U. S. Army, and having little food and finding almost nothing to seize from the land, hundreds died along the trail from starvation and sickness. The most conservative estimate I have heard of the number of Japanese soldiers who died along the way was 200, and many said 300 to 400. At any rate, there were dozens upon dozens of piles of whitened bones along the trail, and it took no detective to tell that these were human bones.

By Friday my shoes were beginning to disintegrate. I had lost the left heel, and ragged nails were pushing painfully into my foot. We forded three streams, wide ones, in less than two hours. Our food was gone. We had been hiking since 5 A.M. with empty stomachs. Finally, tired, bedraggled, hungry, but overjoyed, we reached the first barrio of Palanan at 12:30 P.M. on the fifth day of the longest, most torturous hike of my whole life. We had made it! We were still alive! Our first thought was *food*. We tried to buy rice, but we found to our amazement that instead of their having food to sell or spare us, the people of

Palanan were in the midst of a severe food shortage. Some were eating boiled corn only once or twice daily. Here was famine.

We learned that during the war when the 2000 to 3000 Japanese soldiers had reached Palanan, after subsisting on the trail without any food except leaves and grass and bamboo shoots, they stripped it bare as a bone. They ate up all the crops, chickens, and even killed the carabaos (used as work animals). They tore down the houses to make larger shelters, burning the houses of those who were not too cooperative. They took all the boats and fishing nets. Thus, the people of Palanan had been left in a desperate condition. Most of them had only their hands and the barest hand tools to work their fields. They had no way to get money to replace the work animals, since they are separated by the mountains from any market for their produce. The corn-borer insect had destroyed their last two corn crops and they had had five serious typhoons in two years! And since there are no stores to buy food, people there were simply starving. Every pound of soap, every drop of oil, every bite of food has to be brought in on the backs of these pygmy Negritos, who get $1.00 per day for hauling in forty pounds of food over fifty-five miles of the roughest, muddiest mountain trails I've ever been on. Never, even in the Orient, have I seen such grinding poverty, pinched faces, bloated bellies as these people had in Palanan. Tuberculosis was rampant. People were dying almost daily.

The people in the first house, though they had no food to offer us, insisted that we come in. They sent a small boy up a fifty-foot coconut palm for some fresh coconuts. Though the milk was too warm to be palatable, the coconut meat filled up the vacant spots in our stomachs, and we were grateful. They had given us the best they had. This generous hospitality I have found to be the trade-mark of the Filipinos. They give the best to their guests and forget themselves. We thanked those people and set out to look over the town. Passing along a rare field of corn, Brother Inis "borrowed" a few not-quite-ripe ears of corn, and we threw them on a fire, snatched them out, and ate them ravenously, meditating all the while on "the ethics of poverty." Then we continued walking through the Japanese-ravished, typhoon-gutted town of Palanan. There were thirty or forty houses standing, made largely of bamboo with nipa-thatched roofs, with a few old, well-constructed wooden houses in varying stages of disrepair. For every house left, there were the gaunt posts standing of a dozen more that had been destroyed.

In our conversations with the people we learned that Palanan consisted of five or six large barrios, as well as the central part of town, comprising a total of about 5000 people. Our hearts were touched by the serious plight of these people. Skinny children played in the streets. In the hot midday sun people sat silently in the shade, or were indoors. Later that day, we watched a silent column of people wind their sorrowful way through the streets of this war-scarred village, carrying a small wooden box. A man near us said, half to himself, "Another child." With the serious lack of food, eating only one or two skimpy meals per day, the children soon became prey to the first disease that came along. I saw many fresh mounds in the small cemetery. I asked, "Isn't there a doctor or a dentist here among these 5000 people?" "None." "Not even a nurse?" "No. . . ." "What kind of medicine is available?" "None." No medicine! No food! And here we were in the midst of a serious famine! We were there—but what could we do? At that moment I knew I would have to come back. The resolve was born in me. Somehow —some way—I *must* bring help to these people.

Saturday morning, in spite of a drizzling rain, we called on the various town officials. I happened to ask one of them how often a priest or a minister visited Palanan. He replied, "We have never had a Protestant minister here. One Catholic priest visited here in 1930." It seems that a priest used to come to Palanan once every year or two on the big boats that come yearly to haul the hogs to Manila. However, it had been more than ten years since the last one had come. There was practically no religious activity of any kind in this remote place. Here were people who were facing not only hunger of the body. They were also spiritually hungry. We determined to make plans to bring them the Bread of Life.

I talked at length with Mayor Bernardo about the problems of Palanan. He and I hiked all over the town to see if we could find any spot suitable for landing my small ambulance plane. The river bank was the only possibility, and it had all kinds of small stumps and large stones on it. It would be difficult, if not dangerous. He promised me he would have it cleared off as much as possible; I promised him I would fly back and bring help for Palanan.

That afternoon Brother Inis and I went down the Palanan River to the mouth of Palanan Bay by banca (dug-out canoe) to see the vast indigo-blue Pacific. There we met an interesting old Spaniard, Don Buensocesso. Upon seeing strange people approaching his large bamboo house set back in the trees, a child ran inside shouting, "Americano! Americano!" After shaking hands all round, we discovered that Don Buensocesso spoke Spanish and Tagalog. Brother Inis spoke Ilocano and English, and I, with several college degrees, was fairly fluent in English only. However, Don Buensocesso excused himself, went out in the kitchen, and soon appeared with four cans of beer! Upon our refusal, he went back into the kitchen, and came out the next time with four glasses, a bottle of Scotch, and a huge smile. As politely as possible we refused his second offer. Dejected, he went back into the kitchen. The third time, he returned, face abeam, with—believe it or not—*champagne!* We broke his heart by refusing his beloved nectar. He obviously thought we were "nuts." Just as he dejectedly turned to go back into the kitchen, a plump chicken wandered casually in the front door.

43

I pointed to the chicken and to my stomach. Chicken.... A-h-h-h.
... *Now*, he understood. . . . We were hungry. The chicken
disappeared. The smell of meat frying in a skillet filled the air
with pungent odors. And then—after several minutes, we were
eating de luxe chicken, fried in coconut oil. It was the feast
of a king to famished men.

By this time the old man and Don Buensocesso had worked
out a three-language exchange and with the addition of a few
hand signals we found out that Don Buensocesso had charge of
all logging operations for a big lumber mill in Manila. Great
numbers of the primitive mountain people and pygmies worked
for him, on a barter basis. As far as I could tell, one large
mahogany log was worth from one to four cans of sardines
(depending upon the size). It seems these wild people are very
fond of sardines. They must be. After we told Don Buensocesso
our plight in having no food to hike back to Ilagan and civilization, he graciously sold us twenty pounds of rice, two cans of
milk, a tiny tin of peanut butter, and to our great joy, a dozen
eggs!

We planned to leave on Sunday morning at 9:30, after an
early service. We had called a meeting for 8 A.M.—the first
Protestant meeting ever held in this enormous 10,000-square-
mile area. I had hopefully, prayerfully, expected a roomful of
people by the appointed hour. Instead, there was not one soul.
At 8:30, still no one. At 9, just two people. At 9:30, we started
off with twelve people present, but by 10 there was standing
room only. Our faith and prayers had been justified. After a
short song service (they didn't know a single hymn), we explained the nature of our visit, and told them about our willingness to fly in with "The Circuit Rider" to help them, *if*
they would, in turn, get to work to get out the worst of those
stumps, logs, and holes on the beach. At the close of the
service we asked those people, who were deeply interested in
the Word of God and in establishing a church, and who were

willing to *work*, to stay for an additional service. To those we promised Sunday school materials, and Bibles, that they might begin a Sunday school. There were five who stayed. One man showed real ability. He was a public school teacher. We earnestly prayed in closing that out of this small group might come the beginning of a new church for the Master.

In the middle of the morning we donned our packs and were just about to hit the trail again, when we heard a commotion outside the window where we had been having our service. A man was butchering an old carabao, too feeble to work any more, to feed his hungry family. We decided to wait a few minutes to see if we could buy some. Some extra protein might give us extra strength for the long hike back over the mountain! We managed to get three or four pounds of "I-don't-know-what-part" of the animal. We tied it on top of one of the army packs, and then flies by the hundreds immediately covered it. It's hard to tell which weighed the most, the meat, or the mountain of flies that sucked its blood. I was losing my taste for meat rapidly. I wondered whether the meat could last in this muggy, steaming heat.

We were on the trail by 12:30, to begin our long trek home again. We forded seven streams in the first two hours. All afternoon we climbed upward, from the low river bed of Palanan up toward the towering mountains. By the time we reached our first camp site, near a cool spring, it was nearly dusk and we were famished. My companions had salted down our meat and decided to save it for the next day. Our menu for supper was to be rice and freshly boiled eggs. Bless Don Buensocesso's heart for providing us with such a luxury as eggs! I was sending him, via mental telegraph, all sorts of good wishes when, to my horror, I opened one of the eggs and discovered we had, not fresh eggs, but "balots." A balot is an egg that has been placed under a setting hen for about two weeks, and then removed just before it is ready to hatch. It is considered a delicacy among many

Filipinos, especially the Tagalogs. That night Brother Inis, the young pastor, and the cargadores had a wonderful time eating the balots, but for some reason I had lost my appetite. My *mind* told me that if chicken tasted good, and if eggs tasted good, then surely something that was both chicken and egg ought to taste good. But when I saw the tiny little black feathers just inside the shell, my *stomach* said "No"!

Monday was our hardest day of hiking, for we had to climb from a level of about 1000 feet up to nearly the peak of the highest mountain, ford two swift, roaring streams, and then pass between several more peaks on the pass that was 4000 feet high. This went on all day. Mountains . . . mountains . . . mountains. . . . Up . . . up . . . up. . . . For thirteen and one-half hours we kept plugging on. We finished up the meat at noontime, and feasted on the tiny jar of peanut butter. I couldn't eat supper. I had an upset stomach again.

Up at 4 A.M. the next day! We found that sleep was impossible on the rocky, wet trail. Besides, we were all in a hurry to get home again to our families, and so we had finished breakfast and repacking, and were hiking soon after 5 A.M. It was hard going. I was finding that the simple diet was doing funny things to me. After three or four hours on the trail, my legs began to feel like rubber, and every step became an agonizing effort. At noon we found that we had lost contact with our cargadores. They were either lost or, horrible thought, they had run off with all of our things. They had all of the food with them, and so the situation was serious. Fortunately, a little boy on his way to school at the capital of Isabela, Ilagan, shared some of his ground corn with us, and a morsel of his dried fish. We all squatted around his little fire and ate the corn (larger than grits, but smaller than rice), and were very, very grateful. It was most generous of the boy, for he was still two days from his destination.

Two hours later our cargadores appeared. They had been off

"hunting," but brought nothing back. The trail was really rugged, but we kept steadily on all afternoon, thinking of the little clearing we were hoping to reach by dark, where we might find shelter. Then, just at dusk, a tropical storm hit us. Fierce winds bent the trees before them, and drove the rain like bullets through our clothing. Our raincoats were useless. In the pitch black darkness that descended upon us, we lost our way. We were pushing on, without supper, trying to cover the five miles we estimated to be the distance between us and the settlement, and now here we were, lost in the dense forests, in the dark, in the rain. It was a black time—but we kept going. Hours later, we finally saw through the trees a pinpoint of light. Saved! We stumbled and fell a half mile more, and at last came to a small settler's cabin on the edge of the forest. After three nights of sleeping on the trail, we at last were able to sleep in luxury— under a roof! We were on the floor, of course, but we were under a roof. The rain was still pouring steadily outside, but we were *inside*. Praise be!

The next morning we were on the trail by 5:30 A.M. Thoughts of home and family put wings on our feet. We reached San Mariano and the jeep by 8 A.M., and were in Ilagan by 10:30. I drove Pastors Inis and Valdez home, and then headed north for Tuguegarao! At four different rivers I had to wait for ferries to take the jeep across, for the bridges were washed out. Since I had not yet learned the Filipino virtue of patience, I chafed at the bit—so near home, and yet so far. I paced up and down the river banks, asking over and over, "When can we get across?" only to be told, "Mabiit laeng," which means, "In a little while."

A little after dark, though, about 7:30 P.M., I did finally arrive in Tuguegarao. The trip to Palanan from start to finish had been only slightly more than 200 miles, and yet it had taken us eleven rugged days, and I had come home more tired than I had ever been in my whole life. A few days later I was to learn

47

why I had had such stomach trouble. The doctor discovered that I had amoebic dysentery—the "missionary's complaint"!

I came home utterly tired and beat—and yet terribly glad I had gone. I had seen behind the word "Unexplored" on the map. I had caught a glimpse of human need that was to color my missionary service all the rest of my life. And now I was home again—home, sweet home. Truly, it's wonderful. A home is just a building with four walls until it's filled with the sweet smiles and laughing voices of a wife and children. Then it becomes a little bit of heaven.

# 4

# Famine

FAMINE. The mere word brought to mind pictures of hungry babies. What could I do? One lone person facing the need of 5000! I didn't know—and I didn't know anybody else who had had any experience on whom I could unload this responsibility. I was "it"—whether I was trained or not, whether I knew what to do or not.

I jumped in our L-5 ambulance plane, "The Circuit Rider," and headed for Manila. I presented the desperate situation of Palanan to the head of Church World Service. He said, "What do you want, and how much?" I started reeling off the figures that I had prepared that seemed enormously large, but were actually very short: 15,000 vitamin pills; 10,000 malaria pills; 20-30 barrels of powdered milk; several boxes of simple medicines for anemia, skin diseases, and others; vegetable seeds for increasing the local food supply; as many sacks of rice as possible for emergency relief feeding.

The Church World Service really came through in wonderful fashion. From our mission superintendent I was able to get Methodist Committee for Overseas Relief funds to buy two drums of aviation gasoline. From Mary Johnston Hospital I was able to get extra medicines and supplies. We were not able to get powdered milk, and so we had cases and cases of canned milk. It was heavier and bulkier, but still it would save lives, and so we had to find some way to get it to Palanan.

For days in Manila I tried to find some way of getting these supplies shipped by boat to Palanan. I found that the logging company would not have another ship going there for at least eight more months. The Philippine Navy flatly refused my request that they go in. "Absolutely impossible! The weather is too rough in the Pacific at this time. There are dangerous cross-currents around Northeast Luzon." Next, I considered what it would cost to have these supplies carried in on the back of the pygmy cargadores. We would have had to hire almost fifty men, each one to make several trips. The cost was prohibitive. The only way I could see to met the emergency was to fly these supplies in. No plane had ever landed in Palanan before. Could it be done? Safely? More than once? It is true I had found a gently curving river bank that looked like a possible landing strip, but still I was not at all sure whether it would be safe for a steady, continuous operation with heavy loads. However, we had no other alternative. It was that or nothing—and the remembrance of the long, silent column of people carrying the little box steeled my heart to the difficult task.

We now had the materials we needed. In addition to the medicines and milk, the Philippine government responded to my plea for help by giving a large quantity of vegetable seeds. I sent all of these on ahead by bus to Ilagan, Isabela, where there was a small landing strip. It had been used during the war, but was now abandoned and neglected. However, I figured I could use it. Now the next problem was to find not just supplies, but *people* whom I could fly in to help the folk of Palanan. A doctor, a nurse, a dentist, an agriculturist—where would I find these people?

I tried first at our own Mary Johnston Hospital, but I found they were already crowded, and shorthanded. Some of the doctors and nurses were interested, and I interviewed several, but their enthusiasm waned in a hurry when I showed them Palanan on the map, and told them truthfully, "This is a dangerous mission. We have no regular airstrip. We have only a sandy, unimproved river bank. If anything happens to the plane, you will have a five- or six-day hike back out through the mountains."

Leaving Manila, I began to track down nurses in the Cagayan Valley. I had gone practically down my list of possible recruits, always getting the same answer—"No"—when finally I approached Mrs. Juana Loria, of Bagabag, Nueva Vizcaya. Mrs. Loria was a busy mother, with two or three children at home and one away in school. Her husband, a successful farmer, depended upon his wife heavily. He was very skeptical of the idea of his busy wife getting away for a month, which was the length of time I was challenging her to stay in Palanan. Mrs. Loria was a graduate of Mary Johnston Hospital and for several years had been a missionary nurse before she married. She had just the skills and experience we needed. She knew the backwoods from hiking. She was a devoted Christian. I presented the need—the desperate need—and said, "You must go as both doctor and nurse. If you do not go, we have no one else who can bring medical help to those people." We knelt to pray, to ask God's guidance. It was an extremely difficult decision for a mother, with small children at home, with heavy responsibility. It would be a dangerous mission. There were a hundred reasons why she should *not* go. After prayer, she said quietly to me, "I am ready to go if my husband is willing." Her husband, who a few minutes before had been dogmatic and determined that she not go, said, "If she feels God wants her to go, I am willing." There were tears in his eyes. Here was a miracle of the power of the Holy Spirit.

We still had no agriculturist to help the people in the problem of food production. I also wanted a children's worker, someone to grasp the magnificent opportunity of working with the dozens upon dozens of children there, to tell these young minds the story of Jesus. A few days later a letter arrived through the mail from a young missionary teacher up in the mountains of Abra.

He signed his name, "Wilmer Heisey." He had been in the islands for the past two or three years, working among the mountain people in a remote village in Abra. He had experience as well as training as an agriculturist. He wanted to know if I would be able to give him advice about hiking through the mountains of Isabela. He was interested in seeing at firsthand the tribes of Negritos, Ilongots, and Kalingas, and comparing their customs with the customs of the mountain people of Abra. How God answered prayer! Here was our agriculturist for our mission to Palanan.

Miss Mercedes Santiago was about our ablest deaconess in the Cagayan Valley at that time. In her late thirties, she combined quiet leadership, deep devotion and rare courage. When I presented the need of Palanan, she volunteered. Now we had our team! Mrs. Juana Loria, nurse; Wilmer Heisey, agriculturist; Miss Mercedes Santiago, children's and youth worker; and myself—missionary, pilot, and general "flunky." With the help of the Methodist Church members and MYFers in Ilagan, Isabela, just four or five miles from the old government airstrip, we got everything all ready. We had almost 3000 pounds of supplies and people to be transported.

Early Monday morning I started flying in supplies. The first trip I flew in a light load of milk and vitamins, to test out our river-bank landing field. I took off from the 600-yard airstrip of Ilagan, and "Airlift Pee Wee" began quite undramatically. It was simply a matter of climbing up to 7000 feet as I flew eastward, over the carpet of unbroken green mountains that stretched straight ahead for forty to fifty miles below me. By the time I reached 7000 feet, I was right over the heart of the wildest, weirdest, untouched jungle in these 7000 islands. I thought, "If that engine quits, church is out!" There was no strip or clearing in any direction. It would have been a matter of crashing into those giant trees, 100 feet to 150 feet high, and then disappearing in the trackless waste of a land unknown to any except the tiny pygmies who slipped noiselessly across its unseen trails with their bows and arrows. I remembered a story I had read in the newspapers of some natives discovering a plane in the Mountain Province that had been missing over five years, and there were skeletal bones still in the wreckage!

It was during Airlift Pee Wee that I learned a technique that kept sweat off my forehead, fear out of my heart, and ulcers out of my stomach during many dangerous flights in the days and years ahead. I'd take along a few pages from an old hymnal and sing, or rather shout, these hymns at the top of my lungs all during these jungle flights.

> O God, our help in ages past,
> Our hope for years to come,
> Our shelter from the stormy blast,
> And our eternal home.

Over the top of the highest mountains, at about 7000 to 8000 feet, I would pull on the carburetor heat throttle and start the long twenty- to thirty-mile glide over to our river bank. By the time I had circled Palanan once and started into the landing run, the river bank was full of children anxious to see, or maybe touch, a real airplane. I came in over the river with full flaps to slow the plane down to 60 m.p.h., and seconds later the wheels hit the sand. In less than 100 yards the heavy sand dragging against the small tail wheel brought me to a halt. A half-second after the propeller stopped spinning, I was surrounded by a sea of faces, 75 per cent of them children. One or two officials of the town were present and offered to take care of unloading milk and supplies and storing them in a safe place. I got out of the plane and began to walk over our "landing field." It was anything but encouraging. The surface was not even, but rolling, and big rocks stuck up at intervals. There were some huge stumps, rocks, and trees that only a bulldozer could handle. The one thing in its favor was that it was long.

Charting a course to avoid the worst, I took off for the return trip to Ilagan. I was airborne forty minutes after my first touchdown. Back over that jungle again, I could feel my stomach tightening up. "Where's that hymnbook?" I thought.

> My hope is built on nothing less
> Then Jesus' blood and righteousness. . . .

It was touch and go as to which was the louder, the 185 h.p. Lycoming engine, or the voice of one scared missionary.

Back on the ground in Ilagan, I could tell from the looks of relief on the faces of my co-workers that they had been afraid that I might not make it. The smiles of welcome faded to fear as they then realized that *now it was their turn*. Who would it be? There was heavy silence as we loaded the plane and as I gassed up. I guessed that each thought the other should be first. As we neared the end of the loading, it was obvious that each was thinking of some reason why "she" should go back to the half-destroyed cottage at the airstrip for "something" that took her away from the plane. Considering the work to be done at Palanan, though, I decided it would be wisest to take Mrs. Loria, the nurse, first. She was a good sport, and she climbed in without a word. It was along about this time that my L-5 ambulance plane picked up its nickname, "The Chapel," because everybody who got in it always wanted to pray! On that long, lonely flight over the jungle without a parachute, I knew she was praying, and so was I. The second flight was uneventful, and we were on the ground and unloading in Palanan in forty minutes. A whispered comment spread quickly through the big crowd out to welcome us on the second landing: "A *nurse! Did you hear that he brought us a nurse! Maybe she has medicine!*"

I returned to Ilagan the second time. We had some rice and sardines, and a few "pandesal" (biscuits), and then after a little rest it was time to gas up and get ready for the afternoon flights. Shortly afterwards, at 2:30 P.M., we were airborne with Miss

# FAMINE

Mercedes Santiago and another load of medical supplies. Three-fifteen saw us on the ground and unloading cargo. By 3:30 I was flying west again for Ilagan. Shortly after 4:00 the plane touched the ground. "I must gas up and *hurry* . . . last trip today . . . four loads." I was about "beat"—not from the work of loading and unloading or gassing up, but from the sheer nervous strain of hours and hours of flying over those uncharted wastes called jungles, never knowing where some mechanical failure might slam us into a giant mountainside. But God was good, and our last and fourth flight was uneventful.

Just as the sun's rays were gilding the western sky, I returned to the strip at Ilagan, after taking to Palanan in the last load nothing but 300 pounds of cargo. Wilmer Heisey had decided to hike in over the trail, that he might be better familiar with the area and the people. After a small supper of rice and sardines, I lay down on a mat on the floor of the cottage, pulled over the mosquito net, and by 7:30 was sound asleep, but not before thanking the Almighty for His wonderful care and travel mercies in the most dangerous flying of my life. I fell asleep grateful that the Father's hand had supported us, upheld us during the last sixteen hours.

Morning came early. By 4:30, the bones in my hips and shoulder blades were tired of pushing against the floor, so I got up and went outside to start a fire in the damp coolness of the dawn. There was not a cloud in the sky, and I knew the early morning hours, until nearly ten, would be nice flying. Well, back to the job at hand! Breakfast, clean-up, and then in the first lightening of the eastern sky, I gassed up the ship and loaded more supplies. By carrying a light gas load, enough for a round trip plus thirty miles of reserve for trouble, we could load much more cargo. Using this system, our L-5 was carrying as much in *one* load as six strong cargadores could carry on their backs! It was thirty minutes by plane against three days by a fast hiker. It was about $15 to $20 by plane against $40 to $50 for the men. Practically, it would have been almost impossible to find enough men to haul 3000 pounds over those mountains in a one- to two-month period of time.

I took off and flew east, just as God lifted up the sun above the horizon. The words of the hymn,

> When morning gilds the skies,
> My heart awakening cries,
> "May Jesus Christ be praised. . . ."

came easy. The melody brought quietness to fears and to worries. Never had that Lycoming sounded so smooth! Ah-h-h, how beautiful the mornings in the tropics!

> O God, O Lord, our Christ, may we have Thy
>   mind and Thy spirit;
> Make us instruments of Thy peace;
> Where there is hatred, let us sow love;
> Where there is injury, pardon;
> Where there is discord, union;
> Where there is doubt, faith;
> Where there is despair, hope;
> Where there is darkness, light;
> Where there is sadness, joy.
>
> O Divine Master, grant that we may not so much
>   seek to be consoled as to console;
> To be loved as to love;
> For it is in giving that we receive,
> It is in pardoning that we are pardoned;
> And it is in dying that we are born to eternal life.
> Amen.

This beautiful prayer by St. Francis of Assisi was the prayer of my heart this morning. Truly I wanted this plane, wanted *me*, to be used as God's instrument. I prayed so, and peace came over my soul. . . .

Time for throttle back—and carburetor heat. Airspeed steady

on 95 m.p.h. Ten minutes later I was circling Palanan. I could see tiny figures on the ground racing for the river bank. A minute later and the familiar w—r—r—umph . . . w-r-r-umph . . . sounded, as the main wheels hit the gravel and sand. Trip number 5 was over, and 1000 pounds of medicines, powdered and canned milk and 10,000 vitamins were in. Day number two slipped noiselessly away almost unnoticed, as we landed again in Ilagan, gassed up, loaded up and went through the same old routine again and again and yet again. By evening all our food, canned milk, medicines, Bibles, Sunday school literature, and seeds were in. What was left was bales and bales of good used clothes. These were much needed by the poor folk of Palanan too.

About 4:30 or 5 P.M. of the third day, Wilmer Heisey hiked in, completing his rugged trip through those gaunt, tough, and seemingly-endless mountains. What a guy! He was really Grade A. The good Mayor, Mr. Bernardo, invited Wilmer and me to share his house, and we accepted.

The next morning I prepared to fly back to Ilagan to get the bales of clothing. We were all anxious and excited to begin our work in Palanan. After all the preparation and assembling and transporting of materials, we were now ready to really get to know the people and to minister to them in Christ's name and loving spirit. This was to be the day! I took off, alone, just as the first rays of the sun peeped over the horizon. Because of the slope of the river bank, I had to take off facing the sun. I was roaring down the river bank straight into the sun. As I dodged the plane to the left to avoid a sunken log, the left wing tip caught on a small tree stump that stuck up just high enough to catch it. Wham! The next thing I knew the plane heeled hard over to the left and a second later was standing on its nose. The engine was dead, and the prop smashed. I crawled out of the cockpit, amazed to discover that I had not a scratch on me, in spite of the fact that the accident had happened when the plane was going between 40 and 50 m.p.h. The kids and young people reached the plane almost by the time I was out of the ship. We gingerly lowered the tail of the plane to the ground and began to take stock. Four feet of the left wing was torn off. Part of the aileron was chewed up. Well, that took care of that! There would be no more flying in that plane without a new wing and new propeller! Impossible!

We pushed the plane back to the other end of the river bank, where we could watch it, and we all went home. The team—Wilmer, Mrs. Loria, Miss Santiago and I—thanked our Father that He had preserved my life and enabled us to bring in all medicines, food, seeds, Bibles and Sunday school materials *before* the crash! We had the tools to do the job we'd pledged God to do.

The work was divided up into five major aspects. First, the ministry of healing was under Mrs. Loria. Assisting her in dispensing the food and vitamins were some of the local public school teachers. Second, our Daily Vacation Bible School, for the children and also the youth work, was under Miss Santiago. Third, our agricultural work and extension program was under Mr. Heisey. The fourth part of our work was a community recreation program of volleyball, softball, and other sports three times weekly, with a party for the young people every Wednesday. The "singaree" which always followed the party was a "packed-house" affair. We all shared in the leadership of this. Fifth, and lastly, we planned to share the good news of Christ through visitation evangelism and preaching services conducted in each of the five small villages. All the members of our team shared in this work, too.

Our work plan was simple. We got up at 5 A.M. for a quick bath at the river 200 yards away. Bible study and prayer lasted till breakfast at 6:30. Then came preparation and plans for the day till 7:30. At 8 A.M., Miss Santiago met her seventy-five or eighty DVBSers, while Mrs. Loria, Mr. Heisey, one of the local leaders, and I would hike to one of the four or five villages surrounding Palanan Centro. Most were two to five miles away. This way we covered not only the main part of the town, but also all the surrounding settlements.

In each place we held a small clinic under Mrs. Loria's leadership. My! How those people packed the houses where we spread out our medicines and supplies and held clinic! They pushed and shoved their way in, clamoring for pills for malaria, the worst killer in Palanan, for milk for the babies and pregnant mothers, for vitamins for the whole family. Finally, after seeing several bamboo houses almost collapse from the pressure of the crowds of people, all trying to get their share of the food and medicines, we set up tables and benches outdoors under the trees in some shady place, and held open-air clinics. Mrs. Loria bandaged sore after sore after sore. From a stubbed toe to a badly broken arm, every problem received her loving, gentle touch. There was even one old woman who, suffering agonies from an untreated aching tooth, had finally taken matters into her own hands. She had taken a chisel and a hammer and removed her own tooth! She came to the clinic when the gum wound had already become so infected that it had ruptured through her cheek. She had a raging fever. Her face was swollen and red. An old piece of newspaper had been stuck to the running sore, but could not conceal the odor of the foul-smelling pus. Mrs. Loria ministered gently to this old woman, as to all others who came. Later the patient was taken out to the provincial hospital at Ilagan, but the tragedy of Palanan was that in this case, as in so many others, it was a case of *too little* medical help—*too late!* She died. But dozens of others were saved, because Mrs. Loria answered the call of her Lord, "Go—in My name."

After the clinic was over, Wilmer Heisey would take over for the agricultural lectures and demonstrations. The fact that the Philippine Department of Agriculture and Natural Resources had helped us secure some fine, first-class vegetable seeds made the agricultural hour a very significant one in the lives of the farmers and their families. Most of the farmers planted few, if any, vegetables. There was even a commonly held view that "only carabaos and horses eat green vegetables!" The great majority of the people lived on corn, a little fish, and a few fruits. As one part of his relief and rehabilitation program for Palanan, Heisey was able not only to explain the value of vegetables, but also to give out ten packets each of different kinds of seeds. That meant that within forty to sixty days the pitifully inadequate diet of the people could be greatly enlarged.

When the clinic and farm hour were over, we would invite the people back into the house for a Christian service. Usually from 50 to 75 per cent of the people present would respond, so that the small bamboo houses were always filled and overflowing, with people sitting on benches, small wooden boxes, and on the floor—and many more outside, peering through the windows. Some were just curious, of course; but many were genuinely hungry for knowledge of God and of His Word. It was gratifying to see the interest in the eyes and faces of the listeners as we told them the story of the God who, for their sakes, became Man—who, for their sins, was betrayed, arrested, tried in a criminal court, condemned, tortured, and executed upon a cross. We told them how God then broke into human history, pushed back the walls of time, and raised His Son Jesus Christ from the dead, to live with us, to reign in our hearts as Saviour and Lord.

As I spoke these words through an interpreter, my biggest competitor for the attention of the men and women and children gathered together would be—invariably—a rooster! There were always chickens scratching in the dirt under the split bamboo floor of the little houses. Just as I would reach the climax of my message, some rooster would start a crowing and wing-flapping that drowned me out! And yet, in spite of the difficulties, we presented to them the incredible, the undeserved, the self-giving love of God. Through little services in the houses, through visits, and through personal talks we were able to reach the hearts of fifteen or twenty people in each of the different villages of Palanan.

After a bite of lunch, we would hike back to the main base in Palanan Centro, and have a little rest before the afternoon's visitation and recreational activities. The days slipped by swiftly. Two weeks were gone before we had thoroughly covered the different villages. It was a hard life. We slept on the floor. We had very little to eat except ground corn and fish. We were constantly surrounded by people, pressed by the crowds, and deeply burdened by the overwhelming human misery that we were so powerless to relieve. Hiking under the hot sun was exhausting, and we were all losing weight. And yet—we were happy. Ours was a deep and abiding joy, a shared joy, the joy of serving our Master in this faraway place. As we knelt in prayer under the stars, we felt His presence with us and gave thanks.

Then tragedy struck. Heisey became ill with dysentery from drinking the river water, which was heavily polluted. There were no toilets in Palanan. The only one we saw had been in the school yard, but it had been blown over by a typhoon. Consequently, the river was usually "it." There were no wells either, and so clean water was quite a problem. All of us had had a number of stomach upsets, but as our supply of medicine ran out, Heisey got progressively worse. He refused to give in, or admit that he could not do his work. We took him at his word, but I could not help being concerned over his growing pallor. Then down at the river one morning I noticed him stagger and almost fall. I asked him what was the matter, and he tried to pass it off lightly, murmuring, "Same old thing," and patting his stomach. He seemed all right, and we went on with our shaving.

Then, just as we got back to Mayor Bernardo's house, I turned in time to see Heisey collapse, falling forward and striking his head on the sharp edge of a cabinet. Seconds later he was lying on the floor in a pool of blood. I used my handkerchief and applied pressure, Red Cross style, and was able to stop the spurting blood from the artery which had been cut near his forehead. A neighbor ran for Mrs. Loria who was able to bandage him up, but by this time we did not have a bit of medicine left to treat his wound, to prevent infection, or to treat the much more serious, debilitating, amoebic dysentery. It was a dreadful situation. How would we *ever* get Heisey out of Palanan? He could not possibly walk out now. The plane was wrecked. There were no boats due for another year. The rainy season for this area was fast approaching. There was no way to call for outside help, for there was no telegraph office in this place. Even a runner who might cross the mountains to Ilagan to buy medicine would be at least a week in getting back.

We ate our breakfast in silence that day. Our morning devotions were words—just words—and mighty little faith. Each one of us was thinking, "We'll never get him out of here now." Heisey was six feet tall, and *big*. We could never carry him over those giant mountains. The morning wore away slowly. The minutes dragged by. The hours loafed. It was lunchtime at last. Then we lay down for siesta, to try to think—but actually, we just went over the same troubling, worrisome paths in our minds. I dozed, but then a mosquito's droning waked me. "But there are no mosquitoes here in the daytime!" Startled, I jumped up and went to the window. Away to the southwest I could see a small dot, flying leisurely this way and that. The dot gradually became larger and larger as I eagerly watched, until I could see that it was a large, four-engine plane. Closer and closer it came, as it circled back and forth across the carpet of trees that masked the tops of the Sierra Madre range. The sound of the engines became clearer. By this time, we were all crowding the windows, watching. We could tell the pilots were looking for something.

Heisey volunteered, "One of those big planes that flies from Manila to Okinawa must have crashed." The four-engine plane came closer, and now we could tell that it was a B-17. It had a large yellow boat strapped underneath and bore the markings of the United States Air Force. "Why . . . why . . . that's a plane of the 2nd Air-Sea Rescue Squadron, from Clark Field!" I shouted. Clark Field was the big U.S. base about 200 miles south and west of where we were. Soon the B-17, flying at an altitude of about 2000 feet, spotted the settlement of Palanan, and began to circle the thirty or forty houses in the center of town. Suddenly a wild hope—a dream—burst full-blown in our hearts. Heisey's face was aflame with the reality of it. Then the big plane turned slowly northward and continued its lazy back and forth movements, getting farther and farther away, until after about thirty minutes it was completely out of view. A heavy blanket of disappointment settled over us as the last embers of hope died out. Only a sense of hopelessness and frustration remained.

"How can we ever get Heisey out of Palanan? How can we get him through the jungle?" My heart was deeply troubled, and my thoughts ran over and over the problems. "He can never walk out. He is getting weaker and weaker, no matter what he says." The afternoon faded into evening, and I slipped outside the house to watch the stars come out. They seemed to speak to me, to remind me that God was there watching over us. The beauty of the Southern Cross whispered that sometimes the way of suffering *was* God's way.

The next morning dawned clear and cool. We were here in Palanan on the Lord's business, and so we had to get busy doing what we could. I wanted to make a trip to the next little village up the river, where we had started a small Bible study group, to check up on their progress. Immediately after breakfast I got ready, and started hiking. However, I had hardly covered a mile when I heard the faint hum of an engine. I turned and ran as fast as I could back toward the town, scanning the sky eagerly as I ran. I saw in the distant southwest two tiny dots.

"Pretty low," I thought, "and the sound is different from the big one." I kept running, and kept looking, and soon I could distinguish the shape of two small L-5s. *Hope!* Maybe the Air Force was looking for *us!* By the time I got back to town, the two small planes were circling Palanan, trying to find the best place to land. They spotted my wrecked plane on the river bank, and a few minutes later they were lined up with the beach and prepared to land. Seconds later the wheels flashed by, "wh-u-um-p-ed" on the ground, and the beautiful silver ships taxied up to where we were standing, by my plane. Slowly and gracefully a husky, handsome Air Force captain climbed out. He was dressed in neatly pressed khakis, his overseas cap set at a jaunty angle. He ambled over to me, and said, "Your name Spottswood?"

"Yes."

"Well, thank God you're alive!"

We shook hands warmly. By that time the second pilot, dressed in a blue flying suit, came up. He was a redhead, with a big grin on his face, and he began telling me the story.

"That last day you were at the airstrip at Ilagan, you told a fellow you'd be back for supper. When you didn't show up, he told people you had crashed in the jungle. The newspapers have been running stories about you. 'Missionary believed captured by Huks. Plane lost in jungle. Rev. C. L. Spottswood feared killed in crash.' Your wife called the Embassy, and they decided we had better come looking. Mighty glad you're O.K."

I interrupted the fellows to tell them I was all right, but that we did have a real medical emergency on our hands—Heisey. I knew too that the two women would have an extremely difficult time trying to hike out, weakened as they were by sickness and our lack of food. I asked the two pilots if they could possibly fly the two women out to safety, as well as Heisey. Captain Hank Parker took off almost immediately with Heisey and had him in a hospital within an hour. (He recovered.) The two ladies rushed home to pack as hurriedly as they could, while I helped the other pilot refuel from the extra jerry cans he had way inside the plane. It was a risky operation, at best, to take off from the rough, curving, sandy river bank with two passengers, but he agreed to try it. I prayed silently, and soon they were off the ground, climbing up over the mountains. I knew they would soon be home again, safe and sound—two women who had given wholeheartedly of themselves in service, two women who had faced real danger to serve their Master. I thanked God for them. And I thanked God for the U.S. Air Force, for the two brave pilots who had come at just our hour of need and surely saved the life of Wilmer Heisey, a brave, consecrated young missionary.

I was grateful—and yet, as I wandered slowly back to the mayor's house, I also felt strangely dejected. The excitement was over, and now I was all alone. I was left behind, to try to tie up all the loose ends, to try to train the leaders who would carry on after we were all gone, to officially organize our little Methodist Church. I felt tired, depressed, deeply lonely. And yet, I knew I was not alone. God was with me. This was *His* work I must still do, before I could go home.

Thank heavens for work! I planned to stay just one more week in Palanan before hiking back out, and so I threw myself into my work and the time flew. I visited each one of the villages of Palanan again, talking with the new converts and organizing the little congregations into committees and commissions to continue the work after I was gone. Sunday was soon upon us, the day of parting. I conducted the service early that morning, baptizing the new converts, and giving real prayers of thanksgiving to God that He had given us the *power*, the *prayer*, the *presence* of the Holy Spirit, to build a tiny church here in this distant place for the mighty Saviour. This was the first Protestant Church on the whole east coast of Luzon for a distance of almost 300 miles. I almost shouted the benediction, I was so

65

filled with joy—joy that He had made possible this mission to Palanan and that a new church had been established for Him. What a thrill to be a missionary!

A few more good-byes—a lot of hand-shaking and farewells—and then I was on the trail again, ready to start home. I grabbed a few bananas for my lunch, donned my pack, and was ready to go by 10 A.M. A few of the young boys went with me as far as the foothills of the first mountains, to be sure I got on the right trail. Then they turned back toward Palanan, and I kept on going—towards home, and Mariam and the children.

Poor Mariam! Little had I dreamed, as I went calmly about my work in Palanan, what she had been going through at home. Those stories in the newspapers must have been harrowing for her. For three weeks she had not known whether I was dead or alive! I was to find out later that the Negrito whom I had paid ten pesos to take out a letter to be mailed at the post office at Ilagan had just used the money to get drunk. The letter was never delivered, and all these weeks Mariam had had not one word. She did not know whether I was dead, lost in the jungle, severely injured—or what. It got so bad that many of our church members wrote her letters eulogizing "Brother Spottswood." "He was a fine brave, young missionary." *Was*, not *is*. All she could do was *wait*. In the years ahead she was to learn, over and over again, that the hardest part of a missionary wife's job is *waiting*—always waiting for some word to come, waiting for her husband to come home.

Thoughts of home and family kept me walking fast, even when my legs were aching, and my knees almost buckled under me. Then, as the darkness of the gloomy jungle closed around me, the eerie loneliness of the place spurred me on. In the deep shadows of the jungle, my nerves became jumpy. I could just see tiny pygmies, bows and arrows cocked. When I reached the camp site, I built a fire as fast as I could to keep away snakes—and head-hunters, I hoped! I had never felt so alone—alone and at the mercy of any Ilongot head-hunter who might heave a spear into my back. While head-hunters are few, there are some —and I was *alone!*

The next morning at five o'clock I was still alive, alive and hungry. After a good breakfast, I started up the steepest part of the trail. About noon I was near the highest peak of the whole trip. Because of the steepness of the trail, and its slipperiness from the rains, I was on my hands and knees most of the day. But I kept going. The scariness of the dark jungle kept me from lingering long in any one place, no matter how tired I felt, or how deeply my shoulder pack dug into my shoulders. Three days, and more than fifty miles later, I reached the first vestiges of civilization, San Mariano. There I was able to catch a jeep to Ilagan, and then a bus for the Cagayan Valley. The hike that had taken Pastor Inis, Pastor Valdez, and me five days before had taken me only three days this time. For this time I was alone— and scared!

God was good. I had gone to Palanan. We had made a start in meeting the physical and the spiritual needs of the people of Palanan. We had started a church. And now I was out, alive, and healthy, and headed for home. Truly, God had been good to me.

# 5

## Home

THERE ARE AS many types of missionary homes as there are different missionaries—and these run up into the thousands—but in all of them there is "a heap o' living." For the house of a missionary out in the remote places in the provinces is much more than just a residence for the missionary family. It is also the "mission station," the literature distribution center for the whole area, a sort of glorified "warehouse" for materials for the area (which, in our case, had to be shipped up clear from Manila), a lending library, often the recreation hall for the M.Y.F. and local church groups, and last but not least, the school for the missionary children. Our home in Tuguegarao in the days and years ahead became a real beehive of activity, morning, noon, and night.

Our days began early! Cecilia Orpilla, our "assistant mother" whom we had found to help Mariam in caring for the house and the three little boys, was a ball of fire from the word "Go!" Between 4:45 and 5 A.M. each day we would hear the back door open, and then a few minutes later the rattle of pots and pans as Cecilia started breakfast. A few minutes later the rhythmical scraping of a coconut husk being "skated" across the floor woke us up thoroughly, and got us started on the day. In the Philippines, as in most of the tropics, floors are not just swept. They are also "skated." The girl places one bare foot on the coconut husk, and the other foot on the floor. Then she

68

shoves off, putting her weight on the coconut husk, stepping, continuing a back-and-forth motion until the strong, stiff fibers of the coconut husk scrub the floor spotlessly clean and give it a high gloss. The steady "Whoosh, thump, whoosh, thump," of Cecilia's skating the floor was a wonderful alarm clock six days of the week. But whenever we could plan a day off, there was no way to turn off the alarm! In the Philippines it is the custom to skate the floors early in the morning, and Cecilia knew only one time to get up in the morning—*early!*

Cecilia was a very real addition to our family. Her tremendous energy and selfless hard work in spite of the hot, humid weather were a constant inspiration to us. Without her, Mariam would never have had the time to share in so much of the work of the church in the Cagayan Valley. She shared in all of our family devotions, and many times in our prayers we gave thanks to God for sending her to us.

Cecilia saved Mariam not only time, but money. She was one of the original Scots; she hated to spend money. She did 95 per cent of all our buying for us. In the market, where there is seldom a "fixed price" for anything, an American is at a great disadvantage in the daily game of bargaining, or haggling over prices. For an American there is only one price—high. Cecilia knew all the "ins" and "outs" of buying, though, and would not spend even one centavo more than she thought a thing was worth. We might go hungry, but we would never eat food that cost too much! Cecilia typified one of the best traits of the Ilocanos, thrift, reminding us often of the old New England Yankees. We were glad to learn that she was saving all her earnings from us, and before we left the Cagayan Valley, she had built a new home for her father in their village farther north.

Breakfast in the Spottswood household was never later than 6 A.M. We soon learned that in the tropics the best time of day to work is in the early morning, before the oppressive heat settles over us. Usually the family had been up and busy for an hour or so by the time we sat down to breakfast. Often we were not alone, either, for visitors would drop in early in the mornings, in time to join us at the table. A pastor's wife would hike in from a far barrio, walking in the early morning while it was still cool, and stop at the mission house to give us a gift of a few eggs, tied up in a handkerchief—eggs which she and her children sorely needed, but which out of her love she wanted to share with her missionary. Or a group of students would come to say good-bye before taking the early Red Line bus to their homes for the week ends. Or the district superintendent would come by to talk over some coming district meeting, before starting out on his journey. And so it went. We found that one of our richest joys as missionaries was this steady stream of visitors to our home. We loved these warmhearted, friendly people. We found that the "fellowship of the table" was the heart of our Christian witness, giving visible expression to the bonds of love which united us as brothers in Christ.

It is true that Asian people—all 1,500,000,000 of them—are very race conscious. Orientals have read in the newspapers that Americans are prejudiced against colored people. They have heard of "Jim Crow" laws in hotels, trains, buses, and theatres. The Communist press has played up every possible incident in the United States, raising the question of America's hypocrisy in preaching democracy. Even our Filipino co-workers—with their beautiful dark eyes, and warmly tanned skins—feel a troubling, though unspoken, question in their minds as they approach the home of a missionary for the first time: "How will I be treated? Will they think of me as somehow inferior because of the color of my skin?"

Thus, the missionary home is very crucial. If the lady of the house genuinely welcomes visitors, and with a warm, friendly, gracious smile urges them, "Won't you come in and sit down? Have a cup of coffee with us," she can build real brotherhood. If the missionaries' co-workers—pastors, deaconesses, laymen, students—feel a warm welcome in the home of the missionary, the news swiftly gets out and spreads through the church and the community. If not, the most eloquent sermon can not erase the barriers which these humble but wise people feel. We learned that brotherhood begins at the table—or it doesn't begin at all. The home, and the fellowship of breaking bread together as Christ did with His disciples in the Upper Room so long ago, is truly a means of grace, and can do as much for the cause of Christ as a hundred sermons.

Morning devotions were usually held in the Spottswood family right after breakfast. Mariam and I both felt a grave sense of responsibility in rearing these sons whom God had entrusted to us, so that in trying to help other people's children, we would not neglect our own. Curran, David, and Stephen sang lustily—in fact, everything they did they did lustily, so that we had a noisy household, to put it mildly. The boys made friends easily with all the neighborhood children, and seemed to enjoy living in Tuguegarao. Sometimes we caught glimpses of their growing awareness of spiritual truths, and their growing sensitivity to spiritual matters. At other times we were not so sure.

For example, one morning during devotions, after a period of robust hymn-singing, Daddy read a section of the Holy Scriptures about sharing, and then told a story and preached a bit about it. In our prayers we each asked God to help us learn to share that day, to share our toys, and our possessions, in a Christlike way. Then we left the table, Daddy went off to the office to work on letters, Mother got ready to teach the boys' home-study class, Cecilia took Stevie into the kitchen with her, and things settled down to the muffled roar of a routine morning. Suddenly, an ear-splitting scream rent the air. I reached the front porch just in time to see Curran knock David to the floor with a fast "right." He stood over his fallen, sprawling brother, and yelled defiantly, "Gimme that ball! What's the matter with you? Don't you know God wants you to share?" There was no

71

guarantee that because these boys were sons of a missionary they would automatically become good! No, it was a long, day-in, day-out process of slow growth, just as in everybody else's home.

We had not been in Tuguegarao too long before Mariam became good friends with Dr. Iderlina Manuel, a beautiful, dark-eyed Spanish woman physician. She became our stand-by in all of the thousand and one emergencies that came up with the children—cut fingers, measles, sore throats, and the countless bruises and bumps that active boys receive—and give. In treating their minor illnesses, and examining them in between times, Dr. Manuel discovered a far more serious symptom. Both Curran and David were having continuing low fever, and this fever, together with leg aches, pointed strongly toward rheumatic fever. She urged us not to be alarmed, but then went on to recommend that the boys stay in bed for quiet bed rest for at least half of every day. Quiet bed rest? For those two wild Indians? Mariam dropped everything to try to carry out the doctor's orders, but those two active, wiggling, restless boys crawled *over* the beds, leaned on their heads *under* the beds, jumped *across* the beds, and did everything in the world except stay *on* the beds. It was all Mariam could do to keep them down. The doctor dropped by to see us regularly in those days, as much to keep up Mariam's morale as to check up on the boys' condition. Her friendly smile became a commonplace around the mission house.

Before many months had passed, Mariam went to see Dr. Manuel at her office, and this time she was the patient. The doctor examined her thoroughly, and then startled her with this question: "Mrs. Spottswood, are there twins in your family . . . or your husband's family?"

"Why, yes, doctor. My grandmother had. . . . Good heavens! Do you mean. . . . I. . . . Oh! . . . My goodness! Do you mean that I am going to have *twins?*"

"Well, it's too early to be sure, but it looks like it."

"Oh, no, doctor! This is just a big American boy. I always have big American boy babies."

"H-m-m-m. We'll see. You can have some X rays taken later on."

We had some exciting times as we awaited the coming of the babies. At the height of the rainy season we had four very important house guests, visiting U.S. college presidents and professors who were making an educational survey of our Methodist schools in the Cagayan Valley. A severe typhoon hit northern Luzon during their survey trip, and when they got back to Tuguegarao, where they were supposed to take a plane to Manila, they found they were marooned. The airfield was flooded, and all flights of the Philippine Air Lines had been canceled. They waited at our house for a day or two, but when there were still no flights, they began to try to find some other way to get out. The bridges over the rivers had been washed away, and there was no possible overland transportation. Buses and cars had been lined up at the rivers for days, waiting for some way to get across. Our visitors waited and worried and chafed at the bit. Mariam by this time was having to spend many of her daytime hours resting, and so she welcomed the presence of those educators. Their conversation was a stimulating change from the constant chatter of four- and five-year-olds which was her daily intellectual fare. She would sit in a big chair on the porch, with her feet propped up on cushions, and reign like a queen over this interesting household, completely unconcerned over the rain which poured steadily down in solid sheets outside the house.

But while Mariam was enjoying our visitors and the pleasant break they made in the loneliness which so often engulfs the missionary wife in isolated places, the good doctors were getting more and more desperate. They waited. They discussed the rain. They made plans. They worried. They *had* to go to Manila. Finally, they thought of sending a telegram to the American Embassy: "Medical emergency. Please send small plane to

73

Tuguegarao." They figured that even though the airstrip was still too soft for a large plane, a small one might be able to land safely. Mariam was to be the "medical emergency." It was true that Dr. Manuel had advised her to go to Manila to have X rays taken. Our visiting V.I.P.s hoped that if a plane came to take her out, at least Dr. Davis, the chairman of the Educational Survey Team, would be able to get a ride out too. The U.S. Air Force promised to send a plane the next day, if it didn't rain. However, the field drained off so much during the night that Philippine Air Lines scheduled two flights the next morning. Since these were to be their first flights in almost two weeks, there was a long line of names on the waiting list. I knew that Dr. Davis was badly needed in Manila for a Seminary meeting, and so I graciously suggested that he go along with Mariam on the first trip, and I would wait and take a chance on getting a seat on the second flight. That good gentleman—I don't remember whether he was a bachelor or not—took one good look at Mariam's bulge, and quickly declined. "Oh, no! No! I think you'd better go ahead!"

Two X rays were made in Manila, but they were inconclusive. Worse, they were disturbing. The shadows of two little heads could be seen, but no backbones or leg bones. Mariam began to have horrible fears. Suppose these were joined twins, or there were some other deformity. She was faced with a tremendous decision. The doctors recommended that she stay in Manila to await the babies' birth, where she would be in a modern hospital that could offer oxygen, blood, and expert medical care in case of any emergencies. And yet—Tuguegarao was home, and Tuguegarao was where Mother was needed, to look after the little ones she already had. She wanted to be with Curran and David, both still in bed. Then there was Stephen to be considered, not quite two years old, and too young to understand if his mother stayed away for at least six weeks. She had to do what her own mind and heart dictated. I could only promise to back her up in whatever decision she made.

She decided to have the babies in Tuguegarao! And what an easy, happy time it turned out to be for all of us the day the twins actually made their appearance! The whole neighborhood perked up in anticipation when they saw Mariam and me hop into our little army jeep and rush down the street towards the provincial hospital. Dr. Manuel arrived breathlesly a few minutes after we got there, looked at Mariam, and said, "Can you still walk?" "Sure," Mariam replied, and so she walked back to the operating room, where Dr. Manuel was planning to deliver the babies.

Mariam climbed up on the table, and the doctor began scrubbing up, when all of a sudden Philip John Spottswood announced his arrival with a lusty yell. Within ten minutes the nurse, "Miss Cab," was shouting, "It's another boy!" as Paul Gregory pushed his way into the family circle. Mariam raised herself up on one elbow to be *sure* there wasn't some mistake about his sex. (We had ordered *one* girl, and here we were, getting *two* boys!) Somebody outside the hospital window began cranking up the old army weapons-carrier that was to serve as an ambulance, for Dr. Manuel had decided that Mariam would be happier in her own room at home than in the old, battered, half-cement, half-bamboo hospital, which had not been restored since the days of the heavy fighting during the war. As soon as the babies were cleaned up and dressed, and Dr. Manuel took off her one glove (she never got the second one on), Mariam was carried out to the truck on a stretcher, with a baby boy tucked under each arm.

When we rolled up to the mission house again, just one hour after we had left in such a hurry, there were hundreds of people lined up around the fence to see Mariam and the babies. Mariam smiled and waved happily to them all, and in a few minutes she was safely back in her own bed—still with the same dress on.

We had not bothered with the niceties of hospital routine that seem so necessary in America—the pre-delivery preparations, drugs, the starched white uniforms, the frilly nightgowns—but we had the babies, and that was what counted.

The crowning joy for Mariam was the reaction of our three boys when she got home. They tiptoed timidly into Mother's room, lined up beside the bed and with round, incredulous eyes stared from Mother over to the crib, where two little black heads cuddled side by side, and then back to Mother, and then finally whispered in awe-struck gasps, "You *did* have two, didn't you, Mother?" They knew she was *supposed* to have twins, but they had not really believed such a miracle was possible. Now, with great joy and thanksgiving in our hearts we all began to delight in these two pink, roly-poly little bundles that God had given us.

Life never grew monotonous in the days that lay ahead. If Mariam had thought she was busy B.T. (Before the Twins), she was doubly and triply so now. We found a wonderful helper in Flora Dulin, a cheerful, sunny-dispositioned girl, who was to wash hundreds and hundreds of diapers in the days ahead, but whose contribution to the family could never be measured in terms of work alone. She gave us love and loyalty—and the memory of Cecilia and Flora, each with a twin perched jauntily on one hip as they went about their household chores, is etched indelibly on our minds as we remember those early days of our life in Tuguegarao.

Mariam was finding that the life of a missionary wife was varied, but always full. As the "missionary for Tuguegarao," she did regular visitation to the sick and the shut-ins of our community. I remember particularly Nena, whom Mariam used to visit every week or two, taking along a chicken or other gift of food, some medicines, and some reading material. I remember vividly the first time I met Nena. She was as thin as a rail, so skinny I wondered how on earth she had stayed alive. She was about thirty-five years old, but had had tuberculosis for the past five years. Nearly five feet tall, she weighed only about seventy-five pounds. Her head seemed to be too large for her thin, tubercular body. Yet she was a joyous Christian, and though she was bedridden much of the time, she never complained. She felt a real sense of responsibility to *work* for Christ, and so, since she was not strong enough to go out visiting in the neighborhood, she had conceived the idea of holding a Sunday school class for children on her front porch on Sunday afternoons. One of the most inspiring sights of my life is the picture of that scrawny, sickly woman with big brown eyes and a radiant smile, sitting on an old army cot, teaching five or six little barefoot children about the love of Christ.

Besides working with the women of the church, Mariam also found that she was the counselor for the Methodist Youth Fellowship. Working with these able high-school and college students proved to be a very rewarding experience, for they were eager and alert, and took readily to suggestions for activities for Christian witnessing and sharing. Before long Mariam had four different teams of MYFers going out each Sunday afternoon to different neighboring barrios, or small villages, to teach Sunday school classes for children. What gay times they used to have! Mariam used to fill our army jeep with young people. They would drive out to a barrio, circle around the paths and road-ways while people stared curiously at this strange "Americano" and the laughing, singing, shouting boys and girls with her, and then stop the jeep in an empty, cleared field somewhere. Within seconds the jeep would be surrounded by a group of twenty to thirty children. Our MYFers would hop out of the jeep, offer to teach the children some games, lead them in pep songs, and then tell them some stories. Our Sunday school was on! Then they would ask the children if they wanted to do it again the next Sunday, and the answer was always a chorused "Yes!" Through these Sunday afternoon outdoor classes were laid the foundations for several of our strong village churches that exist today.

Another of Mariam's home-town responsibilities was the holding of religious services in the provincial jail. She inspired some of the young adults of the church to join her in visiting the young men there. Most of them looked so young and innocent, and yet Mariam knew that the group included robbers, murderers, and Communist-led "Huks" who were actively fighting the government forces all up and down the Cagayan Valley. The services had to be held in the open courtyard in the center of the jail, the men seated on backless board benches, free to get up and wander away if they were bored. To hold the interest of these men a speaker had to have a real message, a genuine experience of Christ to share. It was a challenge! The remarkable thing was the number of men who stayed for the service each Sunday, who asked for Bibles, and who wrote Mariam letters, even after we moved away.

However, Mariam's biggest responsibility was always her home —and what an exciting, sometimes frightening, but always satisfying responsibility it was. Our home life consisted of one crisis after another. One day the twins ate black shoe polish, and had to be rushed to the hospital to have their stomachs pumped. Another day, I was delirious with the fever of malaria, and nearly scared Mariam to death by repeating over and over again, "Who am I? What's my name? I can't think. I can't *think!*" She was sure I was mentally deranged for life. Another day a severe earthquake so shook our house that Mariam sprawled flat on the floor in trying to round a fast corner to grab the boys and lead them outside the seemingly about-to-collapse house. One of our more hectic memories was the day the jeep, parked just outside the kitchen door, caught fire. I was testing the motor generator, which was loaded in the jeep for a trip to a nearby church for a showing of religious movies. A spark exploded in the leaking gas from the carburetor, and in a matter of minutes the whole jeep had gone up in flames. Why the house did not also catch fire from the fiercely burning jeep, just a few feet away, I'll never know!

# HOME

Five restless, active, bouncing boys kept things hopping around the house. Mariam and I were fairly accustomed to the daily recurring crises that descended upon us and could keep reasonably calm. But occasionally our family crises spilled over into our church life, and then there was some explaining to do. One day I was feeling pretty satisfied, after having made some calls on the mayor, the governor, and other government officials, and came home with a good feeling that perhaps we "Protestantes," usually looked down upon in Catholic communities, were beginning to win some respect in the eyes of the people. I passed through our back yard, filled to overflowing with our boys and a group of neighborhood children, riding tricycles, pulling wagons, swinging, and I thought with pleasure, "We are really becoming accepted by our Filipino friends."

I had not noticed anything amiss as I walked through the group of children and entered the house. I had not seen that Curran, who was then about six years old, had surreptitiously taken the big kitchen knife out of Cecilia's drawer, and was busily transforming an old wooden block into what he hoped would look like a real army jeep. Some of the other older boys in the group were also trying to make a jeep, and as they got more and more engrossed, the big knife was more and more in demand. It passed from boy to boy, but not always peaceably. Curran was getting increasingly annoyed, and finally, he grabbed the knife from another boy. In the fight that followed, the boy's arm was cut. The boy screamed, and Mariam came running. She saw a gash about half an inch long. It was quite shallow, but fearing that the boy's parents might not dress it properly or keep the wound clean, Mariam took him down to Dr. Manuel's office to have the cut treated. Everything was settled amicably and Curran and his companion parted friends, Curran a bit awestricken over what he had done, and the other boy quite proud of his visit to the doctor and his beautiful bandage. We thought the matter was ended. But we reckoned without gossip. The next day our back yard was empty. The story had spread like wildfire all over town. "The missionary's son stabbed a Filipino boy! He had to be rushed to the doctor to save his life!" It took us quite a while to live that one down.

Much of the time Mariam was left at home with the children, while I traveled up and down the Cagayan Valley with the superintendents, visiting churches and attending district meetings. One district conference stands out particularly in my mind —the conference where I got my A no. 1, super de luxe stomach ache. I was up in Sanchez Mira, a little town on the far northern coast of Luzon. I was sitting in the little bamboo church, fighting off mosquitoes, and wiggling on the hard bamboo bench. Gradually I became aware that my discomfort had spread to the front of my anatomy, where I was feeling occasional sharp twinges of pain. "Those green bananas we ate for supper," I thought, and tried to get my mind back on the Ilocano sermon that was being given in the little chapel.

The pains could not be pushed aside. During the night they got steadily worse. "Boy, those bananas have done terrible things to my digestion!" I tossed and turned on the floor where I was sleeping, and finally, about 3 A.M. the horrible thought crossed my mind, "Suppose this isn't indigestion? Suppose it's appendicitis!"

In the morning I approached Brother Tovera and suggested that we start back to Tuguegarao, but he was horrified. The conference was not over. He could not think of leaving early. I did not like the idea of driving the jeep alone for a whole day. I knew that if I should get worse—the pain was now drawing my right leg up in spasms—I might not be able to drive the jeep. Yet the thought of having acute appendicitis in this desolate place, where there was no doctor, no nurse, no hospital, made me realize that I just had to get home. I started out early in the morning, driving just as hard and as fast as that little jeep would go. And God was with me, for I crossed the ferry over the rushing, rain-swollen Camalaniugan River just minutes before the huge steel cable snapped! I learned later that mine was the last car to get across the river for two weeks. If I had not started just when I did, I would have been trapped on the other side of the raging river.

I reached Tuguegarao late in the afternoon. Mariam took one look at me and sent for Dr. Manuel. She took me to the hospital for a blood count, stuck me full of penicillin and streptomycin and intimated that an operation might be necessary the following morning. She decided to keep me in the hospital overnight, just to be safe, but assured Mariam everything was under control and she could go on home to put the children to bed. I breathed a sigh of relief. The medicines she had given me had relieved the pain, and after the long drive and the sleepless hours the night before, I was beginning to feel drowsy. The attendants kept coming in and out, and occasionally a nurse would stick another needle in me, but I wasn't paying too much attention. Then I suddenly heard the doctor's voice bark out the command, "Send for Mrs. Spottswood. I'll operate at once!"

I bolted upright, and cold chills went down my spine. I knew the situation must be getting serious, or Dr. Manuel would never risk an operation at night, with the only light in the temporary bamboo hospital a flickering bulb powered by a used army generator that sometimes ran, and sometimes did not.

An orderly came in, and said, "Let's go." I went, with fear in my heart, and a tight, apprehensive coldness in my stomach. We came to a room covered with screen wire, almost completely bare except for a dilapidated table in the center. I crawled up on the table, and the orderly began to shave my side, and paint it with iodine. Then he said, "Put your arm here." I obeyed, and within seconds that arm was strapped tight. Then the other arm was strapped down, and next my ankles and thighs. A heavy strap was tightened across my chest, so that the only thing left on me that could still move was my eyes. Cold sweat broke out on my forehead as I remembered that in this out-of-

81

the-way place there was no general anesthesia. Pictures of medieval torture chambers flashed through my mind.

The doctor came in, followed by Mariam, looking white and scared. First, the doctor injected a large dose of pain-killer into the abdomen, then smiled reassuringly, and set to work. I saw her reach for a scalpel. I winced and gritted my teeth. I could just dully feel the knife as it cut through the first layer of tissue, and then another. I was remembering the names of the parts of the body I had learned back in my old physical education days, and wondering if the doctor knew as much as I knew. Mariam, who was standing by my shoulder, says I began to talk and talk, telling all about an appendectomy I had once watched. I remembered that it had taken only about thirty-five minutes. "Well, if it doesn't get any worse than this," I thought, "I can take it."

The snip, snip of the hemostats as they clamped off the various blood vessels sounded re-assuring. The minutes wore on. The humid heat of the tropics began to show in the glistening faces of the doctor and the surgical nurse. It had been nearly an hour now, and I knew they ought to be beginning to close the wound. The local anesthesia was wearing off and I began to twist and jerk in pain as the doctor continued to probe. I whispered to Mariam, "What are they doing?" Her answer appalled me, "Still looking for the appendix. It's hidden, and there are many adhesions." The search continued, and the operation went on for another hour. By this time I was in agony. I bit my lip until the warm, salty blood seeped into my mouth. I knew something was wrong, for the sweat was now pouring off the doctor's face, and she looked distinctly worried. I learned later from Mariam that the appendix was already gangrenous, so that every time the doctor touched it with her instruments, it ruptured. I had now been on the operating table in this dimly lit "chamber of horrors" for two hours.

Just at the height of our anxious waiting, as I began to despair of ever getting out of there alive, an orderly opened the door of the operating room, and as he did so, a large black bat flew into the room. "Omen of death," I thought, as I watched the orderly grab a fly swatter and begin to chase the bat back and forth across the room. Round and round the operating table it went, and I could just imagine the millions and millions of germs that were dropping into the open wound. With a final, well-aimed blow the orderly knocked it down, and fortunately it landed over to the right of the table. With an audible sigh, the doctor got back to her work. I closed my eyes again, but not before noticing that Mariam was still there beside me, praying silently.

The hands of the clock pushed on toward the third hour. About 11 P.M. I felt the sharp sting of the needle and the bite and tug of the sutures. The ordeal was over. Thanks to the skill of Dr. Manuel, and the miracle powers of modern medicines, four days later I was up and by the next week life went back to normal.

About a week later, we were just sitting down to breakfast when a hesitant tap-tap began to sound at the front door. Breakfast time in the Spottswood household is not a time of light and joy—at least not until we've had that second cup of coffee. As the knocking at the door continued, I glanced at my watch —6:02 A.M.—and grumbled, as I stalked to the door, "I wish people would wait until at least 7 A.M. before they start pounding on our door."

There, standing at our door, was one of our oldest, most loyal accepted supply pastors, the Reverend Mamerto Agustin. His wife was standing a little behind him, and the children were seated on the front steps. They were flushed with fever. I repented of my inhospitable feelings, and urged them to come in. Mariam rushed forward and began talking to them in their own dialect. Sensing the seriousness of their condition, she put them in the jeep and rushed to the provincial hospital. The resident doctor admitted them to the ward, a wide open room thirty by forty feet, with about twenty metal cots. The patients were separated from the corridor by a thin white cloth stretched over a metal stand. Pastor Agustin and his family were put to bed, and the doctor began first to examine the twelve-year-old boy, who seemed to be the weakest. Mariam told the nurse she would be back later, and then went back home to finish her breakfast and get the "Spottswood School" under way.

Later in the morning she returned to the hospital, carrying a large chicken, some milk, and some vitamins. This extra food was necessary because about 90 per cent of the hospital cases were charity cases, and the government appropriations could not provide more than the smallest amount of rice and soup for them. Mariam took her gifts to the kitchen and then looked for the attending physician. He greeted her smile with a somber, serious look. "All of this family are suffering from beri-beri and severe malnutrition. The boy's the worst. He has an advanced case of nephritis. I don't know whether we can save him or not."

The story came out slowly. Pastor and Mrs. Agustin were assigned to a little rural church near Baggao, way up the river in the foothills of the Sierra Madre mountains in a barrio called Tallung. The church was new and the members few, so the pastoral support was meager. The situation got steadily worse, for a severe typhoon hit northeast Luzon and destroyed all the crops. The next time the rice seedlings came up they were again destroyed by heavy rains and floods. Pastor Agustin and his family, having no means of support but the gifts of the members, got less and less food to eat as the farmers got less and less crops. Finally, they were down to a few handfuls of dried corn a day and some green bananas when they could find them. His wife urged him to quit, to leave his assignment and go to live with their relatives in the lowlands. The old pastor was sorely tempted. But he was a true shepherd of his little flock. They stayed at their post, and daily they grew weaker.

Mariam stayed at their bedsides all afternoon. Late that afternoon she came home. She walked in slowly, silently, her eyes red from weeping. She began to answer the question in my eyes, saying, "The little boy died." Then she choked up.

We went around and told the members of the church in Tuguegarao of the plight of these devoted Christian workers, and many people contributed from their own none-too-plentiful stores of rice, chickens, and eggs. Mariam gave milk and vitamins, and the other members of the Women's Society gave fruits and vegetables, and presently the future of the rest of the family looked more hopeful.

The next day we loaded a plain, rough wooden box in the back of the jeep, and the pastor and a few friends rode out to the graveyard to inter the mortal remains of the little boy. As we rode back, silently, sadly, a four-word refrain kept pounding on my brain: "He died of starvation. He died of starvation. . . ." Standing beside the shallow grave, I had felt the rubber tire of fat around my own waist, and been condemned. I had come out to the Philippines to *preach* the way of the cross. Pastor Agustin *lived* it.

Many times in the years of my missionary service I have been tempted to quit. When the going was tough, when the outlook seemed so hopeless, I have been strongly tempted to go back to comfortable America. But always the picture of Pastor Agustin standing beside the grave of his son has flashed before my eyes, and the memory of his utter commitment to his Lord has kept my feet steady on the "strait and narrow way" of the high calling of a missionary of Jesus Christ.

# 6

## Crash in the Jungle

She was a tall, blonde, efficient-looking nurse, spic and span in a stiffly starched, freshly pressed white uniform. She was just three months out of the Brooklyn Methodist Hospital in Brooklyn, New York. Her name was Miss Dorothy Edwards, R.N.

"So you have come out to be the director of the Methodist Mobile Medical Clinic, to be located in the giant Cagayan Valley?"

"Yes."

"Got your doctor?"

"Yes, Dr. George Ros."

"Who else is on your staff?" I asked her.

"Another nurse, Miss Josefina Cabanilla," she replied, "and a driver-mechanic, Camilo Toledo."

"When will you start your work?"

"Just as soon as our medical supplies arrive. They are on the way up the valley now in our new truck."

"Would you and your staff be willing to start your work with a really tough and possibly dangerous assignment?" I challenged her.

Dorothy's eyes widened, "What is it?"

I began to tell her about the need of Palanan. "A few months ago, just before the rainy season last year, two very severe typhoons hit a community of about 5000 people over on the east coast, along the Pacific Ocean. The food supply was just about wiped out. Last year I went in with a nurse, an agriculturist, and a deaconess, and we gave emergency help, but we need some professionals to go in and do a thorough job of ministering to these people. This is a tremendous job. It will call for everything you've ever learned—and then some. It would mean that you and your medical staff would have to spend at least a week in each of the barrios, where no doctor has ever penetrated before. You will meet all the diseases stemming from malnutrition, or semi-starvation . . . people eating only two meals a day, of dried corn, a few bananas, a coconut, or an occasional fish. Tuberculosis will rank high on the list. Almost every person you meet will have malaria in one form or another. I doubt if ever again in your life you'll see greater need."

"How would we get there? Isn't that way over on the other side of the mountains?"

"In my plane."

Again her eyes widened and she asked slowly, "Is that the same plane that was wrecked there seven or eight months ago?"

I admitted that it was, but assured her that it was still a good plane, not more than five years old. I told her the remarkable story of how Leland Archer, a Caltex executive and a wonderful friend, had flown a new propellor over to Palanan for me. And I told her the even more incredible story of the cooperation of the U. S. Embassy, the U. S. Air Force, and the U. S. Navy in getting a practically new wing carried in to Palanan to replace the damaged one. I pulled out a newspaper clipping from the *Manila Bulletin* and began to read the story under the heading: "Plane Wing Shipped to Flying Missionary": "The U. S. Navy Fleet Tug *Molala* departed from Cavite last Wednesday for Palanan Bay on the northern coast of Luzon with an airplane wing for C. L. Spottswood, flying Methodist missionary. The arrival of the *Molala* tomorrow morning will mark the culmination of a cooperative effort by the U. S. Air Force, the U. S. Army, the U. S. Navy, and the American Embassy. Rev. Mr.

Spottswood badly damaged the wing of his L-5 airplane several weeks ago landing at the northern Luzon port with a cargo of medicine and supplies for the people of the area. Because of the lack of communications, he was reported missing for several days. The same lack of communications made it impossible for Rev. Mr. Spottswood to arrange for transportation of a new wing after he had secured one through the aid of Major General Howard M. Turner, Commanding Officer of the 13th Air Force at Clark Field. The possibility of flying the wing into Palanan was explored and found to be impossible, since the small field could not accommodate a large plane, and the wing was too bulky to be carried by a small aircraft or helicopter. The PBY planes at Sangley Point could carry the wing, but could not land on the water without damage to both plane and wing.

"Chargé D'Affaires Thomas H. Lockett explained the situation to Vice Admiral Badger during his recent visit and asked for his suggestions. The Commander of the Western Pacific Fleet offered to permit the seagoing tug *Molala* to drop the wing off at Palanan on its projected northward voyage. General Howard Turner had the wing flown to Sangley Point where it was loaded on the tug."

The fact that my small plane was again flying was a marvelous tribute to a lot of wonderful military persons, both officers and men, who are not usually thought of as being particularly interested in missionaries or religion. First of all, the men at the base at Clark Field turned the place upside down trying to find a wing. They finally got one from the junk yard. Second, there were all the unnamed men who voluntarily spent countless hours of their free time to rebuild and re-cover the wing.

With the new wing I had a plane in good flying condition. Now I was presenting the challenge to Dorothy and her medical team for a real mission to Palanan. She said she would pray about it. A week later a telegram from Dorothy arrived with

88

these thrilling words: "Medical unit volunteers Palanan mission four weeks."

We had the plane. I now had the medical unit to go. But I still needed money for all the gas and oil that would be required to take in all of the personnel and supplies. I flew down to Clark Field and told Chaplain Warren Ferguson of the Base Chapel the story of our mission the past year to Palanan, and of the present need there. I told him about the clinic's being willing to go, but our need for about $300 for plane and trucking expenses. He and Captain Hank Parker, our "Good Samaritan" pilot of the previous summer, were both interested and enthusiastic, and said, "Listen, you come to the service tomorrow and tell these people about Palanan, and we'll see what happens."

In the chapel the next morning, after a careful preparation by Chaplain Ferguson, I stood up to present to the assembled men of the base, and their wives and families, the burning need for a mission to Palanan, the magnificent opportunity to take in a real medical team, and the need for the money for expenses. I presented the amount needed with great fear and misgivings. Could we get that kind of money from these "hardhearted" service people? We needed a genuine miracle to find $300 in the next twenty-four hours. I say miracle, because the chaplain had told me the usual Sunday offering was about $100, and from this they had certain regular expenses to be taken. After my plea for help for the people of Palanan, the ushers came forward and took up a special offering. A few minutes later an awed young man rushed up to Chaplain Ferguson and whispered, "Sir, that offering was over $250!" The chaplain turned to me quietly and said, "I'll give you a personal check for the balance."

Here was a real miracle of love! As I turned to go toward the back of the church, the chaplain said to me, "Don't forget the men and women of the Base Chapel will be praying for you." There were tears in his eyes. Suddenly something happened to my throat, and I could not say a word. I bobbed my head up

89

and down, and turned quickly to hide the tears of thankfulness in my own eyes. Truly, it had been a miracle of love. Yesterday, I had no money for this mission. This morning I had all the money that was necessary. God, moving the hearts of ordinary men and women, and a dedicated young chaplain, had done all that was necessary.

That experience taught me a great lesson about U. S. Service and Embassy personnel. They are all hemmed in and bound up by red tape and service responsibility, but show these men and woman a great human need and red tape goes out the window. From General Turner, Admiral Badger, and Chargé D'Affaires Lovett down to the last USN bos'n's mate who had the extra tough job of floating the new wing, (measuring 16 feet by 6 feet), up the narrow, shallow stream from Palanan Bay into the town, the entire project had called for a lot of extra volunteer effort on the part of many, many people—tough-skinned twentieth-century Americans, who showed that under the surface they hadn't changed much from their eighteenth-century pioneer cousins. They got the job done!

As soon as the drums of aviation gasoline arrived at the Ilagan, Isabela, airport, we started flying. It was the same old routine— 3000 to 4000 pounds of supplies and personnel to be transported to Palanan, about fifty or sixty miles over seven ranges of mountain peaks rising up between the Cagayan Valley and the Pacific Coast. Dorothy and the team and I got all the boxes of supplies moved to the airport, and we were ready to start. The clinic was eager to tackle the first assignment. I knew how desperate was the need for their services, and I was eager to get them there. With full hearts we all knelt in prayer on our mats on the floor of the little shack there at the airport, where we had decided to sleep to get an early dawn take-off for the first flight. We thanked God for giving us this opportunity to serve, and prayed for His strength to take us through.

But then came *rain*! The drops began pounding on the tin

roof of our shack in the middle of the night. The rain became harder, and continued all the next day. The second day, while we restlessly paced the little airport shack, anxiously scanning the sky, the rain continued to pour. By the third day we were getting desperate. We had only thirty days to cover the four or five barrios of Palanan, and it meant a tough schedule of packing and unpacking a hundred or so boxes of medicines and supplies and hiking from place to place. We had to get moving.

Just as our nerves were at the breaking point, the sun came out and we got started. On the first flight I took in Dorothy Edwards and 100 pounds of the most needed medical supplies. We landed safely, and she immediately began to make the necessary arrangements for the clinic, while I returned to the Ilagan airstrip for a second load.

This time I decided to take Miss Josefina Cabanilla, and another load of medical supplies. "Miss Cab," as she is affectionately nicknamed, is a jolly, roly-poly person of boundless energy, and an even bigger heart. She was still joking as she crawled into the plane for this, her first plane ride, but as I began to strap her in tightly, her eyes widened with fear. Just before I started the engine, I asked her, "Would you like to say a short prayer for us, Miss Cab?" She would—and she began to pray with great earnestness. How she prayed! She prayed for the pilot, she prayed for the engine, she prayed for each wing, she prayed for the gas, and most of all, she prayed for the weather. I relaxed. I knew I was flying in the most prayed-for-airplane in the Philippines. I would be flying over those rugged, trackless jungles, with God's hands holding up the wings.

With such a beginning, and with Miss Cab's continuous minute-by-minute prayers, we made it! As the plane zipped across the river, and the wheels hit the sandy gravel and began to slow down in the deeper sand of the river bank, I was startled to hear a mighty *"Praise the Lord, Praise the Lord! We made it!"* And now Miss Cab's face was lit up like an electric signboard with a huge smile of relief and thanksgiving. On the safety of level ground, no longer timid nor afraid, she began giving instructions to the men to unload the plane, with all the assurance of a top sergeant—and a voice to match!

Other flights back and forth from Ilagan to Palanan followed in quick succession. On the second or third day Dorothy asked me casually if I thought we could carry the complete audio-visual unit in the plane. This included a 2500-watt motor generator weighing about 300 pounds, the 16 mm. movie projector, cables, microphone, large outdoor loudspeaker horn, and about 100 pounds of films. I examined the motor generator, and found it could be disassembled. "We could sure try!" I answered, and then we began studying the equipment and calculating the weight, piece by piece, to make doubly sure. The list was formidable and added up to over 1000 pounds. Camilo Toledo, the driver-mechanic of the Mobile Clinic, began to take apart the motor generator. Laboriously we got everything loaded into the plane, and after two trips the whole A.V. unit was flown in and unloaded on the beach at Palanan. We were really excited talking about how happy the people would be to know there would be movies. We wanted to see the looks on the faces of people who would be seeing movies for the first time.

There was just one more flight to be made and the job would be done. My companion on this last flight was Camilo, the young mechanic. He was just out of the National School of Arts and Trades in Manila, a friendly, happy person, with a sunny smile that made children love him. But behind this smile was the rowdy, restless, roustabout soul of a young man who turned up his nose at "authority," who laughed at church, who had been thrown in jail for drinking and gambling on more than one occasion. However, he was really a hard worker, and a good mechanic. He knew a jeep like the back of his hand.

The gas tanks were now full to the brim, and it was time to go. Camilo was very quiet and thoughtful as we tied down the last odds and ends of equipment and medicines, but he was a tough "man of the world" and was not going to come right out and admit that he was scared to go with me. Minutes later we taxied out on the airstrip, waited for a few carabaos to wander off the runway, checked the magnetos, and then I turned to see if Camilo's safety belt was tightly fastened. He was sitting bolt upright, his hands gripping tightly the metal tubing along the sides until his knuckles stood out white and bold. We had a prayer together, and then were off, beginning our gradual climb over the thickly wooded Sierra Madre mountains which separated us from Palanan.

Ten minutes later I yelled back at Camilo to look at the beautiful, peaceful Pacific in the distance. We could see the white horses of the waves as they galloped into the shore at Palanan Bay. For the first time on the flight I saw Camilo loosen his deathlike grip on the metal tubing. He took a deep breath in appreciation of the beauty of the scene before us, and began to relax. I was humming "This is my Father's world," and I could see Camilo smile momentarily, as he remembered too those beautiful words: "Of rocks and trees, of skies and seas, His hands the wonders wrought."

However, as we approached Palanan, and I began to lower the plane for the river-bank landing field, Camilo grabbed the metal tubing again, and took care of his main business—holding on! As Palanan came more sharply in focus, I was noticing the beauty of the day—the cobalt blue sky, the rich green countryside, the low white clouds scudding across the horizon. "Oh, what a beautiful day!" I breathed. But Camilo wasn't talking to me. As I banked into landing position, a glance at Camilo told me he was really punishing that metal he was holding so tightly. His eyes were closed, and his lips were moving. I pulled on flaps, steadied the needle at 70 m.p.h., and we were right on the beam. Full flaps now, and we were right over the river, just seconds to go before touchdown.

Suddenly . . . right over the center of the river . . . the plane abruptly dropped . . . hit the water . . . bounced . . . nosed over . . . and was upside down . . . half in the water . . . and the tail out. I hung upside down for a second or two, noted all arms and legs were in working order, unhooked my safety belt, landed on my head, righted myself and crawled out. I walked around the plane. "O my gosh . . . Camilo!" I got down on my hands and knees, opened the ambulance door, and there was Camilo, upside down, hands still frozen to the metal tubing, eyes closed, still praying. I got him out, and in minutes the river bank was alive with people trying to get near to see the plane. Dorothy, Dr. Ros, and Miss Cab came rushing up to bind up our wounds, sew up our gaping holes, reduce the fractures. But search as they would, they could not find anything to sew up or repair, for—unbelievable as it sounds—we had lived through a plane crash at 60 m.p.h. into a river, and had only one or two small bruises and scratches to show for it. Camilo was as white as a sheet—but the doctor could not find any injury at all, external or internal. I guess it was a good thing he was holding on so tight! I had one small cut and that was all—except for one badly damaged ego.

After studying the crash very carefully, I finally decided the cause must have been a very simple one. The plane was coming in at the hottest part of the day, about two o'clock in the afternoon. At that time there was an updraft caused by the hot air rising from the hot white sand of the beach under the noontime sun. Conversely, when the plane went from the hot air over the beach to the cold air over the cold mountain stream, there was a sharp downdraft, which sucked the plane down and caused the wreck. The effect was disaster. A $5000 airplane was utterly destroyed. Well, anyway, we were there. All of the members of the team were in, we had our supplies, and we had a tremendous job to do. "Let's get going!" I said to the clinic staff—and we did!

# CRASH IN THE JUNGLE

While we were busily starting our work in Palanan, Mariam was going through the same old story at home—the agonizing wait for news of our safe arrival. I had promised to send out a messenger with a letter reporting the last flight in. Well, I sent out the letter, but it never reached Tuguegarao. Rumors did, though—rumors of a plane crash, of the wreck. All sorts of garbled stories filtered out. Once again I was "missing," presumed crashed in the jungle. I had planned to fly back to Tuguegarao soon after we got things started in Palanan, and so when the little red and silver ambulance plane did not show up on schedule, the folks in town began thinking, and whispering, and then saying aloud. "Reverend Spottswood's had another plane crash. He was supposed to return yesterday, but he didn't." In a small town bad news travels like wildfire, and before nightfall of the second day the whole town was buzzing with the news.

As the tension mounted in the mission house, Mariam tried to keep cheerful. She carried on bravely, but all the while the question kept nagging at her, "How can I rear five loud, husky, jumping, running lads, without a father? How. . . . How?" Oh, the sleepless nights, the red-eyed mornings! Every morning in family devotions five little heads bowed in quavering prayer that always ended, "And please, God, bring Daddy home safely."

By the end of the first week past my expected visit home, the townspeople and members of the church were certain I was dead. After all, they realized that it was possible for a man to hike out in five days in that season of the year. "If he were alive, we'd have heard," they reasoned. By the middle of the second week members of the church began to talk of the possibility of a memorial service. A funeral service was impossible —no body! The next best thing would be to have a memorial service. The pastor went quietly ahead with plans. The next Sunday when Mariam entered the church, with five little boys following in line behind her, all eyes turned on the stricken family. The pastor prayed a long prayer for those who have given their lives in the Master's service. The fourth verse of every hymn was always about the "Home up yonder." Tears flowed freely during the service.

In the meantime, the "ghost" of the Reverend C. L. Spottswood was very actively at work in Palanan with a top-flight medical clinic staff, visiting from village to village, and eating an astonishing amount of food for a "ghost!"

We found that our biggest job was to minister to those who, because of semi-starvation for many weeks and months, were already victims of weakening and crippling tuberculosis. This horrible illness had affected from 20 to 30 per cent of all those who came to the clinic for examination, and during our one month stay there, there were six deaths from that dread killer. The first week the clinic stayed in the "centro," or central town of Palanan, from which the other villages radiate. At first there were very few patients, not more than ten or fifteen people the first day. The people were quite shy, and afraid of the unknown. However, as news of the friendly nurses, the kindly doctor, and the low costs—even the minimal charge made by the clinic for medicines and treatment could be paid in bananas, eggs, or services, if the people had no money—began to spread throughout the community, the people relaxed somewhat and the daily clinic load of patients jumped.

Our best publicity was the "cine!" The very first night we got the motor generator going, and people appeared from all sides—hundreds and hundreds and hundreds of them—when the news got around that movies would be shown, the first movies to be shown on the barren, isolated eastern coast since the very beginning of Time. Even large numbers of Negrito pygmies had come down from the mountains and from their interior river settlements and were gathered expectantly around the projector, bows and arrows slung over their shoulders, spears held upright in their hands. The excitement was at a fever pitch. The motor generator was already running. Camilo had connected the sound apparatus, and the amplifier was humming softly under its breath. Everybody was almost on tiptoe. "Imagine a real *cine!*" Excited whispers ran around the group of packed, steaming men, women, and children. Camilo started the projector—and found that he had inadvertently turned the sound to highest volume. Suddenly the screen was filled with running, leaping figures, and a thunderous noise was coming out. The tiny Negritos were scared out of their wits, and immediately drew back their spears, and their bows and arrows, and prepared for war. Only the quickest action kept the screen from being slaughtered. Camilo turned off the sound, stopped the film which he was only testing, and pandemonium subsided!

The first film was a technicolor cartoon, "Malaria," one of the very excellent health films prepared by Walt Disney for educational use in South American countries. We learned to appreciate very much the skill with which these health films presented important truths in cartoon, easy-to-understand form. The next film was one on "Infant Care." After each picture Dr. Ros or Miss Cab gave an explanation through an interpreter, and then opened the "floor" for questions. And there were always plenty. Then we showed our first religious film, a Cathedral picture entitled, "No Greater Power," the story of the conversion of Zaccheus. This was followed by a brief message, explaining the story and relating its message to Palanan and to them. The huge audience that turned out for this film "cine" was surprisingly quiet for an outdoor audience. As a general rule, children make up a large percentage of any audio-visual audience, and they are apt to get very noisy and undisciplined the minute the films stops. When fifty to one hundred children start running around and playing, bedlam is a mild word for the confusion. Outdoor preaching under these conditions requires careful preparation, with plenty of illustrations right out of the lives of the people, and words that touch them, their families, their problems, hopes and dreams and aspirations.

The next day many more people began to crowd into the

clinic. These excellent health films make people conscious of disease and its dangers, and as the news of the doctor and the nurses and the clinic spreads through the barrios, more and more people become bold enough to come in. And so it went—clinic all day, visitation in the homes in the late afternoons, the holding of Bible study and prayer groups in homes where people were interested, "singarees" of pep songs, gospel choruses, and easy hymns before every evening program of movies. We mixed in educational and agricultural movies with the health and religious movies, so that everybody who came was bound to learn a little. We learned that Camilo had been reared on a farm and was a very versatile lad. In the mornings when the mothers and children thronged the clinic, Camilo would take seeds out into the fields where the fathers were working and, side by side with them, help them plant new seeds, demonstrating the proper distance between rows, the depth the seeds should be planted, or the making of seed-beds, if necessary. The days fled by on wings of work, as we visited each of four different barrios.

By this time the Philippine government had been able to send in some tubes and condensers, by the bi-weekly mail carrier, for the repair of the telegraph equipment. A few days later, we had connections again with the outside world. The station played an important role in sending out warnings to the Weather Bureau of approaching typhoons, and the government kept a man assigned to Palanan full time. However, the equipment was old, and every time anything broke down, there were many weeks of delay before new parts could be brought in, so that communications with the rest of Luzon were impossible a good part of the time. It had been our luck every time we had been in Palanan to find the machine broken down, with no way to send out messages. When news reached us that it was working again, we thanked the Lord for our good fortune, and immediately began sending out messages. We sent an urgent wire to Leland Archer telling him of the plane crash and asking if he could fly out some of our heaviest and most expensive equipment. Several days later "Art" showed up in his L-5 plane. Without wasting any words, he looked over what was left of my plane, and then began to study the equipment we had that needed to be ferried out. What a friend! We selected the most expensive and most delicate audio-visual equipment, the motor generator, and the doctor's microscope. Thirty minutes after he landed, we had his plane loaded. He promised to fly to Tuguegarao to report to Mariam, and then, with a big smile and a wave of the hand, he gunned the plane down the river bank, and was off.

We breathed a sigh of relief, and began to make plans for getting the rest of our equipment out. We recruited eight Negrito men, and they started making their back-packs out of bamboo and rattan strips. All of us worked feverishly, trying to do as many jobs as possible before we left Palanan, treating as many patients as possible, counseling with the leaders of the new church about how to carry on the work of visiting and teaching and winning men and women to Jesus Christ—and always packing, packing, packing, trying to make everything fit into as small and as comfortable a pack as possible. There was a lot of stuff to be carried across those mountains!

Finally the great day came. There were eight Negrito cargadores, the four members of the clinic staff, and I, each loaded to the ears with army back-packs, clothing, medical equipment, ready to start the long trek back to Ilagan, and home. Grateful patients and friends gathered close around us, helping us tie things together and adjust our packs. We prayed together, thanking God for what He had been able to accomplish during our month together, and asking His blessings on these good people who would remain in Palanan, and then we sang together "God Be with You Until We Meet Again." It was a moment packed with emotion. Then we broke away, and started slowly on our way.

It was slow going with such a large party, for every few minutes somebody's pack needed adjusting, or somebody's shoestring broke, or a piece of equipment slipped loose. The first two hours were relatively easy for us old-timers in spite of the steaming heat, but they proved extremely difficult for the tenderfeet. Dorothy began to limp after a few hours. Her white nursing shoes, fine for a hospital ward, were not at all suited for the gravel or the large stones which made up our trail, mile after mile. She grimaced in pain every time she took a step, until Camilo insisted we must stop and look at her feet. Sure enough, there was a blister. That blister—a bad one, even though still small— showed us the bigness of Camilo's heart. Since his feet were small, he took off his own tennis shoes, and insisted that Dorothy wear them. Dorothy said she couldn't take his shoes. She refused. She argued. She balked. Finally, I bluntly told her, "Dorothy, unless you do as Camilo says, you'll never make it. You must do this, for if you do not, you delay the trip and endanger the lives of all of us." That stubborn, hardheaded nurse, just 100 days off the sidewalks of New York City, finally gave in and put on Camilo's shoes. He walked barefooted. What a guy! He tried to be hard and tough, on the outside, but on the inside he was pure gold. His was an act of pure unselfishness, for his feet were soft, too. He had been living in the city, wearing shoes all the time like the rest of us. God taught me a great lesson in sharing, through the so-called "tough guy," who gladly gave up his own shoes so that another might walk with less pain!

That afternoon, about 3:30 P.M., it began to rain. First the rain came slowly, but steadily, and then it began to really pour, coming down in great torrents. There was no possible shelter along the way—the nearest house was at least a mile or two farther along the trail. We sloshed and squished on for more than an hour before we reached it. About 5 P.M. we finally reached the house, looking like drowned, shaking puppies. The little hut was sixteen feet square, made of bamboo, with a grass roof, with a small lean-to for a kitchen at the back. Small though it was, it looked like a castle to us. The occupants of the house didn't stop and ask questions; they just asked us in. They were not "civilized" enough to question our right to be there and to ask for their hospitality. They did not know much about life in the cities, and they were not accustomed to having set "guest rooms" and saying, "Sorry, but we have room for only two!" They just grunted and took us *all* in, in spite of the fact that their small house was already crowded, and thirteen more people would well-nigh push out the walls.

We climbed the eight slender rungs of the bamboo ladder, went inside and took off our wet clothes. By hanging up a blanket in the corner of the room, the girls were able to find a measure of privacy for changing into dry clothes. The place was so packed with the family, their belongings, plus the thirteen of us, with all of our packs, and two wet dogs that wagged around, that we had to take turns sitting down. When we saw how small the little kitchen lean-to was, we wondered how in the world we could feed all of us. We had one small smoky fire, built on a heap of dirt piled in one corner of the lean-to. First, the family put on their rice pot. Then we added a few sticks to the fire, and put on two more pots of rice for our group. We started heating some of our sun-dried fish over the flames. By 7 P.M. most of us had eaten some rice and fish, using banana leaves for plates, so that at least we had no dishes to wash!

Our next problem was harder: How could nineteen people sleep in a house that was meant for six or eight people, when we were crowded while still standing up? I don't remember exactly how we worked out all of the details, but I do know that we all were tired and wanted to sleep—and sleep we did. I remember vividly that on one side of me a tiny pigmy lay; on the other side a young American nurse was squeezed in. We didn't argue about having this or that. We were all just deeply grateful to God that in the middle of a very hard rainstorm these kindly, so-called "uncivilized" people had taken us in out of the downpour and given us a warm shelter over our heads. When I awoke in the morning, the small Negrito's arm was thrown across mine; the handsome young Filipino doctor whose body was touching my feet was sleeping peacefully; and the American nurse on my left purred quietly. Looking out through the open door, I could see clear blue sky and the hint of the morning sun as the eastern sky flushed pink.

After a quick breakfast of rice and more dried fish, we read a few verses of the New Testament, prayed with these little people who had cared for us so graciously, and started moving out on the trail by 6:45. This was the hard day, for the trail sort of wound around two of the smaller mountains for a mile or two, and then at the foot of one high mountain just went up, and up, and up. The trail got smaller and smaller, until finally we just followed our guides almost blindly, trusting that they knew where they were going. Much of the time we were on hands and knees, pulling ourselves up the steep mountainside.

To make matters worse, Miss Cabanilla was sick with dysentery, and was having severe stomach cramps. As we struggled forward, she became weaker and weaker as the morning wore on. About 11 A.M. we reached another very steep place, where we could inch forward only by using our feet, knees, and hands. We took one step up, slid backward, held on to a root, grabbed for a handful of the grass, which was becoming very sparse in this high place. Nobody said a word. The only sound was the panting of our heavily burdened bodies, or the occasional groan of someone who stumbled and fell. Suddenly, Miss Cab fainted and started to roll down the steep incline toward the rocky stream just 100 feet below. I lunged to catch her, but I was too slow. Then I saw George Ros, several yards behind me, stop her headlong plunge by throwing himself down flat between her fast-moving body and the river below. I caught my breath as I heard the heavy thud of his body hit the rocky path, and I heaved a great sigh of relief when I saw Miss Cab come to a stop. We all rushed to her, and administered first aid. After a bit of rest, she was able to go on—and indeed we *had* to go on, for there was no place to stay in that wild, mountainous spot. I marveled at her grit and determination as she plodded on. But most of all, I kept re-living in my mind's eye George's heroic and completely selfless act in throwing himself down to save Miss Cab. I, the missionary, who had come out to the Philippines to teach others about devotion, was fast learning the meaning of devoton and self-sacrifice from those whom I had come to teach.

The third day on the trail was just like the day before, a steady climb up one mountainside and down another. We were always thirsty and had no water to drink. We felt hungry for something substantial, but had to subsist on our standard diet of rice and dried fish. We were all beginning to feel the drain of three days of exhausting climbing and hiking, but somehow we kept going. About the middle of that third day we again faced a crisis. We came to a steep cliff jutting out over a rushing mountain stream below. Great jagged boulders covered the river bed. We found to our horror that our trail went right across that forty-foot expanse of rock. The drizzling rain of the morning had left the trail wet and slippery. Every foot that walked across that rocky path left more mud and made the way more slippery and hazardous for the person following behind him. We sent the Negrito guides off in every direction trying to find some other way around that cliff jutting out over the raging torrent so that we would not have to walk on that slippery rock ledge, but they all came back shaking their heads. This was the only way across. We had no choice. I prayed as I had never prayed before, as the tiny, sure-footed pygmies, balancing their heavy loads on their heads and backs, padded silently across. One by one we inched out into the rocky ledge, hardly breathing for fear we would lose our balance and go crashing down into the rocky abyss below.

Finally, we all got across, except Dorothy and Camilo. Dorothy was worn out after three agonizing days through this leech-infested terrible terrain. She was near the breaking point. She said, "I can't do it. I'm too afraid. I *can't*. I'll slip down. I know I will." Quietly Camilo talked to her, trying to give her self-confidence, but it seemed a hopeless impasse. This New York City girl, who had been such a good sport about everything all along the way, had finally come to a step she just could not tackle. She was completely paralyzed. She could not move. I was wondering what in the world we could do. We could not go forward without her and it was too dangerous for anyone to try to carry her. As I agonized over this new problem, I saw Camilo once more talking, calmly and confidently, with Dorothy. And then, we saw Dorothy stand up, take Camilo's hand, and start across. Even sixty feet away we could see the trembling in Dorothy's hand. They moved forward very slowly, inch by inch.

Reaching the narrowest part, where the path was only six or eight inches wide, and where the roar of the water dashing against the boulders below was a terrifying, thundering reminder of what would happen if she fell, Dorothy stopped again. "I can't, I *can't*," she repeated over and over again. Camilo then turned his body so that his back was out over the cliff. Everybody stopped talking. He placed his right foot near her two shaking feet, and we heard him say quietly, "Now put one of your feet on top of mine, and you *can't* slip." We held our breath as Dorothy, knees shaking, inched her left foot on top of Camilo's foot, and hugging the cliff, moved slightly forward. Camilo moved his left foot a few inches, then his right. Dorothy put her left foot on top of Camilo's right, and inched forward again. The silence was intense, so that every heart beat pounded in my ears, and every breath sounded like a sigh. Miss Cab's eyes were closed, and her lips were moving. She knew that now the slightest jerk, the least little sudden movement, and two bodies would go crashing down to the rocks below. Inch by terrifying inch Dorothy and Camilo moved across the ledge. *They made it!* Suddenly, everybody was laughing and shouting and talking at once. We had passed through another trial, and made it.

The fourth day we began to get out of the mountainous jungle. By now Dorothy had three blisters as big as a quarter on each foot. How she moved I don't know. George, the city-bred doctor, was limping badly, with a twisted knee, but he never complained. Camilo's feet were raw from rubbing on the jagged rocks, and occasionally we saw drops of blood as he hiked on ahead of us on the stony trail. Of all of us, perhaps the one who had the hardest time was Miss Cabanilla. She was the oldest of the group, very heavy on her feet, and still weak from her serious bout with dysentery. She limped along in a dress that had been shredded by the hundred fingers of many trees, shrubs, and rocks. Miss Cab, plodding along with one hand on her hip, grunting as she got to this hard place, or climbed over that rock, looked very innocuous and weak. But the minute we stopped to rest or eat lunch, "manang," or older sister, sat down under a tree, and organized us all with the full aplomb of a commanding general. Her voice cracked out like a pistol. Five minutes after she sat down, she'd have the camp organized. One Negrito ran for water, two cut wood, a third built a fire, someone else washed the rice. Miss Cab had us all hopping around like trained fleas! We might grumble, but we obeyed for she was the one who got us all fed.

On the fifth day I decided to leave the rest of the group behind and hike on faster to get to the first little village and try to find a carabao. Miss Cab was growing progressively weaker from her continuing dysentery, and Dorothy's feet were bleeding. George could hardly limp along, with his twisted knee. We were a pretty beat-up, sorry-looking lot. We were reaching the raw edge of our limit of endurance. I was lucky, though, and could hike much faster, once I left the others behind. I soon reached the little village, and was able to rent a couple of carabaos and take them back the trail to the rest of the gang. Finally, on the evening of the fifth day, just as the sun was setting, we reached San Mariano—and *civilization!* There we were able to get a jeep and ride on home. We were a tired and bedraggled group—but a joyous and thankful one. We knelt and thanked God for our safe journey home, for our deliverance from all the crises along the way, for His guiding care over us. We thanked Him for the work that had been accomplished at Palanan—for the lives that had been saved—for the sick bodies that had been made well— and most of all, for the more than 100 converts who had found Christ as Lord and Saviour, and who were now banded together into this Evangelical church, the first on the east coast for a distance of more than 300 miles. We were glad we had gone, in spite of the cost in physical effort and pain, and we thanked God that He had called us on such a mission.

However, the most important thing that came out of the Palanan expedition was not what happened to the people in Palanan. It was what happened to us, the people who went. Years later Dorothy wrote to me, recalling her trip to Palanan ten years earlier: "I don't believe you will ever know how important a part you played in getting this green missionary started out on the right foot. Palanan set the whole tone of our clinic, and had a guiding influence on everything we did after that."

Camilo wrote up his experience this way: "While we were in Palanan, I had the great privilege of witnessing for Christ. I would accompany the Reverend Spottswood to the barrios where he preached the gospel to the people. I was ignorant of what he was talking about, but in some way I began to grasp that what he was telling the people was about the wonderful news of salvation. I was with the 'Saint,' but I was a sinner. After my experience in the plane crash, and during my hikes with him to the barrios to preach the Word, I came to realize that I was a soul who needed Christ. This was the turning point in my life, when I was changed from a sinful man to a redeemed

106

man. Palanan is the place where I found God. It was in this place that I realized that God needed my life. At first I thought that serving as the mechanic and helper in the Mobile Clinic was the calling that God had for me. But as I continued to work and pray with the clinic staff in the year ahead, I came to realize that God wanted me to become a minister. I had to resign from the clinic and enter the Seminary."

Camilo *did* enter the Seminary, and without any help from his family or church, worked his way through his three-year course, and graduated. Today he is one of our finest young ministers, serving in Mindanao. He continues to hike through hard places, to give himself sacrificially, to continue the Palanan tradition of self-giving, uncomplaining service. As he wrote me recently, "We have to go across rivers and mountains hundreds of times. In ordinary hiking, this would be very strenuous, but we are happy, in spite of the strain, because we are serving the people, and we are moving out to serve in more and more places where the people have need of us. It is a joy to witness for Christ."

George Ros, Miss Cabanilla and some of the others were asked to tell of their experiences from the pulpit in Knox Church, that great, historic old church where Protestantism was first born in the Philippines. As they told stories of their Palanan service, the members of Knox received new inspiration to go out to open new work in new areas where there were no churches. Today that church has a great missionary outreach, sending "missionaries" into the suburbs of Manila, into Mindoro, and into Mindanao. The "Palanan spirit" lives on. Palanan is not just one place, not just a small town on the east coast of Luzon. Palanan is *any* place where daring, courageous, self-sacrificing young people are willing to go, to give of themselves to the very uttermost, in obedience to the command of Christ, "Go therefore and make disciples of all nations. . . ." Palanan is not just a place. Palanan is a spirit—a spirit of devotion, of courage, of obedience.

# 7

## Lost at Sea

THE LETTER FROM Brother Tovera, the district superintendent for Cagayan Province, said that the need was *urgent*. The needs always are urgent, it seems. This time, typhoon "Louise" had swept across the northern coast of Luzon and then sideswiped the northern islands of Fuga, Dalupiri, and Calayan, laying waste crops, and wreaking wholesale devastation. Buildings were blown down by the eighty-mile winds. Trees had fallen everywhere. Many of the bamboo homes of the people had collapsed. Several people had been drowned in the swollen rivers as they tried to make their way to safer, higher ground. Brother Tovera wanted me to visit Calayan and to take the Mobile Clinic along, to minister to those desperate people. Since they were cut off from the mainland, and very few ships ever stopped there, they were in dire need of supplies, medicines, and food.

In answer to a telegram from me, Dorothy Edwards wired me that the Methodist Church Mobile Clinic staff were willing to try to go to Calayan Island. I began the formidable task of trying to find a boat which we could rent for the trip. Over and over again I received the reply from the various people I approached, "Sorry. That is a rough, dangerous channel. This is the typhoon season of the year. I would not like to try it."

At last I found a young American man, manager of a lumber mill on the northern coast, who said he knew of a boat we could rent. Paul said, "I can't guarantee this boat, but the owner says

108

it is new." It seemed like a good choice—and since it was the *only* one we could get, I didn't spend too much time making up my mind to take it.

We left Aparri, northernmost town of the Luzon Island, at 4 A.M. of the day we started our trip. We were fortunate in being able to cross all three of the ferries across the rivers that bisected the national road going west from Aparri to Claveria, our starting point for the sea voyage. We reached Claveria about 9 A.M., and all ran excitedly out on the shore to examine our boat, the *Winifred*. It was a nice looking boat, freshly painted. It was about twenty feet long, with a canvas awning thrown over the front, a small lean-to in the rear for the helmsman and below, a cockpit with several open portholes for the engine and the mechanic-operator. The engine was a husky, rebuilt Chevrolet truck engine. A quick once-over of the boat was encouraging. It looked good. Yet . . . there was something that seemed to be lacking. I had sort of an uneasy feeling, but I could not figure out what was bothering me. "Well," I thought, "it must not be important. This fellow knows more about boats than I do. He must know what he is doing." How I was to regret my careless, overconfident thinking later on!

We started unloading our boxes of supplies. This was a task that required everybody's help—man, woman, and child—and we had a bunch of children looking on who were pressed into action. We laid a plank across from the bank of the river over to the boat, and began pushing the boxes of medicines, food, relief supplies over our makeshift "gangplank." Fortunately, the boat had a good-sized hold and we could store all but the heavy motor generator in the space below. We tied that heavy piece of equipment as well as we could on the back end of the open deck. Then, our unloading finished, we began trying to find the owner of the boat, to tell him we were ready to start. He was nowhere in evidence, and there were no signs of any preparedness for a voyage that day, although our arrangements had been very clear and specific that this was the day we would start. Finally, after asking around at all the stores and meeting places in town, we located the man. I told him we were all ready and asked him what time we could start. His answer was, "Soon. Very soon."

We trouped back to the boat and started waiting. Fifteen, then twenty, and then thirty minutes limped by. Finally, an old truck drove up alongside the boat, and unloaded three drums of fuel. The Chinese driver and his assistants slowly hauled them to the rear of the little boat, and tied them on behind the cockpit. We were carrying a heavy load! The *Winifred* was really packed. Besides the freight, we had the eight people of our team, plus the crew of two. There was Dorothy Edwards, Miss Cabanilla, Dr. Ros, Camilo Toledo, and Dr. Juan Aragenes, a young Christian dentist who had volunteered to go along, to help Christ and these needy people. He was not to receive one cent for his month of work. In addition, there was a young American, Gordon Christiansen, and I. Gordon was a young paratrooper who, at the completion of his last year of service in Japan, had written me and asked if he could help in my work in the Philippines for a year. He had worked in San Francisco for months and months to earn his boat passage back across the Pacific, and now he was going to serve for at least a year without any pay. He was paying all his own expenses for the privilege of serving Christ in the Orient. He was crazy, literally a fool—a "fool for Christ's sake." The eighth member of our team was a young Christian nurse, who was also volunteering her services because of her great love for the mighty Saviour. A more consecrated, determined group of young people I have never seen.

By the time we were all on the boat, that front deck was overflowing with bodies. Then, when we felt we could not possibly squeeze on another person, the two crew members arrived, and with them were *four more men!* "Jumping Jehoshaphats!" I thought. "Where in the world can we put this gang?"

This worry slipped to one side as I heard Dorothy yell out, calling a "meeting." "Over here, everybody!" she commanded. Irked a little, I wondered what was coming up. Then I noticed a bottle in her hand. "Here they are. Guaranteed! Take one, everybody. What? Why, seasickness pills, of course." I snorted. Only Gordon, whom we had promptly nicknamed "Flash," and I declined to take any.

We got aboard and were ready to start. Every square inch of the cockpit was filled with men, and two leftovers sat up on top of the kerosene drums. These two, plus the eight of us sitting upon the front deck, made the little boat definitely top-heavy. However, the weather looked calm and clear and so I decided we would not need to worry about that problem. The men cranked up the engine and we were off. It was just about twelve noon, and we still had a six- to eight-hour trip ahead of us, and so I was relieved to be on the way at last. Just as we were nearing the mouth of the river and preparing to venture out into the ocean, we saw a long, slithering form that looked like a shark. I yelled, "Shark!" One of the crew grinned, and I could almost hear him think, "Landlubber!" It wasn't a shark, just a large fish, but that fish surely had a Pepsodent smile, with a mouthful of teeth. Then the helmsman began to tell a story of a boy who had been bitten by a shark the year before, lost his leg at the knee, been chewed up horribly, and then died. Ugh! He cheerfully gave us just one more thing to worry about as we began our journey.

We were now out into the sea channel, and the boat began to pitch up and down like a chip on a rollicking sea of swells. The worst part of these rolling swells was the sickening way the boat would roll to one side. I realized with a sense of utter frustration that this little boat, which had looked all right sitting straight up in the river, newly painted, was not at all suitable

111

for the open sea. It was built too high up out of the water. The heavy load, with so many people high up on the deck, accentuated the problem. As we got farther out into the North China Sea, one of the roughest bodies of water in the East and the bane of every ocean voyager, the boat rolled more and more. The edges of the deck were alternately touching the water, or perched precariously high up in the air. Whew! I had hardly begun worrying in real earnest before I noticed one of the nurses, green around the gills, lie down on her stomach, hold on to one of the small metal posts, and hang her head over the side. Minutes later, another nurse followed suit. Then the doctor was next. It was gruesome. Our boat smelled like a hospital before clean-up time. Camilo tried to keep up a jaunty banter of joking and teasing, but he was not immune to the prevailing sickness. He would make a wisecrack, laugh "He, he, he," and then suddenly turn pale, hold his head in his hands, and minutes later throw himself over all the prone bodies (laid out like cordwood along the sides of the boat) and dive for the sides.

Oh, how the hours dragged by! The first island, Fuga, was just fifteen miles from the northern coast of Luzon, and yet it seemed like fifty. It took us two hours to reach it. The rough tossing, rolling, pitching of the boat was loosening our heavy motor generator, and it began to slide from one side to the other. Camilo was now too green to notice or care, and so it fell to Flash and me to try to tie up that wet, slippery, sliding hunk of steel.

The weather was still good as we reached Fuga, and we could see the white sand twenty or thirty feet down below the beautiful greenish-blue water. White clouds scudded by overhead. Dorothy, Flash and I— the only three still on our feet—talked over the situation. I decided that we could worry more intelligently if we had more information, and so I went back to talk to the helmsman. I asked him to let me see his map, so that I could calculate more exactly how much longer the trip would take us. We had already used two hours just to pass the first island along the way. The helmsman calmly replied, "We don't have any maps." *No maps!* I was horrified! Then, I began to think that since he was an older man, he had probably made this trip many, many times, so that he would know this route well. It would be as easy for him as finding the back of his hand, I thought. But when I asked him ever so politely how many times he had made this trip before, he replied again, "I've never been to Calayan Island."

"You mean to tell me you have never been to Calayan Island, and you do not have a map—not even a compass?" I exploded.

"No, sir, we have no map or compass." He turned away and went on calmly smoking a hand-rolled cigar, so strong that I knew its fumes could help us out in any shortage of fuel. Now I could worry intelligently. We had a heavily overloaded boat, poorly balanced, with a crew on board who had never been to the island and who had no map or compass. Bro-o-ther! How dumb could you get? I wondered whether I should instruct the men to turn the boat around and start back home. We held a discussion with all the members of the team who were able to sit up and understand. The trip would be desperately risky. On the other hand, we had already sent a telegram assuring the leading men on the island of Calayan that we were coming. They would be worried and terribly disappointed if the clinic failed to show up. To a man the members of our team voted to go ahead.

By this time it was nearly 4 P.M. A wind was kicking up three- to four-foot waves from the southeast. Away in the distance I could see the second island—Dalupiri—far to the west. "Not even halfway there," I thought to myself. A few minutes later Dorothy called my attention to some dark clouds in the east. With a thud I realized what the old-timers had meant when they had warned against a boat trip in this season! About

113

4:30 the rain hit us. The three- to four-foot waves turned into three- to five-foot waves, and by 5 P.M. the wind and the waves were so strong that as the boat rolled over, water was six inches deep over the gunwales. Those sitting or standing on the sides of the boat got wetter and wetter. The hard wind split the canvas deck covering. The wind-driven rain sought out the last and the least dry spot and drenched the entire boat. Our situation looked desperate, for we were just slightly more than halfway to Calayan, and already the approaching dusk sent shivers of apprehension down our spines. Half knowing the answer already, I slipped and slid my way aft to find out if we had any life preservers. Three of the eight people of our team could not swim a stroke. The answer was as I expected, "No, we did not bring any life preservers."

After the first fifteen minutes, when the boat still had not turned turtle or sunk as it wallowed from side to side in the drenching cold rain, the situation seemed a little less hopeless. I marked it down a notch from "desperate" to "very dangerous." We were all huddled together, cold and miserable. We had had no lunch, five of the group were very seasick, our clothes were wet, and the cold rain was still hitting us in driving sheets. In the midst of the darkness of discouragement came a ray of hope—the first slim thread of light showed in the distance to the north. There was only one island to the north of us— Calayan! Even as I rejoiced in this good news, though, I was almost immediately thrown into despair again, for the pound of the heavy waves rocked the boat way over to one side, and it headed 40° to 60° off course to the west. Drunkenly, the boat swung, slowly righted itself, and heavily keeled over to the east. It did not stop when it pointed north, but instead swung about 45° off course, this time eastward into the teeth of the gale. But *thank God! Thank God for that pencil of light in the distance!* We recalled the lines of that grand old hymn by P. P. Bliss:

Let the lower lights be burning! Send a gleam across
the wave!
Some poor fainting, struggling seaman you may rescue,
you may save!
Trim your feeble lamp, my brother. Some poor sailor,
tempest-tossed
Trying now to make the harbor, in the darkness may
be lost.

Never were truer words written than these. Some good, kind person had lit a lamp on the island of Calayan, thirty or forty miles away, and his tiny kerosene lamp held the safety and lives of fourteen people in its flickering flame.

Hours crept by and the wind made the boiling sea channel rougher and rougher. As the boat heeled over from side to side, water was thrown across the deck up to the knees of Camilo and Dr. Aragenes. It seemed impossible that a boat could roll 30° to 45° with such a top load and ever straighten out again, but it did—again and again. In the pitch-black darkness of the night I kept remembering the words from one of Paul's letters in the New Testament, "We cast four anchors into the stern, and *prayed for the dawn*." As Miss Cab said later, "Never have so few prayed so hard for so long!" More minutes crept by. Only one thing kept our hope alive—that weak, flickering light that kept us on course.

Then, about 9 P.M. without any warning, the light went out. We were in complete ink-black darkness. We had no compass, no light to guide us, and the boat was wallowing 30° to 45° off course with every wave that hit us. Why, oh why, had that little light gone out? We were utterly lost at sea, with nothing to guide us but God. As Camilo said, "We surrendered our lives to Him who had given them and tried to prepare our hearts for what seemed inevitable—death."

The boat kept on rocking back and forth in the deep silence of the midnight. Each of us sat quietly thinking his own thoughts. An hour or so later, George Ros shouted suddenly above the wind and the waves, *"Listen*! I hear something!" Sure enough, we could hear something, but we could not think what it was at first. Then it dawned on Dorothy: waves crashing on a shore. There was only one island to the north—Calayan. Yippee! We might make it. The sound grew louder minute by minute. It was now dead ahead. The helmsman heeled the boat around until the wind and driving waves were directly behind us, pushing us onward. We could just imagine those waves crashing on a beach. We didn't care whether the boat crashed headlong on to the beach, since we felt sure it would be nice and sandy. We could gladly jump out and wade ashore. The sound of the waves crashing sounded very loud and near now.

Then one of the mechanics managed to get an automobile light mounted up on top of the cockpit, to flash on. One glance in that sudden light and everybody began screaming "Para! Para!" ("Stop! Stop!"). Just in front of us, not more than thirty feet away, was a solid rock wall. The edge of the island was not sand at all, but rather a precipice of solid rock rising straight up from the sea, and the whole island was a rocky, coral reef. "Stop the boat!" everyone continued to scream, but there was no stopping. Every wave slammed us three or four feet nearer that rock wall, and sudden death. The captain whipped the boat around as fast as he could, but as the boat turned broadside, the waves hit it full force. Water poured into the open port over a laboring engine. It missed, sputtered a few times, quit, caught on again, sputtered, and then ran. We inched away from sudden death. Another wave hit the boat broadside, and once again the engine stopped, spit and sputtered, then roared back into action again.

As the boat slowly limped away from the rocks, I wondered why it was taking so long to turn. I fought my way across the water-covered deck on my side to get back to where the captain was standing. I shouted, "What's the matter with the rudder?

116

Why can't you get the boat turned around?" Then he pointed to the back, and told me that the rudder cable had broken and the helm was useless. He pointed down, and I could see two men lying on their backs, with both feet pressing with all their might against the rudder bar. Above the rear of the stern I could hear the look-out man, perched atop the cockpit, shouting, "Catagid . . . catagid abangir" ("Left—left turn"). With no map and no knowledge of the shore line, we could not possibly land on that rocky island. Our next step was just to get far enough away from the rocks to keep from being bashed to pieces. Slowly we edged our way out into deeper water, until we were about 300 yards from the shore. It was after 1 A.M. before we were far enough out to have passed the crisis.

Then the captain called me to the rear again and showed me the real hero of the whole group. He aimed his flashlight down into the cockpit. There, standing *in the dark* with water sloshing up to his knees, stood the mechanic, watching, listening to the roar of the engine. Then the captain explained, "This man saved our lives. When the boat turned sideways and the rudder cable broke, the boat would have been smashed into kindling if that engine had stopped. Every wave splashed water all over the meter. Several times it almost died. When the spark plugs were wet, this man, standing barefooted in water a foot deep, took out his handkerchief and in the dark wiped off each spark plug. He kept the engine from being drowned out." Only a person who has felt the terrific electric jolt that comes from grabbing a spark plug on dry land can understand the measure of the courage of that humble mechanic who wiped off those spark plugs, not once, but fifteen or twenty times—all the time standing in water that doubled or tripled the wallop of that high-voltage spark. I could only thank God for such a man. I knew that I might have tried it once . . . but no more.

The night wore slowly away, until finally by 4 A.M. there was enough light in the eastern sky for the captain to be able to find the one sandy stretch of coastline which marked the village of Calayan. There, in the pale light of the early dawn, we discovered the incredible, absolutely amazing guidance of God. In the hours between midnight and four we had completely circled the island at least twice. Without knowing it, we had been weaving in and out between large coral reefs. Oh, the marvelous love of God towards His children! Looking at those jagged, protruding steel fingers of coral, so numerous that the sea looked like a colorful mosaic, I began to understand what a miracle it was that we were still afloat. It was impossible that we could have gone in and out among those hundreds upon hundreds of coral reefs in the dark, guided by men lying on their backs, unable to see ahead. It was absolutely impossible. I would not have believed it if I had not been there. If I had not been awake every single minute of that storm-wracked night, I could not have imagined its being true. When we got ashore at last, in that fateful early morn, we all got down on our knees and gave God all the glory and the praise for His guidance through the night and for His deliverance.

By 6 A.M. we had unloaded all the supplies from the boat. Dotty and Miss Cab cooked us up a whale of a good breakfast, our first food in twenty-four hours, and it tasted like the nectar of the gods.

A few of the townspeople came down to give us a genuinely warm welcome, but most of the fishermen and farmers who passed by the beach at that early morning hour just went about their business as usual, hardly noticing our presence. However, there was one woman who came down to the beach especially to greet us. She was a woman about fifty years old, very unprepossessing in appearance, dress soiled, shoes muddy, hair slighly awry. She gushed, "Oh, Reverend Spottswood and Miss Edwards, we have been praying for your coming. We have been praying earnestly for the coming of a real mission to this godless island." I smiled politely, but I was impatiently wishing this "so-and-so" would stop talking so much so we could get on with the Lord's work, now that we were here.

We made contact right away with the local authorities, who graciously gave us permission to take over the entire school building. We broke up into teams and started getting things organized, making the largest and best room the medical clinic, another room the dental clinic, a schoolroom on one side the "Ladies' Dorm," and another room on the opposite side of the clinic the "Men's Dorm." We got through the morning. The rooms were continually full of people. The news had spread like wildfire that a real doctor and dentist had come, and the place was full. The afternoon was just as busy. The doctor and the nurse barely got anything to eat for lunch. They were dead on their feet, but they never missed a patient, and never quit smiling. I don't know how they kept going as they did.

All afternoon Camilo worked on the motor generator. I thought it would never run again, after being drenched by salt spray, drowned in water, and then dropped overboard in unloading. It seemed impossible that a piece of delicate electrical machinery could survive being splashed by salt water fully ten times an hour all night long. However, Camilo's faith was greater than mine, and he went to work. He took the magneto apart and took out the spark plugs, cleaned, wiped, dried, re-assembled them all. He did the same to the carburetor. By 4:30 P.M. I heard that old motor generator spit several times, and then finally settle down into a steady hum. Wonderful! We could show our health, educational, and religious movies in the evenings.

After supper Camilo set up the audio-visual equipment out in front of the school and ran off several test films. Everything ran fine, and with every film the crowd grew in size and in noise. Dorothy was the first speaker and gave the explanation and commentary on the first film, "The Winged Scourge," on the malaria mosquito. Dr. Ros gave the commentary on the tuberculosis film. Then we began the hymn sing, projecting the words in the dialect on the screen. Some of the people entered into the spirit of the singing, but most of them were very noisy and disinterested. However, we kept on with the program. Dr. Aragenes read the Bible, giving the story of the religious film, and then led in prayer. In all the confusion of the milling crowd, his words would have been completely drowned out without our microphone and the large speaker. It was a difficult situation, but the young dentist carried on bravely. Just as he was finishing his prayer, he was startled by a large stone which someone hurled up to the tin roof. The stone bang . . . bang . . . banged its way down the roof, and fell at his feet. The next speaker, Miss Cab, began with a fervent prayer for love and brotherhood among all men. About halfway through her message, "Jesus Christ Is Saviour," a second and larger stone banged on the tin roof and almost hit her face when it fell. Then shortly afterward, there was a third. The stones came from the back of the crowd. Miss Cab finished her talk without a falter or a quaver.

As the next hymn was played and projected on the screen, we held a brief meeting of our own team. The question was, should we go ahead with the evangelistic service, or in the face of such hostile acts from the crowd, should we just stop? I was thrilled to see the group vote unanimously to continue. We decided for caution's sake to send all the girls back to the house, so that in case of fighting or rioting, they would be protected. They protested. They wanted to stay, but since their parts in the service were finished anyway, we persuaded them to return quietly to the house of a friend.

The next speaker began, and the stones again began to rain down. I went quietly to the rear, behind the back row of the crowd of people, to see if I could find out who the trouble makers were. After I got back there, only one or two more stones were thrown. The evening ended with a prayer and benediction, after one of the most tense, delicate, outdoor meetings I can ever remember. We thanked the Lord for His continuing and protecting love.

As we disassembled the equipment, we discussed the events of the evening. Early the next morning, almost before we had finished our breakfast, the Vice-Mayor of the town came over to apologize for the stoning. He assured us that it was the mischief of three young toughs who had been drinking.

Our schedule on Calayan was the same from day to day. Up at 5 A.M., Bible study and prayer, breakfast at 6 A.M., clean up and set up, and clinics open at 7. Work all morning, lunch at noon, a little rest, clinic by the medical personnel, visitation evangelism by the rest of us, and then movies and a short public service in the evenings. After that first night, we had no further difficulty and the days sped by like autumn leaves falling. The relief supplies we had from Methodist Overseas Relief were distributed to the neediest families, who were greatly heartened by the milk and vitamins we were able to give them.

The last week was upon us, and it was time to leave the town and visit the outlying barrios. Packing, hauling, balancing the load on carabao sleds, slipping, falling, wading through mud holes, unloading, unpacking, setting up clinic again—it was all hard work. Everywhere we found the same tremendous need, the same gnawing poverty, the same pitiful pleas for help. How thankful we were that the Lord's heart is not small. Through His children in America who had sent out these supplies, and through the dedicated lives of these consecrated Filipinos who had come to this place, He ministered to these neediest ones.

Finally we had only two days more to serve in Calayan. We packed up all our things once again and moved back to the "centro" or main town, for the closing service. This was to be the big night in which these people who had been touched during the visitation, who had felt the call of the Master, the claim of the Master for their lives, would be baptized. Our last

121

night, the big night, was calm and clear, in spite of rain for the several preceding nights. A great crowd had gathered for this outdoor service. As Camilo prepared the projector for showing the last film we had on the life of our mighty Saviour, I tried to slip away for a few moments of quiet prayer. Just about that time the "old woman of the dirty dress" came up to talk with me. This was the third or fourth time that she had come to tell me that she was praying for this person or that person. I am afraid I did not take her too seriously. I put her down in my book as a "gusher."

As we began the closing service, the crowd was quiet and attentive, in high contrast to the wild and woolly first night we had been there. I gave the closing message and then asked for those people who would like to accept Jesus Christ as Lord to come forward. Nobody moved a muscle. Such a challenge is terribly difficult to answer out in the open. To make it easier for those people who really wanted to make that decision, I asked our team, as well as the local believers who had gone with us from house to house visiting, to speak to some of their new friends with whom they had shared the good news of our Loving Redeemer, who for our sakes became poor. One by one I saw our team go out among that great throng to find their new friends and lead them to Christ. How proud I was to see nearly everyone—George, Dorothy, Miss Cab, all of them—lead somebody forward to stand at our little improvised altar. I was overjoyed to see three men for whom I had labored long and prayed hard come down and take their stand at the front, to make their public confession of Jesus Christ as Lord of their lives.

Then far back in the crowd I saw a startling thing. The old woman with the bedraggled hair, the still unkempt dress, was leading seven people forward. She was only a layman. She had only a second or third grade education. She had had no training in theology, no training in methods of evangelism. She knew only how to pray. She knew how to prayerfully, earnestly, courageously talk to people about Jesus Christ. Out of the fourteen people who were won to Christ during our weeks on Calayan this lay woman had won seven of them. It was a much humbled, chastened, and conscience-stricken missionary who led the prayer of commitment that night, and who fervently prayed for the forgiveness of our sin that night.

I realized then that I had been "lost at sea" in more ways than one!

# 8

## Ambush

In the early days of my missionary service, right after the cessation of the last World War, the Philippines was a land of ruin and destruction. Manila was the second-worst city in the world. Only Warsaw in Poland survived heavier bombardment. It was a heart-rending sight to walk through the streets of the city and see once great cathedrals left only a pile of shattered stone, great government buildings left nothing but empty shells of pock-marked concrete, hundreds upon hundreds of beautiful homes and buildings standing stark and jagged against the sky, gaunt frameworks of their former structure. Packed against every wall that was left standing were makeshift "shanties," shelters put together of old rusty pieces of corrugated iron sheets, packing boards, ragged remnants of army canvas tents. Hundreds of people were crowded into every single ruined building that had even one wall left standing. It was a heartbreaking experience to walk down the torn city streets, past gaping bomb craters, and see all these great jutting walls of ragged stone and cement, pouring out their teeming millions of hungry, homeless human beings from the "shanty towns" at their base.

And yet, as terrible as was the physical desecration of the once beautiful "Pearl of the Orient," the destruction of homes and buildings was not the most serious aftereffect of the war. Something far more precious was destroyed—law and order. Young boys who had learned to steal during the war in order to survive

continued to pilfer and plunder after the war. Young guerrilla
"rebels," who had fought bravely against the Japanese during
the war, still found it easy and commonplace to fight and stab
and kill for what they wanted after the war. The desperate
economic conditions which prevailed during this difficult re-
adjustment period gave rise to pressures which encouraged law-
lessness. Severe agrarian unrest prevailed in the great rice-growing
plains, where too few people owned the land and thousands and
thousands of tenant farmers eked out existence under intolerable
conditions of poverty and debt. It is not surprising that out of
all these pressures and tensions there arose in the Philippines
a group of revolutionaries, called the "Hukbalahaps," or "Huks."

From 1946 on there was continuous fighting between the
Huks, made up largely of poor tenant farmers who had been mis-
treated and exploited down through the years, plus lawless
elements, plus a small percentage of Communist leadership, and
the Military Police Command of the Philippine Government. In
every day's newspapers I read great headlines: "MPC SET TO WAGE
PUNITIVE ACTION AGAINST HUKS"; or "MILITARY ROUTS LARGE
GROUP HUKS"; or "NEW PUSH AIMED AT DISSIDENTS." The government was always having "all-out" campaigns; and yet during those
early postwar years the number of Huks increased, rather than
decreased, and the movement flourished. "Stalin University"
was established in the mountains north of the Candaba Swamps,
and young men and women thronged to join this new revolutionary movement.

In 1947, at the height of the conflict, I made a trip with some
professors and students of the Seminary in Manila for the purpose of investigating the serious unrest in the provinces. At
that time there were nine companies of the MPC assigned to
the task of wiping out the Huks, but they had had little or
no success. We left one Friday afternoon and drove to
Cabanatuan, and thence to Bongabon, one of the centers of the

125

conflict. Though I had traveled over that road before, I found many interesting evidences of conflict along the way.

On the trip we passed three armored cars carrying 50-caliber machine guns, loaded for action, and two light tanks manning 20 mm. cannons. This kind of road patrol was necessary because of frequent ambushes of trucks and buses by the Huks. Every day's newspaper told of a hold-up somewhere along the road, and twenty or thirty people had been killed in ambushes in just the past month. "Ambush" was a word that brought fear to mind in these days, that gripped the heart with cold fingers and squeezed.

Bongabon is located on the edge of a rich rice plain; yet it is close enough to the mountains for the Huks to be able to get away immediately into hiding, in the event of a military attack. Going out from Bongabon to visit in the foothills in the homes of some of the small tenant farmers, we found ample reasons for the continued growth of the Huk movement. First, the average tenant in this area had about 4.4 acres to yield his total livelihood, both for himself, and for his family of from six to eight children. Of the rice grown on those few acres, he had to return one half to the owner for the use of the land. Usury was a common practice so that a poor man, when faced with an emergency need for cash, might borrow money and have to repay interest at the rate of 33⅓ per cent to 50 per cent of the money borrowed. The seminary students figured that with the prevailing prices for rice, the average income of these farmers varied from $200 to $500 a year. With postwar inflated prices, these people could never have an adequate diet or sufficient clothing. It would be hard for an American to picture the poverty of the people in the barrios. It is hard to believe they can be so poor and still live. The answer, of course, is that they don't really live; they just exist.

A summary of the battle situation in that particular town was succinctly given by a farmer who said, "The MP's rule by day, and the Huks rule by night." One of our accepted supply pastors who lived and worked in this area that was so heavily infested with Huks told us of his experience. One night about 2 A.M. there was a loud knock on his door. His heart froze as he heard the mufflled voices of many men outside and the clank of weapons being lowered to the ground. With great fear and trembling, he opened the door and peeped out. The voice of the leader comanded, "Come down. Come down." They then forced him to lead them to the house of one of the church members who owned a small store. On the way they passed within a few yards of the soldiers' barracks. As the Huks restlessly fingered their guns, the young pastor held his breath, knowing that one false step would awaken the soldiers and start a barrage of bullets coming in his direction. When they arrived at the store, the Huk leaders roused the owner. They explained that they were very poor and that they had nothing to eat, and then they asked if he would like to share some of his supplies with them. Looking around at the ring of hard-eyed men surrounding him and at the muzzles of all those rifles pointed carelessly in his general direction, the store owner decided to make a contribution. The Huks cleaned out most of his wares, leaving him bankrupt. On the way back they questioned the pastor, "How many pairs of trousers do you have?" When they found he had four, two work pants, and two for use on Sundays in the pulpit, they made him "contribute" three pairs. They also took his shirts and underwear, everything except what he was wearing, and then within an hour they had slipped away again into the dark recesses of the mountains.

In the attempt to meet these serious problems, the government had made some steps in the right direction. First, they had passed the Land Tenancy Act, putting the proportion of sharing between owner and land tenant at 30—70, instead of the old 50—50, provided the tenant furnished the tools, seeds, and carabao. However, this ratio was difficult to enforce, for there were many and devious ways of getting around the law. The tenants were usually so deeply in debt to the landlords that they were not in any position to bargain or to argue over terms. The government had also begun to buy up a number of large haciendas, or plantations, to sell them to tenants at reasonable costs. However, this program proceeded very slowly. One of the plantations within three miles of Bongabon was bought by the government and at the time we were there was in the process of being made over into small, highly mechanized cooperative farms. However, the conflict there was so intense that with every tractor that went out to the field there also went a small military jeep, carrying a light machine gun. Just a few days after we left this place, three MP's were ambushed along the road to the plantation and two of them were killed.

We talked with the Mayor of the town, who helped us understand the Huks a little better. He said that to properly evaluate the Huks we needed to remember that they began with a real cause for complaint. Many of the Hukbalahaps were soldiers who had fought the Japanese almost from the day of Pearl Harbor up to VJ-Day, suffering great hardships. Then, after the Americans landed and after the situation had been brought pretty well under control in 1945, many new resistance units or companies were organized to fight the Japanese. Great numbers of these "Johnny-come-lately" units were recognized as guerrilla outfits, subject to veterans' benefits after the war, while many of the Hukbalahaps were not recognized. These unrecognized units, continuing to fight up in the hills, began to take on, in the popular thinking, somewhat of the glamor of "Robin Hoods," out to avenge the wrongs of the poor. Many of these Huks, now living up in the mountains like kings, well fed, with great prestige in their units, had no land to go home to, no positions, no security apart from the Huks.

It was a difficult situation, and our hearts were heavy as we started homeward realizing the amount of suffering and bloodshed that would occur before these real military, economic, and agrarian problems would be met and the needed reforms made. We had an experience on the way back to Manila that aptly illustrated the temper of the people in these trying times. As I drove the jeep through one of the small barrios, we saw a large crowd of people just ahead of us on the road, yelling and talking excitedly around a passenger bus. A man ran out and frantically flagged us down. As I slowed the jeep to a stop, this wild-eyed, barefooted individual came runing up to me, waving a cocked .45 automatic at me, and talking so fast he was incoherent. He leaped beside me on the driver's seat, hit me in the ribs a couple of times with the .45 and motioned down the road. Under the inspiration of the cocked .45, though I still did not know what was happening, I drove hurriedly on. By this time, dozens of people were running along the edge of the road and instantly we understood what had happened. The crumbled figure of a woman lay inert on the edge of the concrete. Less than 400 yards ahead a large bus was disappearing over the hill. It came to us in a flash that the bus ahead had struck the woman and killed her and then had gone on. The driver was afraid to stop in this section of hot blood and loaded automatics. The man sitting beside me on the driver's seat was possibly the husband or the brother of the woman on the road and was intent upon shooting the driver of the bus up ahead. We were all afraid that as soon as I caught up with the bus there would be a running gun battle, as all drivers in this territory are armed. However, the bus driver showed eminently good judgment. He drove just as fast as he could to the nearest MPC station, and leaving his motor running, made a dash and a leap into the front door. We got there just as he was going into the door. My companion with the automatic jumped off the jeep and dashed after him, but he was stopped by two policemen. This whole incident revealed the tense explosiveness of the people, their highly volatile feelings made much more dangerous by the presence of many guns and other loose firearms in the hands of civilians.

In the years that followed, due to the punitive action of Secretary of Defense Magsaysay and the Philippine Armed Forces, the Huks were more subdued. However, as they were driven out of the central areas where they had once been strongest, they migrated northward and became much stronger in the Cagayan Valley where we lived. In much of the country-side in the north, when the sun went down the area was dominated by Huks. For awhile, no buses traveled at all at night. There were curfews in most of the major towns in the Valley. However, after setting up a number of military check-points all along the national road, each one with a mound of sandbags hiding machine guns, the government forces began to let the buses go through. The trip from Manila to the northern towns took fifteen to eighteen hours and could not be made without a part of the journey's falling during the evening hours. Every morning's newspapers brought new stories of buses am-bushed along the road, of passengers robbed, or raped, or killed.

During those hot, horrible days of constant fighting between the Huks and the government troops, I received a message from the Bishop telling me to come to a meeting in Manila. Since the rivers were flooded and jeep travel was very doubtful, I decided to take the good old dependable Rural Transit, the regular passenger bus between Tuguegarao and Manila. I got to Manila without too much difficulty, after a sixteen-hour trip, crossing five rivers by ferry, and covering 300 miles. When the meetings were over and I began to make arrangements for the return trip, I called the Rural Transit station, and found I would leave Manila at midnight. The only way to make the trip in one day was to leave at midnight, travel all next day and arrive about dark the next afternoon.

I ate lunch with a group of fellow missionaries, and just happened to mention that I was taking the bus that night to

# AMBUSH

Tuguegarao. One of them handed me the morning paper and said, "Look." There on the front page was the headline, "RURAL TRANSIT BUS HELD UP IN MOUNTAINS OF VISCAYA." The story went on to tell that three men were wounded and two women raped in an ambush of the bus near Dalton Pass. And I was to leave on that bus at midnight! On the outside I appeared calm and nonchalant, but inside I was scared.

I got down to the bus station around 11 P.M., to be sure I got a seat. To my surprise, the bus was already full. Not only were all the seats taken, but the aisles were full, and all the space under the seats was packed. There were endless packages, sacks of supplies, boxes of one sort and another, and in between, a friendly chicken or two. The only seat I could find was right next to the bus driver, squeezed in under his left elbow. I sat down, and found to my surprise a six-month-old pig nestling under my seat. In the next eighteen hours that pig and I really got well acquainted.

Promptly at midnight the driver cranked up his engine and away we went. The next few hours were eerie ones, as we rode through the Huk-infested areas in the dark. At one place we came to a washed-out bridge where the river had overflowed its banks and the bridge was only a memory. We all got out of the bus and stood around in the stillness of the pre-dawn for at least an hour. Then the men decided to take off their shoes and wade across. We all tried it back and forth in several different places and finally decided on a place where the bus might get through. With the men leading the way through the rushing waters of the swollen stream, the bus driver put the motor in lowest gear, pushed the gas pedal all the way down, and started over. He hit a big hole, almost stalled, and finally got through, to everybody's great relief.

We continued on through the night. Every light we saw made us jump. Every car parked on the side of the road made us wonder if there were going to be a hold-up. An uneasy silence

131

settled down over the passengers, replacing the lighthearted banter of the beginning of the trip. I noticed that many of the passengers were squeezed down into their seats, to present as small a target as possible to any guns that might be aimed their way. A few slept, but not many. Most had read the same paper I had read, and they were as aware as I of the danger. Every hill or clump of trees might be "it." However, nothing happened—and soon it was daytime. With the rising of the sun came light and laughter. Everybody breathed easier and became warm and friendly. We began to laugh and talk together as we unwrapped our "baen" (or lunch bags) and ate breakfast. Cabanatuan was behind us and ahead lay San Jose, the gateway to the winding Cordillero Mountains that divided the Cagayan Valley from the central plains of Luzon.

Leaving San Jose, we also left behind the paved road, and hit the rough, "washboard" gravel road that wound round and round through the mountains. For the next two hours we climbed up toward the Dalton Pass, the 3000-foot pass where so many American lives had been lost during the war in the effort to dig out the Japanese soldiers who were hiding in the caves and had to be cleaned out one by one. As we approached this historic spot, a peculiar chill of apprehension settled over us. Coming up, we had all been carefree and laughing, but as soon as the bus started down the other side of the mountain, everybody became silent. We were remembering the story of the ambush that had occurred just a mile or two from where we were. The bus driver had obviously read the newspaper story too for instead of driving slowly over that narrow, torturous mountain road, he speeded up. He was racing down headlong, forgetting such ordinary safety precautions as blowing his horn around curves, or staying on the right side of the road. I found myself ducking down lower and lower into my seat and tucking my head down on my chest. And so was everyone else.

Then it happened. Halfway down the mountain we rounded

a very sharp turn, and there were two men holding tommy guns. One stepped out in front of the bus and pointed his gun at us. The bus driver slammed on his brakes and pulled over to a screeching halt on the right of the road. The other Huk came around the bus to get inside, on my side. Then the driver did a startling thing. As the Huk started to put one foot up, he suddenly put the bus in gear, and jammed the throttle wide open. As the bus leaped forward, the man jumped to one side to avoid being crushed. The fellow with the tommy gun started shooting at the driver. I was sitting between the driver and that spitting gun. When the first shot sounded, forty men and women dove for the floor—but I was on the bottom! That was the only time I ever put my arms around a pig and really enjoyed it! Due to the courage—or the foolhardiness—of the driver, who yanked his bus out of range around the next curve, nobody was killed, wounded, or even robbed, though the bus had several extra holes in it not many inches from the place where the pig and I sat.

As we went around the next curve, there were audible sighs as people straightened themselves up again, and we all thanked God again and again that we had not been shot. An hour or so later we reached Bayombong, where we stopped for lunch. My knees were still weak as we got out. The driver was the "hero" of the hour.

After lunch, he "fired" up again and we were off in a swirl of dust. The next town was Cordon, and then Santiago, Isabela, scenes of recent Huk violence. Cordon was a large barrio of Santiago and the headquarters of a "Murder Syndicate" which had recently claimed fifteen to twenty victims. However, I felt reasonably calm, figuring that by the law of averages we had had ours for that day. Santiago, one of the largest towns in Isabela Province, had recently been in the newspapers, following capture by the Huks. One night, just after midnight, a group of Huks had surrounded the fairly strong municipal police force, shot them down, and then to show their disdain for the constituted authorities, burned the municipal building. With the town thus at their mercy, the Huks had systematically cleaned out every store in town and gone from house to house getting "contributions." One man who pleaded poverty and did not give what the Huks demanded was taken out behind his house and shot. We were lucky, though, and drove safely on through Santiago, with no sign of any trouble.

We made our way on further north, picking up more and passengers with every stop. We crossed two more ferries, and by 3 p.m. we were pulling out of Ilagan, Isabela, with the bus loaded to overflowing. Since this was the last bus that day for Tuguegarao, it was really packed, with people standing in the aisles, four people standing on the entrance step with their bodies swaying outside the bus, and twelve people up on top. Yet, when we slowed down at Cabagan, there were at least ten more people waiting to fight their way onto the bus. One of these was a loud, noisy, drunken man. Cursing and swearing, he fought his way onto the bus. In the middle of the aisle he stepped on the foot of a man who was fed up with his loud, rude ways. The victim turned on the drunk and shoved him and cursed him. With that, the drunk pulled out a long knife with a switch blade five inches long. He started stabbing in the general direction of the enemy, but in his drunken, swaying condition he barely missed stabbing another person, who began screaming, yelling "Murder!" The other man now had his knife out. In the middle of this crowded, jam-packed bus, the fight was on. As the two were stabbing at each other, people all around were trying to protect themselves, and in the confusion many were cut on the face and arms. Suddenly everybody began diving out of the windows, literally. I saw one mother standing on the seat screaming hysterically as she threw her baby out of the window. All of this had taken place in less than a minute. I sat there transfixed. Every time I started to move, or climb out

134

of the window myself, somebody would step on my lap, or fall into my lap, in the effort to climb out. By that time ten or twelve people had already crawled out of the windows, blood was flowing freely from a number of wounds and pandemonium reigned.

Suddenly, there appeared a policeman. With three excited women screaming at him, this foolish individual went up to the door of the bus, picked up his tommy gun to shoulder height, and started to fire. At that, the bus just exploded with people! That idiot policeman was waving his gun around like a crazy man, ready to slaughter innocent and guilty alike. I finally got halfway over to the window when a sixty-year-old grandmother, crazed with fear and screaming like mad, beat me to it, kicking me in the chest as she went through. Then the bus driver proved himself really and truly a hero this time. He had never completely stopped his engine. When he saw a slight lull in the fighting, as one of the men stopped to wipe blood from his eyes. The bus driver slammed the bus into gear, and suddenly stepped on the gas. The drunk, who was standing with his back to the door, lost his balance—and fell out.

The bus driver had left twenty to thirty of his paying passengers in Cabagan, but he never looked back. The bus never slowed down until we reached the banks of the Pinacanawan River, and Tuguegarao, where I promptly went home and tried unsuccessfully to eat supper. I couldn't. My hands were still shaking!

# 9

## Into Head-hunter Territory

THE DIE WAS CAST. We would start for Casiguran as soon as we could make the needed preparations.

Casiguran was a tiny town on the east coast of Luzon, eighty to a hundred miles south of Palanan, where we had had the plane crash with the Mobile Clinic during the Work Camp. Between Palanan and Casiguran the map was entirely blank except for the short lines indicating mountains near the coastline. We had information from the Philippine Navy that the coastline itself was extremely rocky and forbidding. We made plans to take the jeep as far as Jones, Isabela, the "jumping-off place," or the end of the road. After that we planned to hike to the river, ride a "banca" up the rapids to reach Pinapagan, and then meet our three companions and several guides. Then we hoped to hike into that unexplored wasteland of jungle and by cutting through the mountains reach Casiguran on the coast.

And then we read the news in the daily paper: "VICE-MAYOR OF CASIGURAN MURDERED YESTERDAY BY ILONGOT HEAD-HUNTERS." In smaller type the story went on, "Mayor describes situation as critical. Hundreds of families are evacuating the barrios, where the Ilongots are said to have gone on a killing rampage. An all-out punitive expedition against the band of Ilongot head-hunters urged by Governor of Nueva Viscaya. Governor told Philippine Constabulary Commander that only force will stop wild tribesmen from their orgy of head-hunting." A band believed to consist

136

of three hundred Ilongot tribesmen had already taken several Christian heads during the past month in what was believed to be a retaliation against "land-grabbing" on the part of some new settlers in the area. A week before they had also killed a town councilor who had been on a hunting trip in the mountains near Casiguran.

Pastor Eduardo Garcia and I postponed our trip a few weeks and used the time in gathering additional information on the area between Jones, Pinapagan, and Casiguran. From the town officials of Jones we learned that during the war Filipino guerrillas had once or twice hacked their way through this forbidding forest. The area was largely unpopulated, except by nomadic Ilongot tribesmen. Our purpose in wanting to make the trip over the mountain range to Casiguran was purely exploratory. We wanted to see for ourselves what lay on the other side of the giant Sierra Madre Mountains. We wanted to see what kind of people lived over there; to learn what kind of faith they had, if any; to see what churches were at work, if any; and to open up a new area of Christian work for the mighty Saviour in this place.

After several weeks of intensive hunting, the Philippine Constabulary found and killed one or two of the Ilongots, whose major crime seemed to be resenting being pushed off their land by new settlers. The other Ilongots retreated into the interior, and the situation returned to normal—a normal that continued to be an uneasy peace, a period of sudden, isolated raids on individual settlers, of a head taken here or there. Shades of the Apaches! This was the old Wild West all over again, the main difference being that instead of taking a scalp, as the Apaches did, the Ilongots on a raid were more selfish. They took the whole head!

Since trouble, when it flared, always seemed to be in retaliation for specific grudges, we felt we would be relatively safe as passing strangers, not land settlers. We decided to push on with our plans for the trip to Casiguran. I kept a diary of the Casiguran trip, which follows:

*Tuesday, March 14:* Left Tuguegarao by jeep at 7 A.M., with four army back-packs, canteens, bolos, and thirty cans of sardines. Took two packs full to overflowing with medicines (5000 atabrine pills, 2000 multivitamin tablets, and assorted simple medicines) and New Testaments, Gospel portions, and copies of *The Upper Room* in the dialect. Four ferries later and 130 miles further on I arrived in Jones, the end of the line. About 3 P.M. I parked the jeep under the house of one of the church members and went to look for Pastor Vinarae. We held a service in the little chapel that night. Preached to a good crowd on "The Stewardship of Life." The Spirit of Christ was there, and about twenty people re-dedicated their time, their talents, and their money to the service of God.

Received another warning *not* to go out into this countryside. One of the members who has been helping Magsaysay's scouts in the area warned, "You will pass through the territory of two wild tribes between Jones and Casiguran—the Negritos, who are friendly and helpful, and the Ilongots, who are sometimes friendly, but are more often than not fierce, wild, and treacherous." He told me that a year before the government had put a small school in one Ilongot settlement near the edge of the mountains and sent in a young teacher, in a program to help educate and civilize these primitive tribes. One day he had to whip one of the students for disobedience. Several days later his head was found atop a tall fence post, as a warning.

*Wednesday, March 15:* We crossed the river by dug-out canoe, and fortunately caught a ride on a ten-wheeler logging truck. There was no road. The big truck just followed the footpath. The truck was loaded with a heavy diesel engine for a rice mill in the next barrio, and consequently was top-heavy. Tragedy struck. In trying to cross a narrow bridge the truck veered over to one side, and plunged into the stream. I was able to leap off the other side

138

as the truck went down, and so escaped being crushed by the engine. Began having an attack of malaria in the late afternoon, in the barrio of Palacion. Lay down on a mat on the floor. Dosed myself with camequin, and also gave myself an injection of quinine.

*Thursday, March 16:* Was able to travel with my pack by this morning. Went from Palacion to Pinapagan by banca. It was a continuous fight against the roaring rapids, exciting, but strenuous and dangerous. Magnificent trip through a deep gorge out by the rampaging Cagayan River, which was so swift the boatmen could not paddle. They poled the banca upstream by hugging the quiet water near the shore. The current was so swift in some of the rapids that pushing the banca upstream against the raging torrent required the combined strength of all eight of us. The river was so huge, and the force created by the rapid drop of the tons and tons of water (five to ten feet in every 100 yards distance) was so great, that our greatest efforts as puny men seemed infinitesimal. After leaving the river, we hiked ten kilometers to reach Pinapagan by noon. Ate lunch with Pastor Emilio Posidio. Then went on six more kilometers to Pastor Tuguiere's house in the next barrio, where we were to meet our Negrito guides. However, the guides he had hired for the trip had gotten tired of waiting for us and gone home. Pastor Tuguiere left us to rest at his house while he hiked ten kilometers to the Negrito camp to find some more guides and cargadores. He spent the night there.

*Friday, March 17:* Pastor Tuguiere got home early, reporting he had found guides. They arrived later in the day. After much palaver and getting ready, we finally made definite plans to leave early tomorrow morning. Keep hearing stories of the Ilongots. Two more instances of heads being taken. One of the church members loaned us an old 7 mm. Japanese army rifle and four bullets. Wonder if I'd ever be able to use it. Held service last night in our small church. Preached on "Advancing with Christ and His Church." Eighteen decisions.

Saturday, March 18: Worse luck! It began to rain this morning, long before dawn. However, since this is the dry season, we decided to go ahead, hoping that the rain was just a local shower. We were on the trail by 7 A.M. It always takes longer to get started when there's a group. I like to get going by 5 or 5:30, but the Negritos cannot be pushed—no Filipinos can, for that matter. They move when the spirit moves them. After a three-mile hike, we reached the Manglad River, a wide, swiftly flowing stream about 100 feet wide. We were already in the mountains and the trail continued to climb. We ran into huge rocks about 10:30 A.M. They varied in size from three or four feet across to the size of a small house. Climbing over or around these tremendous obstacles with our heavy, rain-soaked packs, thirty-five to forty pounds in weight, proved extremely difficult, and sometimes dangerous, as we slipped backwards and stumbled. The rocks were covered with green moss and fungus and were slippery as grass. Rice and sardines for supper. One can of sardines was our ration, for eight people! It had rained all afternoon, but the rain finally stopped just as we ate our supper, and we were able to get a good night's sleep. Crossed the river about sixty times today. Covered approximately sixteen to eighteen miles.

Sunday, March 19: Moving very slowly on the trail. This steady rain is making the river wider and swifter. The rocks are slippery and treacherous to cross. No trail any more. In bad places, we have to hack our way through jungle. One hard whack with the machete at shoulder level in each direction, one hard cut at knee level, in both directions, and then we take one step forward. Many hours we are fortunate to make even one half of a mile. We stopped at 11 A.M. on the banks of a small, crystal-clear stream, while the Negrito boys hunted fish with homemade goggles and a "gun" made of a steel rod and rubber bands cut from tire inner tubes. One of the boys caught an eel after about thirty minutes. We devoured it with gusto—head, tail, eyes, and all. As we walked deeper and deeper into the forest primeval in the deep gloom of the dense rain forest, I could hear all sorts of peculiar noises. Flitting shadows made the hair rise on the back of my neck. These Ilongot head-hunters might resent our invading their hunting grounds! I slipped in crossing one of the rivers this morning, and my 35 mm. camera got wet. The sun came out this afternoon for the first time on the trip. I feel stronger today. Guess the malaria is gone for good. Have seen many beautiful birds—one of the most beautiful is a yellow-billed, green-coated bird, shaped somewhat like a duck. Saw many fossils bearing imprint of sea shells, indicating this area was once part of the ocean floor. Covered approximately twelve to fifteen miles today.

*Monday, March 20:* This was our best day's hike, even though it rained lightly all day. Our guide estimated we were already more than forty miles out from Pinapagan. As we hiked deeper and deeper into Ilongot territory, we all became more and more apprehensive, and tried to make as little noise as possible. About 3:30 this afternoon, as we were stealthily creeping through the jungle, we suddenly rounded a sharp turn, and encountered a big hunting party of about thirty to forty men. Since they were all in G-strings, I did not have the slightest idea whether they were Ilongots, or from some other tribe. We did not know whether they were friendly or not.

Being the leader of our group, I stood uncertainly for a minute or two, and then I walked over toward their group and approached a tall, dignified old warrior who stood at their center. He said not a word, but his eyes followed my every movement. I managed to stammer out, "Naimbag a malem," which means "Good afternoon." He looked at me impassively, without a word, until the silence was electric. Then he quietly replied, "Good afternoon to you, sir," in perfect English.

I was flabbergasted. "Where did you learn to speak such good English?" I inquired.

He drew himself up another inch, and with great pride answered, "I was a lieutenant in the American Army." It seems he had enlisted in the U. S. Army at an early age and had been a scout. Being an expert in tracking and in jungle lore, he had progressed rapidly up the ladder of promotion. However, after many years of service in the army, he had grown lonely for the old life in the jungle and had left the army and come home. He was now the chief of this large tribe of Negritos.

The Negrito hunting party had just killed and butchered four deer and three wild hogs, and they graciously invited us to share their feast with them. During the next half hour, as we talked around the campfire, one of the men staggered in with one of the largest wild boars I have ever seen, in real life or in pictures. Its tusks were tremendous. We had a wonderful supper—venison, pork, and the heart of a wild pig generously presented to us by the chief. Our dinner table, as usual, was a large flat rock. After pouring clean water over the stone to clean it, we then dumped out the steaming hot, fragrant rice, and every one dug in. Everybody ate with his hands, except plutocrat Spottswood, who had an army spoon in his back pocket.

After supper I took this opportunity to ask one or two of the Negrito women about their way of life. "Yes," they said, "we believe in a God." When I asked the chief's wife how they knew there was a God, she replied, "We cannot tell." I then asked her what were the main things a mother in the Negrito tribe would teach her children. She replied that when an old mother lies dying, she always calls in all of her children and pleads with them never to steal, to give her their solemn promise never to steal. Pressed for other important teachings, she continued, "We teach our children to tell the truth at all times." Asked for their teaching about adultery, the old woman did not understand the word at all, and replied firmly, "Negrito women have but one husband." How utterly amazing to be five days out in the wildest part of the jungle among primitive tribes who have had almost no contact with civilization and then to find these great moral teachings "written on the tablets of their hearts" by the invisible hand of the Living God!

We were interested to learn how the Negrito marriage ceremony is accomplished. The people told us that when all the tribe is gathered together, the elders give a few words of advice to the young people about to be wed, and then the ceremony itself takes place. The man gives the woman a handful of rice—symbolic of his willingness to provide her with food for the rest of her life—and then she gives it back to him, and he eats it. Thus, she signifies her willingness to prepare and cook his food for him. Through this simple exchange he promises to be her hunter and provider, and she promises to be his homemaker. Then there is a great tribal feast. After the feast, the ceremony is completed.

*Tuesday, March 21:* This was the longest day of my life. The steady rain that started at 9 P.M. last night turned into a deluge by morning. Great sheets of rain came pouring down. In spite of the enormous difficulties, slipping, sliding, falling, rolling, we were able to climb up the steep slopes of the mountain and reached the top of the Sierra Madre range by 9:30 A.M. The jungle was terrible. After we left the river, the Negritos had started into what seemed to me to be an impenetrable jungle. It was steady climbing at a 30° to 40° angle of slope, sometimes even steeper, and always in the rain. Thorns and bushes ripped clothing and skin to shreds. Arms and hands were bleeding from leeches. Going down the side of the highest mountain, we hit another mountain stream. It was normally just a small stream, but the steady all-night downpour had turned it into a raging torrent, with giant rocks crashing down at random. We had to cross this stream to continue our journey toward the coast, and yet it was extremely dangerous, since we might be dashed against

143

the giant boulders, or swept off our feet and drowned. By now it was obvious that we were in an "out-of-season" typhoon. To cross now was dangerous, and yet if we waited for the river to subside, it might become worse instead.

We tried to hold a "pow-wow" to decide what to do, but the sound of the rocks crashing down the river, the roar of the raging torrent, the wind whipping against the giant trees and bending them over like toys all made so much noise it was difficult to talk in the storm. The typhoon picked up the rain and flung it into our faces so that we could hardly see. To top all our difficulties, the guides decided to quit. They were afraid. They simply disappeared, after telling us they refused to go on. What a spot we were in! We were in the middle of the wildest unexplored jungle in Luzon, in the middle of a terrible typhoon, and without guides. There was no turning back. It was three or four days' hike back to the nearest civilization in that direction, while if we pushed on forward, we might make it out of the jungle by nightfall. We decided to go on, to try to make it to the coast, even without our guides.

The only trail we could follow was the river. We knew if we stayed by the river, we would reach the coastline. Yet, the overgrowth was so thick that following the river meant that we had to cross and recross it dozens of times every hour, to find passable places to walk. Half a dozen times in the next seven hours I held my breath as my companions started out into that swollen, surging, screaming stream, with huge boulders crashing down on all sides of them, grazing them, knocking them down. I felt it was utterly impossible to get out of there without the loss of one or two lives. Twice in the swift stream I was swept off my feet and slammed into rocks below. My hat, glasses, film, and knife were lost, and both movie and 35 mm. cameras were submerged again and again in the rushing waters, but I was so glad to be still alive that I never gave them another thought.

It was easier hiking now that we were out of the jungle,

though it was still raining. We hiked until dark, and reached the Pacific coast. Then, to our dismay, we learned that Casiguran was still about thirty or more miles north of us, up a barren coast. Though we had not had a bite of food since breakfast, we could not eat, since all our matches were wet, and there was no way to cook the rice. Cold, wet, hungry, we were still thankful that we had reached safety. At last it stopped raining about 9 P.M., and we lost consciousness in our wet clothes, under our soggy blankets, and slept.

*Wednesday, March 22:* The sun came out blistering hot this morning and dried our spirits and our clothes (but *not* our matches!). We began hiking northward, but it was slow going through the soft sand of the beach. Our feet sank deep with every step, and picking them up again and again became quite an effort. We managed to reach the first barrio of Casiguran—Dilalengan—by about 1 P.M. While we were still more than twenty miles from Casiguran proper, we were glad to be in a village of any sort. We agreed that two of the pastors would stay here to distribute the atabrine and vitamin pills, to give out Gospel portions and talk with the people, and to try to have a service of worship in the school building that evening. Pastor Garcia managed to hire a small banca, and he and I started out to follow the stream up to Casiguran. It was a dug-out canoe, with an outrigger on it. He and I took turns paddling all night, and fourteen hours later, at 9 A.M., we reached the town.

*Thursday, March 23:* After a quick shave and a bite to eat, Pastor Garcia and I started out to explore the town. We called on the Mayor, the chief of police, the supervisor of schools, and the health authorities. We found Casiguran to be a veritable oasis in an erstwhile wilderness. It was a small town of around 3000 people in the centro, with a total population of 7000 including all the outlying barrios. It was practically untouched by war. There were three elementary schools still functioning. There was a doctor, with a small clinic. Compared with Palanan, just

145

eighty to one hundred miles up the coast, this place is a veritable city. It has two or three general stores, run by Chinese merchants. The big difference is due to the fact that a boat stops here at Casiguran once a week, while in Palanan there is a boat only once a year. Here in Casiguran they have a doctor to treat the worst diseases. However, as in much of the Philippines, the chief problem is still malnutrition caused by the unbalanced diet of the poor people, and the subsequent illness, tuberculosis, which so often follows malnutrition. We distributed our atabrine and vitamin tablets. Since malaria is still the most prevalent sickness, and the clinic is very short on drugs, the people accepted our medicines with open arms.

It is only within the past month or so that there has been an active religious program of any kind in Casiguran. The Roman Catholics have just sent in an Italian priest, and he is beginning to build a small chapel. However, the interest of the people in the Gospel portions we have given out, and the large requests for New Testaments and Bibles have convinced us that this place is open to the Gospel of Jesus Christ. We strongly recommend that the Bishop send some one in to serve in this frontier situation, to bring Christ's saving work to those faraway people.

After a quick lunch we jumped into our small banca and by 1 P.M. were on our way back to join our companions in the barrio. We made a sail out of a blanket and were able to make much better time. We reached Dilalengan by 1:30 in the morning.

*Friday, March 24:* The other men reported a fine meeting, with more than sixty people attending. When Pastor Tuguiere asked, "How many of you are interested in accepting Christ, and in being baptized when we come back next time?" Almost the entire group responded.

The weather was perfect as we started the homeward journey. We started out about 9 A.M. and had reached the top of the mountain and started down the other side in slightly more than three hours, the same distance it had taken us more than nine hours to cover during the storm. I was amazed at the stamina of the men who kept moving at a marvelous pace, in spite of the fact that in the past four nights we had had only ten hours sleep in all. In the past three days we have had only five meals. By 3 P.M. we had reached the Negrito hunters' camp. We made wonderful progress, and we did not stop until almost dark. Our guides and cargadores were far behind, and so we wrapped up in our blankets and went to bed without any food.

*Saturday, March 25:* No breakfast, as we wanted to hike while it was cool, instead of waiting for the Negritos to catch up. We hiked steadily until about 9:30, when we stopped to rest. The guides caught up with us then, and we had a *de luxe* banquet of the two cans of sardines, plus one fresh fish which was cooked on a stick in the coals of the fire and seasoned with wild orange. Um-m, it was delicious. We covered sixteen to twenty miles a day on the return trip. Partly, our faster speed was due to the lighter loads we had to carry. Mostly, though, it was because we were sick of the eerie jungle trails, where every unusual noise made us jump behind a tree and every shadow reminded us of the head-hunters. Noted many small rocks and stones impregnated in the large boulders, indicating this terrain was probably of volcanic origin. Many trees along the way were suffering from some kind of blight.

*Sunday, March 26:* This steady rice and fish diet is getting me down. My clothes hang on me like bags. We got off to an early start this morning. By traveling fast all day, we were able to reach Pinapagan by 1:30 P.M. By almost a miracle, I was able to catch a motor boat right away, and after an exciting, breathtaking ride down the rapids, I reached Jones by 9 P.M. I bade my fellow pastors a fond farewell—we were truly close now, for we had all faced death together and we were one in spirit and in consecration to the Master's service—and then I hopped in

147

the jeep and started out immediately. I was able to reach the mission house in San Mateo that night. There Dorothy Edwards, Miss Cab, and Ruth Atkins were all up, prepared for a grand welcome party. We ate, and talked until 1 A.M. No food in the world ever tasted as good as the fruit-cake-saved-since-Christmas that we ate that night!

I was up at 5 A.M. and on the road by 5:30. By 9:30 I reached Tuguegarao, and *home!* In exactly two weeks we had covered almost 300 miles through some of the wildest, most primitive country left in the Philippines—and in a storm.

I went to bed for two days—that glorious, glorious bed—but not before thanking God again for my life. *Praise be to God for His unfailing guidance, strength and blessing.*

# 10

## Move to Mindanao

THE CARABAO PLODDED slowly up. A young farmer slid off the side and went back to help to his feet a young Moro man, wrapped in a brilliant, scarlet-hued robe, who was lying on a bamboo sled at the rear of the carabao. The young Moro, twisting in agony, limped into the medical clinic and crawled up onto the crude wooden plank that served as an examining table. He had a huge carbuncle on his right groin. It was angry, bloody red, and needed to be opened immediately. As the doctor's hand reached for the scalpel, the Moro's eyes widened with fear. After the doctor's quick thrust, pus gushed out of the carbuncle, nearly a cupful. The Moro's face was now ashen, and beads of perspiration stood out on his forehead. But, an hour later, he was back on his carabao sled, ready for his long, bumpy ride back home. This young Mohammedan, sworn enemy of the Christians, had been treated by Christian doctors and nurses with loving care, and given the best of medicines that money could buy. The first patient of the Mindanao Work Camp had been treated.

Mindanao—Mecca of the Mohammedans—the "land of opportunity"—the "Golden West" of the Philippines—the very name spelled adventure to every young, daring, venturesome young man in the Philippines. Mindanao, second largest of the islands, was still 30 per cent to 40 per cent unexplored. It beckoned to all the landless of the archipelago, and its ports welcomed two to three thousand settlers a month, at the height

149

of its influx of immigrants. There were men, women, and children, with their bundles of clothing, baskets of chickens, rope-tied hogs, and most important of all, their hopes and dreams for a better life for themselves in the future. After the war, when the island of Luzon was grappling with its problems of agrarian unrest, of absentee landlordism, of poverty-pressed tenant farming, the magic name of Mindanao spelled "land" and brought people to its shores by the thousands. Selling their houses, their carabaos, their jewels, whatever possessions they had, whole families and even sometimes whole villages pulled up stakes and moved to Mindanao.

What an exotic land they found upon arrival! Fed by the constant tropical rains, the land was a deep, verdant green, with giant, towering trees, thick, lush, tangling undergrowth, wild orchids and brilliant, beautiful flowers of all kinds. This was the "land of the forest primeval"—and only superlatives could describe it. Mindanao was the home of the colorfully dressed Moros, or Mohammedans, the earliest settlers of the island. In addition there were the primitive Atas from the mountainous interior, the distinctive Bagobo and Manobo tribes with their bright, hand-woven costumes, Cebuanos, Boholanos, and settlers from all the various islands of the Philippines, so that Mindanao was a veritable melting pot of races and cultures. It was a land of contrasts—of lovely, mile-long coconut haciendas along the three to four thousand miles of jagged coastline; of small, native villages high up in the mountains; of vast *datu's* mansions where a hundred or more beautifully dressed Moro wives, mothers, cousins, aunts, uncles, brothers, friends might live, together with countless shaven-headed, naked children; of tiny, make-shift huts of new settlers, struggling to get a start in this new land; of vast fields of rice, of corn, of ramie, the newest crop of the island; of small outrigger canoes from which the divers skillfully bring up some of the world's most beautiful pearls.

As I watched my young co-workers go calmly about their work,

on this first day of the Mindanao Work Camp, my mind went
back over that fateful day when Bishop Valencia had first talked
to me of Mindanao. His note had been brief and right to the
point. It read: "Will you and Mrs. Spottswood please come to
my office at 9 A.M. tomorrow?"

We went. The Bishop was warm, friendly, approachable. He
began with several casual remarks about the church, but our
ears were tuned for the question we knew was coming. It came,
slowly. "Brother and Mrs. Spottswood, we have more than 400
Methodists in Mindanao. There are four congregations already
organized, and other groups are petitioning me for pastors, for
guidance, for help. Immigrants are pouring into Mindanao every
month, and many of these are our people. Would you be willing
to move to Mindanao? Would you be willing to recruit and train
young people for church leadership?"

There it was! *Wham!* We were being challenged to move
1000 miles to the south, from the northernmost mission station,
Tuguegarao, to the southernmost outpost. We would move to a
new land, a land of many towns and cities it is true, but also
of mile upon mile of wide, unsettled areas—to a vast frontier
land. The Bishop, a man of prayer, told us, "Don't answer yet.
Take this question home with you and pray about it. Let me
know your feeling later."

We knew we had reached one of the major turning points in
our lives. We were deeply involved in the work of the church
in the Cagayan Valley, and we were challenged by the opportunities for growth which we could see there. On the other hand,
here was a great, yawning open door before us, an evangelistic
opportunity to minister to these thousands upon thousands of
new settlers. Should we enter that door? We began to pray,
earnestly, fervently. We tried to heed the leading of the Spirit.
After several weeks of intensive thinking, discussion, prayer,
we wrote the Bishop, "We are willing to be used of God in
Mindanao." It was a decision we were never to regret. In the

years that followed we had the great joy of seeing the jungles receding and the frontiers being pushed steadily forward, with Methodism in the vanguard, carrying the cross of Christ.

The next step in the move to Mindanao was a brief, exploratory trip to that island, to visit our existing congregations, to study the opportunities, and to report to the Central Conference. I took along two of our most aggressive, pioneering pastors, Felix Grospe, and Adriano Cabotaje. We took off early one morning in my small plane, "The Circuit-Rider," and were soon winging our way over beautiful Lake Taal. We had a breath-taking view of the volcano which in 1913 had taken so many lives, but which was now peaceful and majestic. We flew out over Lipa, and then out over the straits toward Mindoro. As we flew down the east coast of the island, we rejoiced in the changing colors of the countryside, green rice fields turning brown with their heavy heads of rice, promising a good harvest. Leaving Mindoro, we had to fly out over the open sea about sixty miles to Panay. Butterflies kept hopping up and down in my stomach, as I thought, "What would we do if this single engine should quit on us?"

It didn't quit, and we kept on going from Capiz to the island of Panay, where we landed to get gasoline, on to Negros Oriental, where we touched down at Dumaguete, site of Silliman University. Finally, we were out over the open sea heading toward Mindanao. Those butterflies continued to flutter inside me as I remembered the schoolbooks' stories of the "Mindanao Deep," the deepest ocean spot in the whole world. "What a place this would be to go down!" I thought. Soon we spotted a waterfall, the majestic Maria Cristina Falls, where the Philippine Government is putting up a dam, power plant, and fertilizer plant. A few hours later we spotted the three rivers of Cotabato, and a few miles later we were circling the large, well laid-out city of Cotabato and coming in for a landing. (The Mohammedan word for Cotabato means "stone fort.") My two passengers and

# MOVE TO MINDANAO

I thanked God for the safe journey of nearly 1000 miles. Since regular air maps were not available, much of this island-hopping trip had been made entirely by road map, and a good number of its miles had been flown over water. We were deeply and earnestly sincere in thanking God for our safe landing!

We were cordially welcomed to the beautiful city of Cotabato by two active laymen, who took us to the top of the hill where the provincial hospital, capital buildings and Philippine Constabulary headquarters were located. From this high vantage point we had a breath-taking view of the countryside, of this much-talked-of island of Mindanao. Our hosts pointed out to us the vast Liguasan Marshes stretching off to the east, the great Allah Valley to the south where so many of our Methodist people had settled, the rugged mountain ranges stretching northward toward Lake Lanao and the heavily Moro-populated areas, and the small national road cutting through the foothills over to the rich rice-growing plains of the central part of Mindanao. It was a land infinitely rich in natural resources, in possibilities for future growth and development, and in opportunities which whetted our imaginations.

From Cotabato we took a bus along this road to Kabacan, where our largest church in Mindanao was located. Here we stayed in the home of Mayor Catalino Guzman, a Methodist minister who had come down to Mindanao with his fellow townsmen from Luzon and had organized the church. His Christian character and leadership were so marked that he had been elected mayor in a land where the Moros, as the Muslims are called, make up 40 per cent to 50 per cent of the voters.

After visiting with our members in Kabacan, and speaking in the evening church service, we then hiked through the mud to the barrio of Bannawa, about eight miles away. There is no mud anywhere in the world quite like the mud in Mindanao. It is the deepest, stickiest, slipperiest, "mostest" mud in the world. Because of the daily tropical downpours, or deluges, the

153

carabao trails and footpaths become a series of long mud holes, from ankle deep to sometimes hip or even waist deep, and negotiating our way across these muddy areas became a very tricky matter, requiring a toe-dancer's sense of balance, as well as infinite patience. Many times as I gingerly lifted one foot from the sucking mud and tried to balance myself and find the next good place to put it down, I narrowly missed taking a nose dive headlong into the mud. I had to walk barefooted, as my shoes would not stay on my feet, and it was my bad luck to step on some broken glass and cut my right foot badly. However, the joy of the people in seeing us arrive made all the agony of that "purgatory road" seem worthwhile. Tears of joy and hope streamed down the faces of our members there in the little chapel that night.

The mud and dirt and manure of the trail had done their work well, so that by the time I limped back into Kabacan the next day my foot was a red, swollen mass of infection. The local nurse gave me some shots and put me to bed, but it was two days before I could walk again. By the time I was up again, Typhoon Trix was already beginning to bring her rain, strong winds, and general havoc. Roads down into the Koronadal Valley were washed out, and so we next took a bus to Upi, a lovely mountaintop town where the Episcopal Mission had a beautiful chapel and a missionary rector.

By the time the weather cleared up enough to fly again, I found the plane had some engine trouble. The right magneto was dropping 150 to 200 r.p.m. Shades of night! What else could go wrong on this trip? Just as I was restlessly pacing around the airport—the third day after wiring for parts from Manila, with still no reply and no parts—I happened to meet a casually dressed, but handsome young man. He walked up to me by the plane and asked me what was wrong. When I told him our predicament, he informed me, "I have some spare parts down on our plantation."

154

# MOVE TO MINDANAO

Two hours later, skirting the western coast of Cotabato, we were landing at the small strip of the Kalaon Plantation. This large coconut and abaca plantation was set in a lovely valley made by two mountain ranges, a river on the third side, and the Moro Gulf in the west. It was a beautiful little oasis in the thick tropics which pushed in upon it. While we were there for three days, getting the plane in tip-top shape again, several occurrences reminded us of the nearness of the jungle. One day one of the drivers chased with a tractor a giant boa constrictor which had just swallowed a chicken whole! Jim Strong, part owner of the plantation, killed a wild pig less than 100 yards from his house. Harry Pareet, his brother-in-law, told me that there were still a number of crocodiles in the river adjoining their property. I was invited to go down on a dark night to verify the accuracy of this statement, but since my feet and legs were not insured, I did not accept the invitation.

A few days later Pastors Grospe, Cabotaje and I were back in Manila, after visiting General Santos at the southern tip of Mindanao, Davao on the eastern side, and covering a total of 2500 miles in all, part of the time through one of the worst typhoons in Philippine history. We were unanimous in giving our report. Our one big conclusion: *"The church must act—now!"* We were confronted with the church's greatest evangelistic opportunity in fifty years. Mindanao is an enormous place. Cotabato Province alone is as large as seven provinces on Luzon, and then there are also the provinces of Davao, Agusan, Surigao, Bukidnon, and Zamboanga. Most of the places we visited were largely unchurched, although the Jehovah's Witnesses and some of the smaller sect groups were beginning to move in. The Methodist Church had a real obligation to follow and serve its members, and also to minister to the exploding population of Mindanao, with its desperate shortage of trained leadership. With a deep sense of urgency we reported to Bishop Valencia the things we had seen, the places we had visited, the needs we had found. His response was just as I had expected. He said to me, "Brother Spottswood, get ready to go!"

Moving the whole family to Mindanao, 1000 miles from Tuguegarao, proved to be a delightful as well as an educational experience. We traveled on the M.V. *Victor*, a small inter-island freighter which had been converted from an old U.S. Army supply boat from the war days. It was a leisurely five-and-a-half-day trip, in and out of the beautiful green islands. The ship cruised at around ten knots an hour, and we stopped at every major island for loading and unloading our varied cargo of pigs, chickens, sacks of rice and sugar, lumber, and all sorts of boxes and crates. Those stops of from half-day to two days in the larger ports enabled us to see the important cities of the southern islands, and to gain a little understanding of life on the other major islands. Besides the seven Spottswoods we had the following people along with us, as part of our "Christian Commando" team to assault Mindanao for Christ: Miss Dorothy Edwards, Director of the Mobile Clinic from the Cagayan Valley; Lorie Crisologo, the new doctor of the clinic; Bert Sison, the dentist; Josefina Cabanilla, clinic nurse; Fannie Dewar, visiting missionary nurse; Naty Ngo, nurse; Don Reeves, short-term agricultural missionary; Julie Felix, children's worker and cook; Juliano Martinez, driver and mechanic, and Socorro Carino, one of the finest teachers of the Cagayan Valley, who had volunteered to give her time to help train Sunday school teachers.

The ship had three decks. We were fortunate enough to be on the top deck, open to the fresh air and sea breezes. Here more than 100 army cots were lined up side by side, their edges almost touching. Between the rows of cots there was less than ten inches, so that when one person wanted to pass down the "aisle," anybody coming from the opposite direction had to sit down at the foot of the closest cot and draw his feet up out of the way so that the other person could pass. Each person put his suitcase and bags under his cot, spread his mat or bedspread over his cot, and zealously guarded his own private "domain." Soon the ship was a rainbow of bright colors, as the varicolored mats and blankets were spread out and the men, women, and children of all ages and sizes and descriptions began to make themselves at home on top of their cots, spreading out magazines, crackers, boxes, colored fans, and robes and pillows of one sort or another.

The second deck was also filled with cots, but much more tightly packed and jammed together. Since there was not as much fresh air here, more of the passengers were seasick, and the air soon became heavy and putrid. The bottom deck alongside the crew's cabins, as well as the entire front end of the ship above the holds, was filled with 500 to 800 pigs jammed together, and 2000 chickens in split bamboo crates, stacked one above another ten crates deep. The boys were fascinated in watching the sailors throw the food at the pigs, and hose them down several times a day, but I must confess that their aroma forced itself so strongly upon us that the rest of us would gladly have done without this particular diversion. We sought relief from the overpowering odor of the pigs by laboriously picking our way through the tangle of cots to the opposite end of the ship, where an oilcloth-covered dining table and some chairs provided the ship's only dining room. Here, if we were lucky, we could find a seat among the mahjong-playing passengers. However, the smells here were apt to be just as strong, although of a different nature, as frying garlic, fish, dirty dishcloths, and spoiled garbage all blended together and wafted their way up from the crowded galley below.

The captain of the *Victor* was a family man and made us feel immediately at home by saying to my wife and me, "Feel at home, anywhere on the ship." His hospitable, friendly spirit was a real blessing. The first mate also represented the best of Filipino manhood. He was young, handsome, friendly, and extremely polite. He took our five sons up on top, where he was on duty, and let them "work out" with his bar-bells and other athletic equipment. Here, up on the topside, above the flying bridge, he joined our group in some of the beautiful sunset hymnsings and worship services which we held. As the sun sank into the brilliant western sky, and as the millions of stars came out over the shining, twinkling sea, we all prayed earnestly that God would prepare our hearts and minds for the tasks that lay ahead in Mindanao. God was very near to us under His open sky, as we threaded our way between the many Philippine isles, and prayed for His guidance and His strength and His spirit.

The trip was very restful and peaceful. Much of the 1000-mile journey was made in protected, sheltered waters between the green and purple islands, so that the sea was calm most of the time. Since there was no place to sit down, most of the people lay down on their cots most of the day, reading, or sleeping. In reading an interesting story, what did we care if our elbows were touching our neighbor's elbows? However, even the most exciting book was apt to fall to the floor before long, as the soothing sound of the ship's motors and the lulling motion of the rippling waves rocked us to sleep. We would doze, wake to enjoy the beauty of the Sulu Sea around us, try to recognize the different islands in the distance, wave to passengers on other ships passing by us, exchange a few words with our next-cot neighbors, and then doze again. I brought along a typewriter and a pile of work to be done, but the lethargy brought on by the peaceful lazy life on board the ship was not to be overcome. Even the five healthy, usually active, wiggly Spottswood boys were so completely "tranquillized" that there was not a single discipline problem the entire five days of the trip!

The food on the ship was adequate, though apt to be a mite greasy for our Western tastes. What we liked best was the service—coffee brought to our cots the first thing every morning, and at 3 P.M. every day.

Every time we docked, our tranquil, quiet life would be suddenly shattered, as cargadores pushed and shouted and shoved their way aboard with loads of baggage, as peddlers swarmed all over the ship selling souvenirs—baskets, straw hats, Moro pearls, an all-too-many smuggled items which had been brought in from Borneo or Sumatra by small Moro sailing boats—and as the big overhead cranes whined and whistled, loading and unloading freight. The first time the decks were overrun with people and baggage and crew members at odd hours of the night we found sleep impossible, but we soon learned to sleep through it all, even with huge overhead lights glaring down into our eyes. If we did happen to be awakened, as a passing seaman would accidentally brush our feet as he rushed down the narrow passageway between the cots, we enjoyed sitting up in our cots, or going topside to watch the hustle and excitement of the busy harbor, and then later to watch spellbound as the gay twinkling lights of the town slipped farther and farther away in the distance as the ship pulled away again. The silver moon rising higher and higher in the sky, the Big Dipper to the north, the Southern Cross in the south, the rippling waves reflecting in a million diamond points the brilliance of the night painted indelible pictures on our minds.

We realized that we needed a lot of study and prayer to prepare us for the challenge that lay ahead in Mindanao, but the question was *how?* How could we meet together as a group on the crowded deck, with every available square inch covered with cots and people? Miss Cab, who can do *anything*, I am convinced, soon came up with the answer. Standing three of our cots up on end, she then turned two more lengthwise, and we then had a rectangular bit of floor space in the middle that rightfully belonged to us. We sat on the cots all around the edges, opened our Bibles to the Book of Acts, and began earnestly to study the way the Holy Spirit had led the apostles of old in the first beginnings of the Christian Church. We united in a deep and wonderful bond of fellowship, praying that God's

Spirit would also lead us and guide us and empower us as we began to build His Church in Mindanao in *our* day.

What a hunger there is in the human heart for the Word of God! One of the by-products of our daily times of worship, Bible study, and discussion mornings and afternoons was that others on the ship were drawn to our group, and asked if they might join us in our hymn-singing and worship. Thus, even on the ship, God was leading us and preparing the way. One of the new-found friends on the boat had a relative in Davao City who had a bus company, and he arranged for our transportation from the city inland to Kabacan, when we landed. Another of the friends who joined in our devotional meetings on the boat was a prominent lawyer who helped a great deal in laying the ground-work for the organization of the church in Davao City the following year. "God moves in a mysterious way His wonders to perform!"

We landed early in the morning, just as the giant red-rimmed ball of the sun leaped out of the sea and colored all the harbor in brilliant radiance. Ah-h-h, the early mornings in the tropics are so beautiful! While it becomes hot and muggy later in the day, in the early morning hours, the air is crisp and cool and delightful. Without too much delay or trouble we were soon all loaded on a big bus, with all the boxes and cases of medical, dental, audio-visual, and agricultural supplies tied on to the top of the bus, pushed under our feet, and some even in our laps. Some five or six hot, dusty hours later we were pulling up in front of the Home Economics building at Kabacan, Cotabato, the site of our one-month Work Camp. We had chosen this place to begin our work for several reasons: 1) There were many of our evangelical people there who could help us; 2) It was the geographical center of Mindanao, an easy base from which I could go out to visit other areas and churches; 3) It was a large town, combining Moros, Ilocanos, and Cebuanos, and serving a large number of outlying barrios which were in great need. We

160

decided that this was the place where we could best begin to serve.

To the medical team that had come down on the boat with us we added a number of carefully chosen local young people who had volunteered to give Christ one month of their lives, so that we made up a group of twenty-six people in all, young people and leaders, all living together in a small, grass-roofed house, just 30 by 40 feet in size. In its four rooms were a medical clinic, a dental clinic, a complete audio-visual outfit, including large motor generator, projectors, outdoor horn and speakers. Toss in fifty or sixty boxes of supplies piled into the back room where we were supposed to sleep, all of our personal baggage, piles of Bibles and other literature to be sold or given out, several boards laid across some sawhorses to make our dining table, and a make-shift kitchen over in one corner, and you can imagine the little house was already full. Add twenty-six Work Camp members, and a like number of mosquito nets strung up across the floor at night, and the house literally bulged. Add twenty-five or thirty patients waiting out on the little front porch, peeking in the window, their babies screaming and crying, the curious children coming in to look at us and pick up and handle our boxes and bags and you have the atmosphere in which we lived, ate, worked and slept for one month. This was our Work Camp set-up.

Through the window came the dull thud of a pick, the scrape of a shovel, the grunt of human beings lifting heavy loads of dirt. The very first day the boys of the Work Camp were started on their first work project, the digging of a deep pump well for the elementary school. The mayor advised us that this was the greatest need of the community, for dysentery was killing many of the children. Most of the wells of Kabacan were very shallow, containing water that was impure and dangerous. We all took turns in digging and hauling, and many hours—and many grunts—later we reached the water. Then the sand point was adjusted, the long pipe was lowered inch by inch, and the work of grinding down through mud and sand to the clear water was begun. Before the month was over, the pump was installed, the cement mixed and poured, and the job was done. The young people had demonstrated to the people of Kabacan their Christian concern through a concrete act of service to the community. Surely this was "Christ's love made visible."

Another work project was to help the local Methodist congregation move and rebuild their church building in a more strategic location, next to the public market. Hauling lumber, pounding nails, helping to put on the roof, the boys worked side by side with the men of the church in building the new house of worship. The girls of the Work Camp family, not to be outdone, hauled in gravel and made a walk in front of the church, cut the weeds in the church yard, and planted shrubs and flowers. They felt real joy in their hearts, as they made beautiful the house of God.

"How many people will be interested in our Teacher Training Institute?" wondered Socorro and the young people helping her, as they walked over to the school classrooms that first morning. Imagine their thrill when twenty-two people—both adults and young people—enrolled that first morning! This teacher training was an interdenominational project, for there were representatives from every church in town—Methodist, U.C.C.P., Pilgrim Holiness, and Roman Catholic. They studied the purposes of Christian teaching, the principles of learning, methods and techniques of teaching, and child development. For their laboratory experience the teachers-to-be practiced their songs, storytelling, and teaching methods with the neighborhood children in a Vacation Church School in the mornings, and then discussed their experiences in their classroom study in the afternoons. This teacher training was so successful that we were requested to hold the same program in Banawa, a barrio eight miles from the national road. Here ten more young people volun-

162

teered to come every day to learn to be Christian teachers and leaders in their local church. As we hiked the many miles to Banawa and back, our feet were hot and blistered, our faces sunburned, and our backs dripping with perspiration. But our spirits soared within us at being able to do a job that needed doing. We remembered Jesus, hiking over the hills of Galilee, teaching, and we felt humble and proud to be following in His footsteps.

Our two-day Agricultural Institutes, held first in Kabacan, and then in two other nearby villages, attracted huge crowds. Hundreds of people shoved and pushed their way into the school building, where Don Reeves set up the movie projector. First he showed a Walt Disney health film, "Water, Friend or Enemy." Next he showed a picture on rural farmers' cooperatives. In one room Don gave demonstrations in methods of innoculating pigs and chickens against diseases. In another room Dr. Lorie Crisologo held a big audience spellbound as he lectured and demonstrated first-aid measures. Outside under an acacia tree a nurse gave illustrated lectures on prenatal, postnatal, and infant care. Classes in Home Nursing, Rat and Pest Control, Abaca Mosaic, and Fertilizer Use rounded out the Institutes, this vital phase of our Work Camp program. Here we were trying to help people to know how to help themselves. In a land where getting enough to eat is the basic problem of survival this is important business —God's business.

We were all eating dinner one Sunday after church when a child came running in to the little Home Economics house where we were staying. "My mother is dying!" she screamed. "Where's the doctor? Hurry! Hurry!" We explained to her that the doctor and the rest of the clinic were out in the barrio, more than four hours away from Kabacan. But the little girl wailed all the louder, "You must come. My mother is dying."

Finally Mariam and Naty Ngo, a young recent graduate from the Mary Johnston School of Nursing who had come down with

163

us to gain some experience with the clinic, were able to calm the little girl enough to learn what the trouble was. Her mother had been in labor for two days, but had not been able to deliver the child. As she got more and more tired and weak, she would rouse herself occasionally to scream, "I'm dying! I'm dying!" This was obviously an emergency situation, which the native "partrera," or midwife, could not handle. We all turned and looked at Naty. She was the only hope in this desperate situation, the only person who could hope to save the life of this mother and her unborn baby. But Naty was nervous as a cat. She had just finished nursing school and had had no experience. She had no equipment, and only a few drugs and first-aid supplies which the clinic had left with us. She was one small, scared nurse—but she was brave, and she prepared to go.

Late that afternoon Naty stumbled in again. Her uniform was dripping wet, but her face was wreathed in smiles. We knew the outcome: the mother had lived. Naty told us the story. It was a dry birth, and the mother was already weak and exhausted when Naty arrived in the little hut, on the outskirts of the town. All contractions had stopped, and the mother seemed almost in a coma. Naty began to massage the muscles, and after an hour or two of work, massaging, encouraging, and especially *praying*, she got labor started again. After two hours more, during which Naty pushed and pulled—she says she does not remember just exactly what she did, besides praying—the baby was born, a healthy little girl. Naty came back all smiles, because God had used her to help, and had given her the courage and strength and wisdom she needed. Little Naty II was baptized in our church two weeks later.

"We never dreamed we could win people to Christ!" exclaimed our young people, after their first afternoon's experience in visitation evangelism. In the Philippines the young people are unusually shy, and most of our church people were far too diffident to talk to others of their faith. But, after several days

164

of preparation and prayer together with some volunteers of the local church, the work campers began going out in small teams to make visits in the name of Christ. One girl had a truly heart-warming experience. She told us of visiting a backsliding member whose heart was touched by the obvious sincerity and Christlike concern of our young people. The woman began to cry. Viola, not knowing what to do, suggested that they pray, and as they prayed, the woman confessed her sins to God, and gave her heart and life to Jesus Christ once again. The work campers and local leaders continued to go out calling every afternoon. Their enthusiasm, their excitement in discovering how God could work through them was contagious. These young people were taking seriously the command of Jesus, "GO YE . . . and make disciples."

One of the children came running into the room that served as our dormitory, dining room, and storage room, shouting, "A man has been shot! He's bleeding to death!" We all jumped up from the supper table and ran to the front room where the clinic's equipment was kept, just as four men lowered a large bamboo pole, from which was suspended a bloodstained sheet in which the man was lying. The men explained, in answer to our questions, "He and another man got into a fight over their land. He was shot about three o'clock this afternoon, at Pisan. We have been carrying him ever since. He seems to be getting weaker, though." Naty examined the man and found that the bullet had pierced his shoulder and gone into his lung. He had lost a great deal of blood and needed an immediate transfusion, if his life was to be saved. And the nearest hospital was Cotabato! The lone nurse put a compress and bandage over the wound, as I prepared the jeep for a desperate try at saving the man's life. It was raining pitchforks outside by this time, but we decided we would try to get him to Cotabato. Minutes later the patient was stretched out on the back seat. A policeman had been assigned to go along to get all the information he could from the man, since this was sure to be a big homicide case if the man died.

The sharp white eyes of the jeep stabbed into the inky darkness of the rain and mud as we flew along the hole-pocked dirt road. Occasionally the nurse took his pulse. It was very high, and weak. Blood had begun to seep through the heavy army blanket in which we had wrapped the patient and was making puddles on the jeep floor. We threw caution to the winds, ignored the deep holes as best we could, peered intently through the heavy rain, and roared on through the night. Two hours later we reached Cotabato and drove up to the provincial hospital. I picked up the young man, blanket and all, and laid him gently on the waiting stretcher. As we placed him on the operating table, his eyelids fluttered open for a second in the bright light. I asked, "Would you like me to say a prayer?" His eyes, rather than his pale lips, assented, and I thanked God for helping him reach the hospital safely, for the hands of the willing nurses and doctors, and for God's tender care over him while he was passing through the "valley of the shadow of death." The doctor entered the room then, and soon after the operation began.

As I left him, and walked back out to the jeep in the blinding rain, I thanked God silently for His having guided me to come to Mindanao and letting me be at the place where I was most needed on this night. As I got in the jeep, I happened to glance downward. My shirt, my pants, my arms were covered with blood. "But it is the blood of my brother. It is God-given," I thought. And I prayed, "O God, help me always to have a deep concern for the blood, the life, of my brother. Keep me sensitive to the needs, problems, difficulties of all these my brothers. May I see them always through the eyes of my own Older Brother, Christ."

We all went into the Mindanao Work Camp with the idea of helping others, of really trying to meet the needs of the people in Kabacan, in the very heart of Mindanao. And yet, as so often happens in Christian service, we found that we ourselves were helped more than anybody else. As we lived together under the most difficult circumstances, as we ate together, often food which we did not like, as we worked together, often at tasks that seemed utterly impossible and too difficult in our own strength, and as we prayed together, learning to rely on God's strength, we developed a fellowship that truly came from God. We felt His presence in our midst. The motto of the Work Camp was, "Unless God directs the Work Camp, we labor in vain who work here." It was thrilling to learn that God *can* direct our actions, guide our plans, inspire our thoughts, when we come to Him in prayer. He can work out His purposes through us, if we are willing to *go* where He wants us to go, *do* what He wants us to do, and try to *be* what He wants us to be.

# 11

## Our Neighbors

"WHERE SHOULD WE LIVE?" With the Work Camp over, we returned to Luzon and began to make plans with the Bishop for our permanent headquarters in Mindanao. Our experiences during this one month of serving in this great frontier land had convinced us more than ever that we were needed in Mindanao, that we were called of God to pioneer a new rural center for training rural church workers, to help in the expansion of the church over this island of such tremendous open doors, to meet the needs of the thousands of God's children who had come to this new land full of hope, and yet often met great hardships and problems. This was our "chosen field," and we prayed earnestly for guidance in selecting land for our new missionary home and for the rural center.

Our experiences in Kabacan, while very fruitful and thrilling, had showed us that this location would not be suitable for our permanent base of operations. For one thing, the land was strictly a one-crop area, suitable for rice, but too low and swampy in rainy season for fruit trees, other vegetables, or other grains. If we ever hoped to make our rural center self-supporting, we would need a more all-purpose type of soil, so that students coming to us for training, as well as pastors and church leaders attending conferences, could grow their own food at the rural center, and so that we would have a diversified source of income. Another personal, family reason we could not stay at Kabacan

168

was that Mariam was allergic to something there, and the entire month of the Work Camp she suffered with a skin allergy, so that her arms and legs were covered with an intensely itching rash. Kabacan was definitely not the place for her! We considered carefully each of the port cities—Davao, or Cotabato, or General Santos—but realized that while these cities would have ideal living conditions for the family, with their daily plane service, greater food supply, libraries, and congenial social life, they would not meet the need of the church as a whole for a centrally located, rural, multi-purpose training and conference center.

While we were struggling with this problem of where to live, God answered our prayers—as He so often does—by sending us a man with a vision, Dr. George Mecklenburg. This stalwart man of the church made a trip all around Mindanao, looking at land, and looking ahead to the needs of the church in future years. When he stopped beside the Saguing River, just outside of Kidapawan, looked at the rolling hillsides on either side of the bank of cool, sparkling waterway, and gazed up at beautiful Mt. Apo, towering above the rich green fields and touching the golden clouds of the late afternoon, he exclaimed, "Spotty, this is it!" Here was the ideal site for the Methodist Rural Center! It was centrally located, about halfway between the two major cities of Davao and Cotabato, on the national road, just a few kilometers from the road going south to the Koronodal Valley, and only an hour's drive from the road going northward through Bukidnon to the northern coastal cities of Cagayan de Oro and Iligan. At an altitude of 1000 feet, it was cool and invigorating, a welcome change from the heat of the lowlands, and a restful atmosphere for retreats and conferences. Both upland and lowland rice grew in this area, as well as ramie, corn, root crops, citrus trees, and coffee; and it was a center of the newly developing industry of rubber, which offered a great hope for the future economic development of the area. Most important, it was a

169

beautiful spot. God seemed to be very near to us as we stood there beside the little river that late afternoon, looking up into the purple-tinted mountains, across the deep, green valleys, the rich, fertile countryside, and imagining just how our Rural Center would some day look. I could almost hear God's whispered benediction upon us as we talked and dreamed of getting started on that very spot.

Dr. Mecklenburg, that indomitable soul, having made up his mind where we should settle, set out posthaste to close the deal. We dashed back to town, about two kilometers away, and asked questions. We learned that the land beside the river belonged to "Datu" Cristino Icdang, the chief, or tribal head, of a large group of Manobos who live in the interior hills of Kidapawan. Without further ado—and without so much as one bite of supper—the good gentleman took me by the arm and we hiked back to Mr. Icdang's house, just beside the land we hoped to buy.

We arrived just as Mrs. Icdang, the first of the five wives, and obviously the "No. 1," was lighting the small kerosene lantern. Datu Icdang, though small of stature, was a strong-faced individual, fully conscious of the dignity of his position as head of his people. As we sat around the table in the main room of the little bamboo house, we could see on the wall behind the *datu* a large oil portrait of his father, the original settler of this area. He told us a number of stories of the early days of his people, fascinating stories, and then Dr. Mecklenburg steered the conversation back to the point at hand. Did he want to sell his land? He did *not*! Several times the local constabulary chief had approached him for some of his land, but each time he had refused, as he did not want to have soldiers in the neighborhood. Then Dr. Mecklenburg, a smooth-talking "salesman for God," really went into action and before we left that night, he had persuaded the *datu*, who was already a Christian convert and a

170

member of the Christian and Missionary Alliance, that he would like to sell the land to us and have Christian neighbors!

Neighbors! What a real meaning that word was to have for us in the months and years that followed, as we got acquainted with our neighbors in Kidapawan! We enjoyed many hours of fellowship with Datu and Mrs. Icdang, and their lovely family, as we visited in their hospitable home, just 100 yards from our front door. We soon learned the story of the five wives. It was standard practice among *datus* to have a number of wives, although Mr. Icdang, as a devout Christian layman, actually lived with only one wife, the others being just a part of the household. He explained, "You see, when there is war or hatred or quarreling between different tribes of Manobos, one of the best ways of solving the problem is for the *datu* of each tribe to take a young girl from the enemy tribe as a wife. After the two marriages the two *datus* and their tribes are then united to each other by ties of blood, and so they cannot fight or kill any more." Datu Icdang then turned to me with a shrewd smile and asked, "Can you think of a better way?" I had to admit that it seemed an effective way to stop tribal grudges and fights.

Many of the Manobos like to build their little huts high up on the hillsides, sometimes so steep that I could barely make it up the paths to their doors. I marvel at their agility. I have watched them over and over again come swiftly down the path to meet at Datu Icdang's place for worship on Sunday mornings or for tribal gatherings. I have come to respect their honest faces, with their darkened teeth and pierced ears from which heavy ornaments hang, and to admire their bright, multicolored, hand-woven dress. We have spent many pleasant hours listening to the young men play the "agongs," or heavy metal drums, and watching the men and women go through the intricate dances which are such an integral part of their customs. The agongs are one of the chief symbols of wealth. They come in various sizes, the largest ones costing the equivalent of a horse, roughly $75 each. The more agongs a family has, the greater its prestige in the community.

Although Datu Icdang wears Western style dress for everyday occasions, he and his brother and kinsmen still wear the traditional tight, multicolored short pants, ending just above the knees, with many tightly wound ribbons of metal circling their lower legs. Around their waists they wear broad leather belts, into which they have stuck in a very prominent place a short, curved *datu* knife. This knife, which is standard equipment for the *datu's* formal dress, is curved from handle to blade-point and is often used for preparing the "buyo," or betel nut which they chew. Suspended from their belt there is a small bronze box, or carrying case, for carrying the betel nuts, the green leaves in which they wrap them, and the white lime with which the nuts are sprinkled before they are wrapped and chewed. This concoction is chewed until it is the consistency of strong tobacco juice. It is not long before not only the chewer's teeth are a dark red, but also the floor nearby.

Above the brightly decorated short vests which the men wear comes the most amazing part of the whole costume—the headgear. Around their heads they wrap bright-colored turbans which are decorated with hundreds of tiny little balls of fringe, made meticulously and skilfully by hand from horses' hairs, with a big tuft of the hairs standing up at the back of the turban. Such a headdress might be the handiwork of a lifetime and is handed down from father to son as a prized family possession.

Among our most prized family possessions is a pair of the hand-shaped, beautifully decorated ankle bracelets that the young ladies wear while doing their dances. They were given to us by the daughters of Datu Icdang and they are a happy memento of the happy hours we have had with this family. Rosita, the oldest daughter, is an especially bright and talented girl. Coming from a tribal group where it is the exception rather than the rule for the young girls to go any farther in school than third or fourth grade, this bright girl received a scholarship in college, and is now teaching school and being a real leader to her people.

Again very close to us, just across the road in front of the rural center, live some more of our neighbors, the Blase family. But they do not understand Manobo. They speak a different language—Ilongo—and have very different customs and family patterns. They too are members of a Christian church, the Roman Catholic. One day their middle son, Romeo, was playing with our boys in our front yard, climbing a guava tree to pick and eat the still green fruits. To our horror, the limb broke, and Romeo fell and was pinned under the branch, with his leg broken. The family is too poor to afford a doctor, and so we offered to rush the child to the clinic uptown where there is an X-ray unit, so that the doctor could see the injury and set the broken bone. But, as poor little Romeo screamed with pain, his mother spoke these chilling words to me: "I don't like. I don't believe in doctors. If the doctor uses 'cimiento,' my son's leg will be crooked." No amount of persuasion by us could change her mind. She sent for the village quack doctor, "the man who knows how to fix bones," as she called him. He put bark from a native tree on the leg, tied it with rags, gave the boy a shot in the arm with an unsterilized needle—and today Romeo is hobbling around with one leg shorter than the other, crippled. This is our neighbor, our son Stephen's close friend.

Perhaps the most colorful of our neighbors in Kidapawan are the Moros. A whole colony, or settlement, of the Moros live just opposite the river from us, so close that we can hear their agongs beating and their weird-sounding chants in the still hours of the night. The Moros are direct descendants of the fierce Moros against whom then-captain "Black Jack" Pershing and his Philippine Scouts once fought so desperately. The time was around 1906—1908, and conditions in Mindanao were very troubled. All the Christians were friendly to the government, and the huge, largely pagan tribe of Manobos was generally cooperative—but the Moros were a different story. They were unconquered, after nearly 400 years of Spanish conquest and rule.

In a typical battle, "Black Jack" was leading a patrol in company strength in to a centrally located town in Cotabato. His men moved forward slowly, bayonets ready. The place was ominously silent. It was seemingly empty. Captain Pershing lined up his men in a small area protected by a high wall, one flank protected by another building. In this bivouac he set out watches and built very large forest fires out in front of the camp to light up any enemies. He reckoned without the wiliness of the Moros, however. Shortly after midnight, when the sentries were drowsy and all the other men sound asleep, silent forms slithered slowly forward into the sleeping mass of men. Suddenly a knife flashed in the dark, and there was a groan, a gurgle—and death. Two or three of these daring, dedicated Moros cut the throats of twice as many of the Americans before they were discovered. Then pandemonium broke loose, as over all the rifle fire and the screams of the wounded and dying rang out the battle cry of the Moros: *"Allah is the only true God and Mohammed is his prophet."* From behind every tree, from the tops of the bamboo huts, from everywhere they charged, yelling hideously.

Captain "Black Jack" watched, hard-eyed, firing his .38 as fast as he could pull the trigger. He watched as the soldier standing next to him put three shots from his rifle into the body of a fanatic Moro, who still came on running, screaming, blood pouring out of his mouth, but still wielding his large, curved "kris." With his last ounce of strength he was able to thrust that deadly "kris" into the neck of one more soldier, who went down in a gurgle of pain, as the blood spurted from his cut jugular vein. Time after time that horrible night the captain watched his men die in just such a fashion. First came the wild, fanatical charge of the Moro, shouting "Allah is the only true God and Mohammed is his prophet!" Straight on he came, brandishing his bloody knife. A soldier would pump three or four or five bullets in the chest of the Moro, only to be stabbed or beheaded by that wicked "kris" as the Moro went down. There was a pattern: the soldier killing the Moro would himself be killed before the Moro went down. Finally, in desperation, Captain Pershing wrote back to his superiors in the United States demanding a weapon that would not only hit these wildly fanatic fighters, but *knock them down*. Thus, the famous .45 calibre pistols were created. These famous guns which played such an important role in two world wars were first used by the U.S. in fighting the Moros in Mindanao.

It was with this picture in mind that I first went to call on Datu Molud and the large group of his clan and followers who made up the Moro community near us. Datu Molud was a tall, stalwart man, with graying hair which gave him a very distinguished look. There was about him a quietness and a poise which spoke volumes about his tremendous power and deep sense of responsibility. He had nearly 100 people there over whom he had complete authority. He told them where to work; he collected their wages; he made all the important decisions regarding their families. It was with considerable fear and trepidation that I first visited him. He received me cordially, and his young college-student son translated our conversation back and forth. He was a bright young man, and quite fluent in English. This visit was the first of a number of pleasant exchanges which we have had with this strong leader of the Moros.

However, the Moro whom we know best is Tenka, our closest neighbor, living just beside us. He was the man who had first cleared this land, felling the trees and planting the first crops. Since he did not have any land papers or titles, the land was not legally his, but he lived there many years. When Mr. Icdang bought it from the government, for the sake of peace he allowed

Tenka to keep his small hut on the land and farm a small portion of it. When we bought the land, we inherited Tenka. His tiny one-room house, 8 by 14 feet, was on an eastern boundary of our property when we came. Beneath his house his naked children play, while the young mother sets out the rice pot over an open fire in the back yard. One hundred yards away our friend Tenka, together with two or three other members of his family, are out in the ice-cold mountain stream, clad only in undershorts, digging up five-gallon cans full of sand. They pile canful after canful up on the bank in a big pile, which they will later sell to the local contractors. This is the same river where the mother washes the dishes, cleans the fish, launders the clothes, and where the whole family bathes. Like most of the families living along the river, they also take their drinking water from the river, the same river which is used by all the Moros as a toilet. Is it any wonder that dysentery is the foremost killer of small children?

The tiny house atop the cliff is walled with the bark of trees taken nearby and has a roof of cogon grass. There are three families living in this one room: Tenka, his wife, and four children; his brother and his wife; a brother-in-law who is sick of tuberculosis, together with his wife and one child. In addition there are the old grandmother and two young men who are cousins. Because there are no windows, the small hut is dark, so that the first time we went to visit them, our eyes strained in the semi-darkness. We went to visit them soon after our arrival, to show our friendly feelings and to get acquainted with the family. We climbed gingerly up the small bamboo step-ladder, wondering if it would hold our size 10½s. As we bent our heads to get into the low front door, the little wrinkled grandmother greeted us with a toothless smile and a few words in their Magindanao dialect, which we could not understand but which made us feel welcome. There was not a single piece of furniture in the house—not one table, not one chair. The sound of a continuous low, hacking cough drew our eyes over to the corner of the room, where a wasted form of a young man was wrapped in a dirty sheet. Our hearts rent within us at the sight of this young man so weakened by disease, as well as the realization that others in the family would surely catch the infectious sickness. Since they all sleep side by side on the floor, and there are no windows, the sick man's coughing quickly filled the whole room with the germs of tuberculosis. Our first visit to this family painted graphically for us again, in human figures, the need for our setting up a Rural Center, with a program of medical help for people just such as these.

During the weeks and months that followed, our friendship with Tenka flowered. A big powerful man, with bulging muscles made by his physical labor in digging sand and crushing rock, Tenka was capable of tremendous feats of strength, but he was not actually very fond of work. He much preferred sitting around talking. Since he farmed a certain amount of the rural center's land, we had to have periodic discussions of what seeds to plant, how to divide up the crops, and so on—and what a palaver each time! What could have been said in a sentence or two meant an hour or two of talk, if Tenka had his way. He told long stories in Tagalog, which our co-workers translated into Ilocano and English, and round and round we went. But we got along well with Tenka. He loved to come and watch *us* work. Later, as we got into our international Work Camp and were putting up our first building, he came over one day to the long board table where we were all eating— thirty-three of us that day—and said to me, "Apo (a term of respect which is commonly used and means 'Lord,' or 'Sir,' although it is also the word for 'God'), you must be a *datu*, for you certainly have a big family." Mariam looked daggers at him for the implication that our good-looking girl work campers might be the No. 2 or No. 3 or No. 4 wives. She was having none of that multi-wives business, thank you!

177

Another time Tenka came up to me and after a time of talking back and forth came out with this statement: "You know, Apo, you have been good to me. You're really my friend. I'll do anything for you. If ever you have any enemies, just let me know, and I'll kill them for you." With that he made a motion of drawing his finger across his throat. I thanked him, but assured him I would not have any killing jobs for him.

We reached the height of our friendship, however, after the birth of his baby about a year after we moved to Kidapawan. He had been around our house a lot, and he realized that we had only boys in our family. He sort of pitied me for not having any little girl of my own. When his baby was born, it was a girl. Mariam went to visit the family in their little hut, taking along some vitamin extract and a few little gifts of clothing, as a friendly gesture. While there, limited by the language barrier from being able to say much, Mariam did a lot of smiling, and admiring the new baby. She patted its little head, and called it "Baby," not knowing its real name. Imagine our surprise to learn that it was ever afterwards called "Baby"!

Several weeks later we were quite surprised to look up from our work one day and see Tenka, his first wife, his second wife, his four children, his sister-in-law, and the old grandmother all dressed up in their best finery walking toward the rural center. This was obviously a very formal visit, and so we hastily cleared the wood-shavings off some of the benches, and tried to prepare for company. They sat down, we served some cool drinks, we all smiled at each other, there was an awkward silence, and then finally Tenka took the little newborn baby from its mother's arms and handed it to Mariam. They had talked it over and decided that since we did not have a girl, and since we were their friends, they would give us theirs! We were dumbfounded. What should we do next? Stammering and stuttering, we thanked them profusely. We told them we had never heard of such wonderful friendship, that to give away one's own child was the most generous act we could conceive of, but we then went on to explain that the Board of Missions would not let us have more than five children, because of the expense of transportation to and from America. Thank the Lord for the little blue book—the Missionary Manual. It proved a ready scapegoat that day to get us out of a ticklish situation.

Another unforgettable incident with Tenka occurred a couple of years later. One night after a hard day, our clinic staff and I were sitting out on some benches and chairs in our front yard, enjoying the beauties of a lovely tropical evening. We were watching the Southern Cross wink out at us from an azure sky when out of the shadows loomed an excited, bleeding, limping human form. The "form" mumbled, "Apo" and a few words more that we heard indistinctly. The doctor took him by the arm and led him into the clinic room. In the light we recognized Tenka. He was cut and bruised and bleeding from a half a dozen different places. "Bakit ba?" asked Henry, or "Why?" Silence. The young doctor continued to examine the black eye, closed shut with swelling, the bleeding scalp wound, the cut on his shoulder, the scratches and gashes on his legs and arms, as if he had been dragged over rocks and gravel. "Bakit ba?" he insisted, and gradually Tenka began to tell the story.

Tenka had been one of four men courting a pretty young Mora woman from the province of Lanao. As he became more and more intent upon winning her, he learned the "facts of life"—that her dowry, or price, was 200 pesos. This is a large amount of money equal to all a man could earn in six to eight months of hard work. He also learned that there were four men courting the young woman in question. Tenka alone had the drive and determination, the "get-up-and-git," to raise this large amount of money. So, regardless of which man the girl might have preferred personally, she was given in marriage to Tenka. Now, years later, the other three suitors had finally come to Kidapawan and caught Tenka alone. They tackled him, knocked him down, and worked him over with stones, rocks, and their fists. With his clothes badly torn, his body beaten, and his pride sadly wounded, Tenka came across the river to his new Christian friends to ask for help. He had no money, but we patched him up as best we could—"on credit."

From Tenka and his brother Tangurak I learned a great lesson in stewardship. I shall never forget the time of the first "sharing" of the rice which they had grown on our rural center land. Theirs was just a small plot. Their womenfolk had cleaned off the cogon grass by hand and then planted it in the old manner, walking in straight lines, punching holes in the ground with a stick, and then without any prior plowing of any sort dropping the seeds in the holes. Then everybody sat back waiting for the rain to do its work. In six weeks the rice was about knee-high, and the weeds were almost as tall. Once again the field was filled with men, women, and children, weeding from sunup till sundown. Two months later the shoulder-high golden grain was "heading out." A week or ten days later the field was again swarming with Moros, harvesting the grain with short, curved hand knives.

The next morning at daybreak there was a knock on my door. Outside stood Tenka. "Tapas na," he said. The work of harvesting was finished. I went down to the field with them, for the work of dividing up the grain into the proportionate shares. When I arrived, all the Moros who had shared in the work of cutting and stacking and drying the grains were standing around, watching. I immediately noticed that there were three piles of the cut rice stalk, instead of just two for Tenka and for the rural center. "Bakit ba?" I asked, and held up three fingers. (My knowledge of his dialect was scant, but at least I knew how to ask *why*.) "Oh," he explained, "the padi." Then I got the reason for the third pile. As he measured out his own share of the rice, he took out every tenth handful for the Muslim priest and the mosque. Here I learned a great lesson in stewardship from one of the poorest families I had ever met. He was paying his one tenth to his church, without question, even though within two months his own family would probably be without food.

These Muslims had a loyalty to their faith that would make many of us Christians turn our heads in shame. I never watched them filing by on Fridays, dressed in their finest clothes, walking toward their mosque, without being challenged by their loyalty to their religion. As I have watched the Moros working in the river stop and turn their faces toward Mecca and pray—five definite times during every day—I have realized my own need as a Christian to put more time into each day's activities for turning to God in prayer.

Besides the Manobos and the Moros, our neighborhood also included immigrants from other southern islands, so that five different dialects were spoken in the five houses across the street from us. Directly in front of the rural center was a family from Manila, who spoke Tagalog. Behind them, along a little winding dirt path, was the house of a family of Ilongos, who had come from the island of IloIlo several years earlier. The house mother of our center and her four sons and their families, who lived in small huts clustered together about 300 meters down the road, were all Ilocano-speaking people from northern Luzon. And so it went. What an interesting neighborhood in which to live and work and serve! We had met each of our neighbor families, each of them speaking different languages, holding different religious faiths, having different problems of poverty, superstition, disease. How could we best serve them? What was the Christian approach we should take in this neighborhood? What should the Methodist Rural Center be doing? How could we best apply the command of Jesus, "Thou shalt love thy neighbor as thyself"? These questions deeply stirred us and gave us the guideposts by which we planned the international Work Camp to set up and begin the work of the Methodist Rural Center.

# 12

## We're in Business on Mt. Apo

"METHODIST RURAL CENTER" so far meant only a piece of wild, uncleared land on the slopes of Mt. Apo, the highest mountain in the Philippines. The land was part high, part rolling, down toward a roaring mountain stream. But what dreams we had for the future! "Spotty's pipe dream" one of our church leaders laughingly called it. However, the church in the Philippines had approved our plans for the Methodist Rural Center and we were eager to get started. It was to be a rural training center for the holding of annual short-term schools for accepted supply pastors, evangelistic institutes, teacher-training conferences, farm and gospel school, summer youth groups, and various district meetings of the church. In addition, it was to be the center from which would radiate a regular program of extension service, both in the barrio of Saguing, where we were located, and also in the forty or more nearby barrios. We would bring to the needy people of these rural communities medical and dental, agricultural, educational, and spiritual help. "Christ for *all* of life" was our motto, our goal, our dream.

The job before us was tremendous—well-nigh impossible, in fact—and I knew that I could never realize its fulfillment without help, a *lot* of help. God sent us that help, though, in the form of wonderfully consecrated young people, each one of whom volunteered to give Christ one whole year of his or her life, to serve Him without pay, in order to make our dream of a Rural Center come true.

182

# WE'RE IN BUSINESS ON MT. APO

When we sailed from Manila in the early spring of April, 1954, on a small interisland freighter, we had with us four of these one-year volunteers. They were Miss Viola Bravo, a dentist, and three recent graduates from the Trinidad Valley Agricultural School: Mariano Lacadan, Ignacio Macliing, and Conrado Gayano. Two beautiful young graduate nurses joined us a few weeks later—Naty Ngo and Rebecca Ramos. Soon after a young civil engineer, Esdras Martinez, arrived to add his training and talents to our corps of Christian workers. We were able to find two more agricultural school graduates, Amate Cabotaje and Loreto Caluya, who were willing to give freely their training and their time in order to help their own people to help themselves. Within Mindanao we were able to recruit other consecrated young people who were willing to volunteer their services— Arsenia Natividad, a young elementary school teacher; Federico Puno and Antonio Quesado, both young men who were already slightly interested in the ministry and who were eager to gain experience and to learn more of what would be involved in such a life-changing decision.

Then, to top off our little band of volunteer workers there was Camilo Toledo, our young "hero" of Palanan days. He already knew what it meant to work and to serve, being a graduate of the Palanan Work Camp. That enthusiastic young man graduated from the Seminary one day, married a talented young co-student, Evangeline, the next day, and set sail for Mindanao almost the next. We were ready to go!

When we arrived at Kidapawan, we had a ten-acre site of junglelike, overgrown land to be cleared. We faced the terrific job of laboriously clearing the tall, head-high cogon grass and removing the trees, stumps, and boulders before we could start our buildings or begin our farm. Camilo was our "straw boss," or "capitas." He gave every man, woman, and child of us a small Japanese sickle and told us to go to work clearing the land. When our city-bred young women asked him how to use them, he

183

answered jauntily, "It's easy. You just get down on your hands and knees and massage the grass." And they did. These dainty little Filipino girls (Viola did not weigh more than eighty pounds soaking wet, and the others were not much bigger!) who had never in their lives done a day's work in the out-of-doors, toiled hour after hour under the broiling hot tropical sun, until their hands were blistered and bleeding from the cuts and scratches of the sharp razor edges of the cogon grass, with never a word of whimpering or complaint. With a spirit like that, I knew we would succeed.

Their enthusiasm and their devotion were contagious. One boy said, "Every time I swing my sickle, I feel as if Jesus Christ is right there with me, helping me push my arm forward." One day I suggested that three of the boys who had worked steadily in the hot fields all day long for over a week take a day off to go up town to visit some of the local officials and gather information for us. They asked me, "Isn't tomorrow Sunday?" "Yes," I answered. "Then we will be resting tomorrow. So we don't want to rest today. That would be too much resting. We must get this land cleared." And back they went into the burning sunshine, to work their twelve hours a day for no reward at all except three meals a day and the conviction that they were sharing with Christ in building His Kingdom in Mindanao.

As I bent over the grass, working beside these young people, I occasionally lifted my eyes toward majestic Mt. Apo, and I could feel the power and the purpose of God who had called us to this beautiful place. As I gloried in the rich green of all the trees and plants, watered each afternoon by torrential rains, and as I saw the fertility of this soil, full of weeds now, but promising rich harvests in the future, I thanked God for the richness of the resources He had given us with which to work. I thanked Him not just for the land, but even more for the human resources which He had given us—these wonderfully brave, daring, consecrated young people, who were willing to

184

leave their homes, their families, their good-paying jobs in the city, to come to Mindanao to serve Christ. I was sure the job could be done, because God had touched the hearts of these fourteen Filipino young people, trained in their professions, to give one year of their lives to serve Him without pay to make our dream of a Rural Center come true.

In July six outstanding college young people from the United States joined us, to share with these Filipino young people in a six-month international Work Camp. There was Bob Breihan, a tall, hard-working engineer and student leader from Texas; there was Jesse Clements, a carpenter, Fulbright scholar to Sweden, trained social worker, together with his brand-new wife, Molly, determined to do a man's full share of the work each day; there was Francis Hursch, from Kansas, nicknamed "Inky" because of his fondness for writing love letters home; there was Dwayne Suter, an agricultural graduate from Oklahoma A. & M. and last, but certainly not least, for he was over six feet tall and weighed more than 200 pounds, there was John Eddy, from Minnesota. These six students from America had all been chosen because of specific skills. One had been chosen because of his experience in pouring cement. Another was an experienced carpenter, member of a trade union. One had experience in recreation and in coaching basketball. Each one would have something positive to contribute in his own field, as well as being willing to do anything, anywhere, any time, as we all shared and shared alike in the hard, manual labor of the Work Camp.

We were now twenty-seven in all—fourteen Filipinos, six U.S. work campers, and the seven Spottswoods. We were ready to do business. We had a small rented house in Kidapawan, but we had no furniture. So our two carpenters found some boards and nailed them together for the first table. Back of the house they built what looked like a second table and on it they put some dirt. Around the table they put some dirt. Around the dirt they put some boards. They piled three stones on one end and three stones on the other end, and as the boys said, "We were in business," because we could make a fire on the dirt and cook our food. We had a kitchen stove, even if we did not have a kitchen!

We took a piece of chalk and began to mark off "rooms" on the floor. The two bride-and-groom couples, Camilo and Eve, and Jesse and Molly, got the two corner cubbyhole rooms downstairs, and the other girls in the group got the rest of the downstairs area. They nailed up sheets, bedspreads, curtains, and soon had the ladies' dormitory lined up. Upstairs we put "Ma" and "Pa" Spottswood in one corner, and then spread all the Work Camp boys all over the rest of the available floor space. Each boy could have the amount of floor space chalked off with his name on it, and during the day—if he could find time to sit down—that's where he sat and wrote letters or read. At night, each person had to push his possessions into a corner pile, string up his mosquito net, and stretch out on the cold hard boards to sleep as best he could. We soon learned not to mind our next door neighbor's feet protruding in our territory, the odor of his unwashed socks, or even the tired snoring of some of the fellows. The first night the floor seemed awfully hard. We tossed and turned, trying to find some soft spot in the hard floor where our bony shoulders and hips would fit a little better, and we woke up in the wee hours of the morning full of sore spots and aches. However, later on we learned that a hard day of real physical labor, chopping trees or hauling stones or pulling weeds, made us all so tired that we were exceedingly grateful just for the chance to lie on the floor at night. No bed at home ever felt so good.

Like the early Christians in the first-century church we "had all things in common" in our day-by-day living. It was a rich experience, requiring adjustments on all sides, but it was not easy. Tempers flared. Nerves got taut. We went from one crisis to another, in rapid-fire succession. The very first night, after all the mosquito nets were strung up across the room like a crazy crossword puzzle of lines, with bodies, mats, shoes, and blankets thrown over all in profusion, we finally blew out the candle and settled down for the night. We were all exhausted, for the six American work campers had ridden on the truck with the cement and other building materials, and then we had all joined in the back-breaking task of carrying these supplies on our shoulders from the road the 500 yards into our yard. At last an uneasy peace descended upon the room, as we stretched and rolled and tried to settle into positions comfortable enough to sleep. Then, in the middle of the night after every one was asleep, one of the Spottswood boys got up to go to the bathroom. As he tried to pick his way through the maze of mats and nets, he accidentally stepped on John Eddy's big foot, stuck out across the narrow "aisle." John let out a howl and sat bolt upright, and as he did so, he jerked down the main string to which about six other nets had been tied. They all came down, and we were one writhing, struggling, heaving mass of bodies and nets, out of which roared the most amazing sounds, in both Ilocano and English!

The rising bell pealed out at 4:45 in the mornings—and our Christianity was taxed to the uttermost, as we tried to find our clothes in the pre-dawn darkness and stumble our way downstairs for our Bible study and prayer time. However, this hour of daily fellowship, in which we sought God's will for the day and prayed for his strength for whatever might be demanded of us, proved to be the most important thing we did during the entire Work Camp. This discipline of prayer welded us finally into a unity that would never have been achieved any other way We studied first the Book of Acts, seeking to learn from the experiences of the early disciples God's plan for His church and His resources that would still be available to us as we sought to do His will. Then we studied the Gospels, and some of Paul's letters. We learned to pray for each other. Through God's strength we learned to forgive one another for the 101 irritations which each day brought. We learned to share with one another whatever insights we had gained from studying God's Word. We learned to talk over our problems, frankly, freely, in the spirit of Christ, and let Him guide us to a solution. Always we kept before us our motto, "Christ for *all* of life."

After our hour of Bible study and prayer the next activity of the day was breakfast. And what an ordeal that was! The hardest part of our whole experiment in cooperative family living in our mixed Filipino-American group was eating the food. We were struggling to keep our food costs down to fifty cents a day per person, and so we had to eat Filipino food. It was cheaper. But oh, how my stomach rebelled at that smell of dried fish that filled the air every morning. My mind told me that the small, smelly, hard, brittle little dried fish were valuable sources of vitamins and minerals, if eaten Filipino style, bones and all, chewed slowly and carefully—but my stomach stood up on its hind legs and said, "NO!"

We knew that we could not possibly keep up our physical strength and endure the rigorous twelve- to fourteen-hour work schedule we had set for ourselves unless we ate a big breakfast, and so we made up our minds to eat. First, I tried eating just rice, since I had read somewhere about how much food value there is in just plain rice. I figured that if millions all over the Orient could live on it and not much else, it must be pretty good stuff, and I would live on it too. However, even getting the rice down proved a pretty hard job, for it was always cold, hard, and greasy. Cooking for such a large group on a little outdoor wood fire was difficult, at best, so that we could never have more than one dish hot at a time. Usually even that last-cooked dish would be stone cold by the time we all got to the table. It was the custom to cook the rice the night before, so that no one would have to miss Bible study by staying in the kitchen to cook, and then in the morning the rice would be fried, to warm it up. Then, by the time we had all twenty-seven of us finally seated at the table, it would be cold again, each grain coated with con-gealed lard, with the taste of the wood smoke clinging to it.

The American work campers were getting thinner and thinner, and we were rapidly approaching a state of emergency, when our tall, gangling man from Texas came up with a solution. Bob was a prodigious worker—but he also liked to eat on the same scale. He liked food—and lots of it. To this day our boys, when they want to describe a big eater, will say to each other, "He eats as much as Bob Breihan." And that means the ultimate in description has been reached. Well, Bob experimented with first one thing and another, and finally found that a heaping plateful of rice, cold and greasy though it was, could be swallowed with ease if a spoonful or two of peanut butter were put on it, brown sugar sprinkled liberally over it all, and then canned milk poured over it to wet it down. We "Americanos" began arriving at the breakfast table with our little jars of peanut butter, sent from home, and cans of milk, and the problem of breakfast was solved.

The other two meals of the day still presented quite a problem, though. Dwayne, who was used to eating half a chicken at a time on his family's farm back in Oklahoma, worried about the effect on his health of his ration of only one-half of a drum-stick at a time. Every bit of meat we could afford to buy was carefully measured and rationed, so that it meant a real cut in daily protein intake for the American members of the team. To make matters worse, Dwayne got the "flu" and I thought we were going to lose him—from worry, if not from lack of food. However, about this time his girl friend in the States, who was a home economics major, wrote him that bananas were a valuable source of protein. She saved the day. We began slicing bananas—five or six a meal—on top of whatever else was on top of our heaps of rice, and everybody was happier.

The Filipino young people made up the larger part of our team, and so more often than not our food was seasoned to their

189

tastes, not ours. Vegetables were cooked with a lot of fatty pork, and often liberally seasoned with "bagoong," a liquid flavoring that is made from small fish that have been salted, stored in earthenware jars and allowed to age for weeks or months, until nothing is left but the juice and the smell. After all these years I still have to admit to my Filipino co-workers that while my heart is Filipino, and I love the Philippines and its people, my stomach is still American!

"Partners in Christ" became our by-word as we got down to the business in hand—work. Side by side these Filipino young people and American young people began to put in long hours a day in the hardest possible physical labor, pulling weeds, plowing, planting, hauling stones for the road, digging drainage ditches, hoisting lumber for the building, and all the other jobs involved in clearing the thick tropical land and getting started. It is symbolic, I think, that the first building project of the Work Camp was a bridge to join the Rural Center land to the national highway, for the Christian witness of these young people as they labored together played a real part in building a bridge of understanding between the Rural Center and the community. It was thrilling to see the volunteer labor that went into our projects, not only from our own work campers, but also from interested neighbors, nearby church members, the 4-H Clubbers from the school uptown, and even from the Moros who lived across the river from us. They gave us a whole day of free labor in digging sand and hauling rocks for the cement foundations of the new building. As we all stopped from our labors that day to eat our lunch down on the river bank, holding cut banana stalk plates full of rice and canned sardines, I marveled at the way God was drawing us together, even with our non-Christian neighbors.

The note of partnership in Christ extended into the area of finances, too, as contributions began to come in from various Filipino friends and groups. The Methodist Youth Fellowship in the United States had paid for the food of the six Americans, and this money formed the nucleus of our food budget for all twenty-seven of us. Yet we could never have managed on this without the free gift of eggs, chickens, fruits, and vegetables that began rolling in from different nearby church groups whose imaginations had been caught by the spirit of service of these young people and who wanted to have a share in their work. One wealthy merchant in Manila gave us 2000 pesos toward the cost of our new building. A small barrio Sunday school class sent us a gift of two pesos. From the three pure-bred Berkshire pigs given by a rich man to the few sacks of rice from a poor farmer, ours was a venture of faith. Unlike so many mission projects, this work camp was supported more than 50 per cent by the gifts of the Filipinos themselves.

The second building project of the Work Camp was a kitchen, 11 by 12 feet, and a tool shed, to be used first of all by the work campers themselves, and later by the Pastors School, farmers schools, youth conferences and other such groups that would use the Rural Center. We made a big storage room for our tools, sacks of rice, food supplies, and building materials, and somebody had to sleep here every night to guard. This became the most coveted honor—getting to sleep in the new kitchen right on the property—since the rest of us were still having to hike two miles back and forth to town to our little rented house. The rainy season was now on in dead earnest, and the roads were a quagmire of mud. Picking our way through the sticky, slippery mud holes became an agonizing part of each day's work. The lucky one who was chosen to sleep at the Center could just go down to the river, get a refreshing bath in the stream's icy waters, and then flop gratefully down on the kitchen floor, with no more long hike ahead of him. How we fought for that privilege!

By the end of the first month the basic plan for the Rural Center had been mapped out, the big (30 by 53 feet) main building lined off, and the cement footings poured. We had every possible delay in getting up this structure: important lumber would be unavailable and we would have to wait; all work had to be done painfully and laboriously by hand; we lacked heavy winches and other such equipment. And yet somehow, through the grace of God and the indomitable spirit of these young people, the building went up. We had just one employed carpenter, Teroy, a skilled master carpenter who combined rare skill and high standards of workmanship with the most incredible ability to improvise and find solutions to seemingly insoluble problems. Jesse was a skilled carpenter and his wife Molly was a ready learner, sticking to her hammer and nails until it was too dark to work any more. Bob Breihan had had quite a bit of experience in construction in previous work camps and proved to be a valuable worker. The rest of us hauled boards, lifted things, crushed rock, and anything else we could do to help. I remember with horror one day seeing "Inky" fall from the roof trusses, go sailing through the air, too surprised even to cry out, and then land miraculously on the floor joists for the second floor of the building! He was badly scratched and bruised, but the next day he was right back at work. What a team! No wonder we got that building up!

While one part of the group was slowly working to complete the main building, a second group was busy clearing the land and laying off the ten acres into fields suitable for growing corn and rice, planting fruit trees on the hillsides, and transforming the junglelike wilderness into a beauty spot. Our three boys from the Mountain Province, famous for its gorgeous flowers, even got some flower gardens started for us. Working side by side under the broiling sun, these Filipino and American young people—doctors, nurses, professionals—stayed long hours at their rough, rugged, rigorous tasks. From the hilltop, already planted in coffee trees, down the rolling slopes to the river, they cleared, plowed, planted, pulled weeds, tended until they had most of the land in use. As we all shared in the work of bringing forth

192

harvests of rice, corn, and vegetables, we had a fourfold purpose: 1) to provide food for our own needs; 2) to get food ready for the first Pastors School to be held in Mindanao, during the month of November; 3) to help make the Methodist Rural Center eventually become a self-supporting project; 4) to pioneer in better methods of agriculture, to experiment in new varieties of seeds and in new methods; and to make ours a model farm to be used as a base from which our agricultural help would radiate to all the surrounding villages.

To the orchard of more than 300 coffee trees, thirty coconut palms, and banana and papaya trees already on the land, the work campers added more than 1000 coffee trees, eight new coconut trees, and more than forty fruit trees of different varieties. "Big John" Eddy, in addition to being the basketball coach for the college uptown and being our public relations man *par excellence*, was in charge of the nursery project. One of the indelible pictures painted in my mind is the sight of John, dog-tired, sprawled out under a coconut tree late one afternoon, sound asleep. He had planted just one tree too many that day! When John missed the supper bell, we knew he had really had it! Of course, he was not the only one tired. The whole group did work they were unaccustomed to, and stuck to it long, long hours. I used to wonder, and marvel, at the grit and determination that kept these young people working such long hours, at back-breaking toil in hot, humid weather, under the most primitive living conditions. They were *fools*—fools for Christ's sake!

The work campers also began poultry and piggery projects, tending them with a personal interest and attention that went far beyond the call of ordinary duty. I remember Loreto sitting up with a new batch of baby chicks all night long, tenderly picking them up when they fell, removing them when they were about to be crushed by each other, watching that they did not burn themselves on the kerosene lantern which we had to use to keep the make-shift brooder warm. They were his chicks in a very real sense after they survived that night. And Amante's pigs got the same kind of loving care. I remember seeing Naty give one an injection with the same sterile care she gave to the children in the clinic. We even named our pigs. The two males were called "Dwayne" and "Amante," and females were named after two of our favorite missionary visitors—"Jane," for Jane Williams, a short-term missionary who took her vacation with us and used her time to dig the pit for the toilet, and "Carol," for Carol Moe, a regular missionary who took time off from her full-time duties to spend a month with us and carry rocks to build our road.

We gained quite a bit of community interest and participation as the neighbors came by the river each day to watch the progress of our water wheel, which we nicknamed "Dwayne's Folly." The idea of a water wheel to harness the power of our fast-moving mountain stream to pump water up the hill for irrigation purposes was basically sound. Dwayne constructed a beautiful piece of equipment, and being a tall, handsome replica of Gregory Peck and Gary Cooper rolled into one, he had plenty of the Work Camp girls volunteering to help him each day! The trouble was that the river was too swift, so that large rocks and boulders kept crashing down the stream and breaking up the paddles or knocking the whole thing off base. While the work on the water wheel continued on this on-again, off-again basis, Dwayne was able to build with the help of the other boys some simple bamboo water filters, for making safe the river water which most of the village people use for drinking and cooking. In making and demonstrating these filters and explaining their use he performed a real community service.

Another work project of our young people was the digging of a large fishpond for the growing of "tilapia," a fast-growing, highly nutritious Philippine fish. These fish would not only provide food for the work campers and the forthcoming Pastors

194

School, but would also act as an example to inspire other people in the community and neighboring villages to increase their food supply and raise their standard of living. In a land where the majority of the people are undernourished, this is a much needed service.

What a great day it was when the roof was finished on our Rural Center building and we moved in! No mansion was ever as much appreciated as our new "home." Of course, we still had to sleep on the floor, and the boards were not yet nailed down. We had no walls or windows or doors yet, so that every time it rained, we had to dash up the board ladder to the second floor and rush to move our bedding and clothes from the side from which the rain was coming over to the dry side of the building. We had no "facilities," so that we still went to the river to bathe and wash clothes. We had to sacrifice some of our American ideas of privacy, but we were all so glad to be living right on the property and not to have that long muddy hike every day that we did not complain. In all our experiences in cooperative living we had gained so much in fellowship, in soul-searching worship experiences, in the inspiration of living with consecrated young people, that we forgot all about such concerns as lack of screens, no electricity, poor food. God had led us into simpler patterns of living, as we realized how many of the "things" we take for granted in modern life are really quite insignificant in the face of urgent Christian concerns.

Not content just to build and wait, a team of the work campers, made up of the dentist, a nurse, a teacher, an agriculturist, and Camilo, the pastor, began taking Christ—Christ for all of life—into the barrios. Usually the little villages of perhaps a hundred nipa huts were far from any road and could be reached only by hiking or by carabao sled. Our young professionals—the cream of the youth of the Philippines, where only ¼ of 1 per cent of college-age young people graduate from college—gladly hiked through the miles and miles of mud and slush, off the beaten paths, to bring the abundant life of Christ to the often forgotten people of the inner barrios. It was during our six-month international Work Camp that our Mindanao Mobile Medical and Dental Clinic was born. The word "mobile" meant that we had a lumbering carabao and bamboo sled to draw the boxes of medicines, dental chair, and audio-visual equipment, while the staff members still had to go by foot.

Why were they willing to do it? One incident illustrates the reason. Mariam and I had visited our little church at Salaman Libak, way down on the southernmost part of the Sulu Sea. We had arrived early at the small motorboat that was to take us back to Cotabato, and so got aboard and sat and watched people as we waited. Four men brought aboard an old army cot on which a sick man lay. The cot was placed crosswise on the small boat, and his outstretched foot touched my knee. Suddenly he became stiff, then shook convulsively, writhed in agony, and after that relaxed again. This happened every five or ten minutes. After about an hour he died, just a few inches in front of us. My wife asked his wife what the trouble was and she said, "We don't know." Not long before he had been playing volleyball in his village, and one of the players accidentally landed on his foot, knocking his toenail off. When my wife asked what they had done, the woman replied, "Well, later that day we tied a cloth around it, and it didn't bother him much. But two days later he couldn't swallow anything. Last night he couldn't open his mouth." That gave me a clue. I knew that the young man was a victim of lockjaw, or tetanus. He died in terrible agony, and I thought: a nurse or a doctor and a dollar's worth of medicine could have saved his life.

There are thousands of such men, women, and children in the Philippines who are born, live, and die without ever having the services of a doctor or a nurse. It was for such as these—God's neglected children—that our young people were called to serve. Before we started our medical program in the villages we made a survey. In each village Camilo or Esdras or one of the other team members would ask these questions: 1) When was the last time a doctor was here? The average answer was: once in the past year or two, and staying only four to six hours. 2) When was the last visit from a dentist? We found that where there was a village school (and most of the villages had a primary school, made of bamboo with a dirt floor and grass roof) a dentist came in and stayed a day or so, but he ministered only to school children. 3) When did the government agriculturist come here? The answer was: once every year. How long does he stay? Just one day. Of course he cannot visit many of the farms or become acquainted with the problems.

In such a situation as this—in barrios that were disease-ridden, among people that were often superstitious, poverty-stricken, and undernourished—our team sought to bring the gospel of good health. They set up a temporary clinic and stayed in each place a week at a time, taking care of illnesses, treating emergencies, giving thousands of injections against cholera, dysentery, typhoid, and smallpox. A major emphasis was health education and prevention of disease. Through home visits, health movies, lectures, and classes in First Aid, Home Nursing, Infant Care, and others, they sought to better health conditions among the rural people. Since there are no dentists in the villages, our young dentist was kept busy from morning till night. Arsenia, our young teacher, taught the little children in the school yard in the afternoons, teaching them games and songs and stories about Jesus. She also led the house-to-house visitation through which all the members of the team simply and sincerely witnessed to the compelling love of Jesus Christ. The agriculturist also did individual visiting, counseling with farmers about their problems, demonstrating how to caponize chickens, how to inject pigs and chickens against disease, and how to improve their crops.

As evening fell, the whole team got ready for the audio-visual and evangelistic services. The nurse explained the health movies, the agriculturist the agricultural movies, and then a religious movie was shown, and the young people would take turns in giving a simple message about Christ. It was amazing the way God used these young people to win people to Christ. In one barrio, Bulacanon, our young people felt a real concern for the 150 families living there, without any church, spiritually starving. They prayed hard, they visited, they preached—and today one of our strongest barrio churches is in that place. Of course, the work was not easy, and sometimes there were setbacks. In one barrio, Garsica, they experienced the prejudice and suspicion which so often greets "Protestantes." Our young people had led six families to accept Christ and begin a Bible study and prayer group, but then when one of the small children in the group fell sick and died, the old fears and superstitions crept back in. Our team realized that follow-up was desperately needed after they left the villages, and so they worked out a set of mimeographed Bible lessons to be mailed out to new believers.

By Christmas time, the time for our six American work campers to leave us and return to America, we could all point with some pride to very real achievements. We had the land cleared and the farm well started. We had our new two-story building almost completed, a building easily worth $25,000, which we had been able to build with volunteer labor and voluntary gifts for half that amount, or less. Our medical and dental clinic was well-started, and we had a first-rate staff of volunteer workers to carry on the continuing program of service of the Methodist Rural Center. Because of the efforts of a group of young people who obeyed Christ's command, "Go ye . . ." we had six new Sunday schools started, and one church actually organized and a building completed.

The American young people had come in high idealism, challenged by the idea of a new type of rural reconstruction. In the past the white man had come to the Orient as conquerors; these young people had come as servants. This is the era of great

# WE'RE IN BUSINESS ON MT. APO

American programs for the underdeveloped people of the world, and billions and billions of dollars have been poured into such reconstruction projects. But these young people came out believing that it is not *things*—trucks, tractors, or bull-dozers—which can change the world, but *people*—people who care, and share, people who live like brothers among their Oriental brothers.

Bob Breihan told us of his experience with a young Communist once at a national student conference in the States. That young Communist had stuck his finger at Bob's chest and said, "We're going to win the people of the world. We're living with the people, sleeping on the floor beside them. We eat the same rice they eat, talk their language, share their privations. *We're going to lick you!* All you Christians know how to do is send money."

How wrong can a guy be? Bob, and the other "Christian revolutionists" who had joined us in this Mindanao Work Camp, had just proved that young Communist wrong. Paying their own way, serving without pay, these young people had pioneered in a new type of rural reconstruction. Because they were willing to labor side by side with Filipino young people, because they were willing to put their lives on the line, in sacrificial service, a new idea has been born and will continue to live in the Philippines—the idea of challenging young "Christian revolutionists" to use all their training, their talents, their resources to help meet the needs and problems of their own country. In the birth of this new idea of service may yet lie the hope of the resurrection of the neglected people of the world, from poverty and despair into the better life of plenty and health and hope, into the abundant life of Christ.

The six American work campers went home, but their influence lingered on and continued to act as a catalyst in challenging young people to volunteer to serve in Mindanao. As one young man from Knox Church said, expressing his call to serve,

"One day the Lord was walking at Midian, and He saw a busy man tending his flocks. He bid him come, that he might deliver his people from bondage. Many centuries later He was walking by the Sea of Galilee and saw fishermen casting out their nets. He called to them and said, 'Follow me. I need you to become fishers of men.' Last year He came to several young Filipino young people, fresh from college, all eager to go out into the world and find a place for themselves under the sun. He tapped them on their shoulders, and looking straight into their eyes, He said, 'Follow me, and be my witnesses in Mindanao.'"

This is as it should be. No number of Americans can ever solve the problems of the Orient; only Orientals can do it. No missionary can ever hope to win Mindanao for Christ; only consecrated Filipinos can do that. I was more than ever convinced that my job was not to do the work of ten men, but to find ten men—or more—who will do the work. My experience in finding wonderful Filipino young people who would put their lives on the line to serve Christ in Mindanao has given me great faith and hope for the future of our church. For example, there was Reby. . . .

We needed a nurse to carry on the outreach work from the Rural Center, so I went to Mary Johnston Hospital in Manila. I found Rebecca Ramos and I asked her bluntly, "Would you be willing to give Christ a year of your life down on the frontier? Would you let Christ use your training and your talents to minister to these people who can't go to a doctor?"

She was embarrassed and hesitated a long moment. Finally she said, "I have a younger sister to educate. How much is the salary?"

To that I had to reply, "I'm sorry, but we won't be able to pay any salary."

I don't know what she thought or what she said to herself; but two or three weeks later she went home to the province and told her mother, "I've been praying about it, and I feel that

Jesus Christ wants me to go to Mindanao as a missionary." Later she resigned a paying job at the hospital and came to the frontier. She served with us in the Methodist Rural Center for fourteen months.

One day Reby went with us to Compostela, a small town located as far north as you can go on the island. We tried to find a place to set up our medical and dental clinic. We learned that there were only three Methodist families in the village. The first one was away; their house was locked tight. The second had gone to the farm, and we couldn't use the house in their absence. The third family lived in their tiny store, too small for our purposes. I was discouraged, but not our nurse. "Let's go see the mayor," she said, and she dared to ask him for room in the market place.

The mayor responded, "Lady, what in the world would you do with the pigs and the chickens running around here?" I thought about the flies, too. But she answered, "Mayor, I have been down on the street today and I have seen children with sores all over their bodies and people shaking with malaria. All we need is a little parking place." Of course the mayor agreed. Reby got a broom, put it in my hands, and soon we had a clean place, with sheets tied up for walls, and we were in business.

The young pastor who had been invited to give the evangelistic message that night began to grow cold on the idea. He had seen people pass by us and spit on the ground and say "Protestante!" We knew that Protestants were despised and hated in that town. After supper the pastor nailed a sheet on the side of a nearby bamboo house, and we set up the movie projector in the market place. Reby started showing the pictures. The first film was entitled, "Water, Friend or Enemy?" Then she showed a picture on infant care, which drew a large group of mothers and children. The young pastor came over again after the question-and-answer period and said, "Reby, I don't think we ought to have an evangelistic service tonight. This is

201

an awfully rough crowd. There is noise and confusion. Suppose we postpone it until tomorrow night."

That little nurse answered, "Reverend Spottswood said we would have an evangelistic service tonight, and we will." The pastor sat down, looking glum and dejected.

Then Reby showed the picture on the life of Christ. Just as she was turning off the projector, the pastor walked over and said, "Reby, there are three drunks down in front. They are causing a lot of trouble. I am not going to try to preach." "Well, then *I* am," said Reby. And she did.

She walked over to the microphone and began: "Friends, a few months ago I was a nurse in a big hospital in Manila. When I ate my food, they brought it to me on a tray. I didn't have to go out in a yard and cook my rice over a smoky fire. I didn't have to wash my own uniforms in the river, as I did here yesterday. They brought them to me starched from the hospital laundry. I got a good salary and I had many friends. There were conveniences like electricity and running water. I had a boy friend, too.

"But Jesus Christ came into that hospital, and He said, 'Reby, I need your life, your talents, your training. I need you as a missionary.' I said 'Yes' to Jesus Christ, and it changed my life. I have a joy, a peace, a purpose in living now that I never had before. And I want to tell you, friends, that He can change your lives, too."

With that, she called for decisions, and hearts were touched. We are "in business" on Mt. Apo. It is God's business, and with people like Reby to work with, we are bound to succeed.

# 13

## The Birth of a Baby

THE JEEP WAS covered with mud and dripping with water as I pulled up into the front yard of our little church at Tagum, a little town just north of Davao. Mariam and I were just returning from a conference farther north, and needed a place to spend the night, as it was already too dark to travel any further. Limerio Garibay, the pastor, and his pretty young wife, Lily, welcomed us with the warm, genuine hospitality Filipinos know how to give so well. They led us into the small living quarters built on to the rear of the church, and soon served us a tasty meal of rice, eggs, and bananas, carefully prepared and nicely served. It tasted delicious to us after our long hours of bouncing over the rocky roads without stopping for a meal.

It was during our meal as we were seated around the little table in the kitchen that I noticed how large Lily was with her first child. Limerio noticed my glance in her direction and informed me, "We're expecting the baby any day now." "No pains today?" Mariam asked. "No, not yet," Lily replied, and I breathed more easily.

We sat around a little while, talking, but since the only lights in the room were two little bottles with twisted rags for wicks, soaked in kerosene and then lit to smoke and flicker in the darkness, our eyes soon began to droop. By 7:30 or 8 P.M. we were all ready to go to bed. Our hosts led us to the upstairs room and insisted that we sleep on the "matrimonial bed," a large wooden double bed which was the only bed in the house. We argued and fussed, but they insisted. There was nothing for us to do but accept their gracious offer. We put on our pajamas, tied up our mosquito net, and stretched out on the "patati," or woven mat, which covered the hard, tightly woven rattan bottom of the bed. The other members of the family rolled out their "patatis" on the floor all around us, until soon the floor was completely covered. Even though we were all together in one room, we each enjoyed the privacy of our mosquito-net sanctuaries, which hid us from others' eyes, and we were soon all comfortably bedded down. (Maybe "comfortably" is an exaggeration, for sleeping on the rattan-bottomed bed was exactly like lying on a cane-bottomed bed. There was no give to it. However, I am sure it was softer than the floor.)

We made one last appeal to Lily to take the bed, but she insisted that she felt more comfortable on the floor. We tucked our heads back under the net, and minutes later we were safe in dreamland—dreaming of wide, smooth, concrete highways; of air-conditioned station wagons whizzing along at an effortless sixty miles an hour, instead of our jeep's crawling pace of twenty-five miles an hour over the rough, rugged roads; of soft Beautyrest beds and fluffy pillows at journey's end.

Suddenly I was wide awake. I heard Lily whispering in a loud and urgent manner, "Limerio, wake up. Wake up! Go get the midwife. Hurry!"

Limerio came to with a start, sat up, and then began a series of murmured questions and answers on the mat, just a foot or two away from the edge of our bed. I was caught in a crosscurrent of confusion and embarrassment. Should I pretend not to have heard anything? Or should I get up, and run away from there as fast as I could? My inclination was strongly towards the latter. By this time Mariam had awakened and gone over to help Lily, who was moaning softly. Limerio, like fathers the world over before the birth of their first child, was excited and flustered, and had gone running out of the room with his flashlight.

Since it was obvious that this room was already designated as the "delivery room," I was making plans to vacate immediately, if not sooner. However, the other members of the family, who were all awake now, "shushed" me up, assuring me that I should just lie down and go back to sleep. One look at the form of Lily twisting in pain convinced me that she was not the slightest bit interested in where I sat, lay, or slept.

The "hospital" was slowly getting organized now. The young pastor had sent one brother out to call for the midwife, and another had borrowed a large kerosene lantern from a neighbor and was busy cleaning and filling it. A sister-in-law was busy preparing the "delivery table." She covered the floor area with five or six layers of newspapers, and then helped Lily roll over on the "table." Various members of the family took turns in alternately comforting Lily and teasing her, and there was a joyous, lighthearted camaraderie within the family. Even the smallest children in the household, Limerio's nieces and nephews, were wide awake now, chattering with excitement. Lily's pains were closer together now, and occasionally a groan of pain would escape her lips. Yet, between pains Limerio teased his wife, and she and Mariam and the midwife would casually chat of babies, or the price of eggs, or new fashions in clothes.

Mariam was assigned the task of holding the big lantern directly over the birth area. As Lily alternately writhed in pain, and then relaxed, I could not help pitying her, having a baby—her first baby—without even so much as an aspirin tablet as anesthesia. By this time I was fully clothed and had joined the rest of the family as they all sat around in a circle in the room, laughing, joking, but constantly showing their tender concern for Lily. Suddenly it dawned on me: having a baby in the Philippines is a *family* affair!

The moment of actual birth was a thrilling one. Amid loud

shrieks of excitement and joy, "It's here! It's a boy! Lily, it's a boy!" the midwife, like doctors the world over, grasped the baby by the heels, slapped him sharply on the back, and made him cry. With a loud "Wa-a-a" the baby made known his entry into the family. The baby born and his wife O.K., the young pastor dashed over to the nearest Chinese "tienda," or sidewalk store, woke up the proprietor, and bought Coca-Colas, cookies, and candies for a celebration. Minutes later he was back. The baby was now cleaned up and nestling in the crook of his mother's arms. Lily's face was aflame with joy at having shared with God in this miracle of new life. Limerio proudly picked up the baby and held it out while each member of the family, including the tiniest children, all came over and kissed it and welcomed it into the family. Then we all bowed our heads and thanked God for this new life. As we sat around afterwards eating and drinking and rejoicing, in the wee, wee hours of the morning, it came over me again, "What a happy way to have a baby! Having a baby is a family affair in the Philippines!"

There is another thrilling story of the birth of a baby—the birth of the Mindanao Provisional Annual Conference, the youngest offspring of the Methodist Church in the Philippines. The baby was conceived in 1951-1952 when Bishop Jose L. Valencia and his wife made their first trip to Mindanao, in response to urgent pleas from many different groups of Methodist settlers. He met with many small groups of Methodist laymen who had made the 1000-mile move south, leaving their homes on Luzon to settle in Mindanao. After breaking with home ties and leaving lifelong friends and neighbors to come to a new land and make new homes for themselves, these people were eager to keep their ties with the one thing that gave greatest meaning to their lives, that gave them strength and courage and direction in life—their church. And so the Bishop had visited them, had corresponded with them, had encouraged them. He had sent us down as missionaries in this great new area. Several of our ministers from Luzon had come down with their people; congregations had been organized; the work had been started. Now at last, on that historic day in April, 1955, in M'lang, Cotabato, the Mindanao Provisional Annual Conference was officially organized. As the Bishop pounded his gavel upon the table and called the conference to order, I realized with deep joy and exhilaration: "A new life, lusty, kicking, full of potentialities for growth, has been born into the Church Universal."

As I sat near the front row of the church in M'lang and watched the birth of this infant, this new conference within the church, my mind went back over the growth that had led up to this significant moment in the church's history. When I first visited Mindanao in 1951, there were only three pastors, and not more than 200 members. Now there were twelve ministerial members of the conference, including transfers from the northern conferences and two area missionaries whose membership was placed in the Mindanao Conference as well as one probationer. In addition, there were twenty-two accepted supply pastors under appointment and three full-time women workers. The Methodists now numbered nearly 800 members in Mindanao, and truly the doors were wide open for further growth and expansion. My heart was full as we rose to sing our praises to Him who had brought this miracle of new life to pass: "Holy, holy, holy, Lord God *Almighty!*" It was through *His* might that this new conference had come into being.

As I watched the birth of this new conference, I remembered the amazing work of the members in building the church building where we were sitting. Camilo Toledo, after the Work Camp in Kidapawan, had been assigned by the Bishop to M'lang, a little agricultural town in the very heart of Mindanao. There were just a handful of members, meeting in a crude bamboo shack with a dirt floor. I remembered the sermon I heard Camilo preach to them: "Let us love God with our hands, with our saws, with our hammers, with our carabaos. Let's build here in M'lang a church building that we can be proud of before God." The members accepted the challenge. Camilo donned his own old work pants, borrowed an ax, and went out at 4:30 in the morning with his church members to hike to the forest and cut the logs for a new church building. They carefully selected only the finest hardwood trees, as they wanted only first-class materials. This building was being built to the glory of God, and nothing second-class would be dedicated to God. They selected *molave* trees, straight and tall, and by late afternoon twelve logs had been cut.

The young people of the Methodist Youth Fellowship began the job of rough-hewing the logs to square them up. Then they tied them behind carabaos and began to slide them out of the forest toward the church site. The enthusiasm of the people gained momentum day by day as the work continued. Some of the men began the job of sawing the logs by hand into the 2 by 6s and 2 by 8s needed for the framing of the church. The big job was on. Every single piece of wood in the structure had to be hand-sawed, as these were poor farmers and they had no money for "store-bought" lumber. They cut their logs the hard way, by hand. Hour by weary hour they sawed. Day by blistering day they sawed. Back and forth . . . back and forth . . . their bodies glistening with sweat. Others hauled sand from the river to mix cement for the foundations. The pile of lumber grew larger, and the idea of building a great church to the glory of God began to catch on in the community. Instead of just the pastor and four or five men working, others began to volunteer. Young people hauled sand, girls carried water for the cement mixture, mothers fixed food for the noon meal for the thirty or forty people, young and old, who shared in the great task of building the church.

Foot by foot the building mounted upward to God. First

208

the square, blunt, rough concrete footings were poured; then the posts were raised up, straight and tall; then the men lifted up the heavy trusses atop the posts. As I watched one day the men beginning to nail on the galvanized iron roofing, I realized that more than just a building was being built. God was using the sweat and toil of these wonderful men and women and children to build a stronger church, the church in their own hearts.

I watched one young man fitting a door frame for the front of the church. Several times he tried it, took it out, refitted it again and again until it was perfect. This door was to God's house, and it had to be just perfect. Standing there in Cotabato watching that young carpenter fit the door, my mind's eye drifted back a few thousand years, and I could see Jesus, the Carpenter of Nazareth, working with that same painstaking craftsmanship. I seemed to be in His presence, and I realized anew that He called everyone who would be His follower to work, to share with Him in the gigantic task of building "God's house"—His church—on the bedrock of utter trust in Him who is the Master Carpenter, utilizing the timbers of love, building from this love the framework of a world of justice and peace. I saw that the man who gives only money to the building of the church does something important, but the man who gives of his sweat, his toil, his thinking and planning and serving does infinitely more.

A few days later the siding was being nailed on the church, and a lofty spire began to point its finger heavenward to God. By the time of the first annual conference, these people were ready with a beautiful house of worship, one of the first churches of Mindanao to be built of strong, permanent materials, to have a cement floor, and to be painted. The people of this town had done their part. They had shared with God in the birth of the new baby, the Mindanao Provisional Annual Conference.

The church was not built without sacrifice, not only of time and work, but also of money. One of the most inspiring examples of giving that I have ever known came out of this little rural church in M'lang. Mrs. Bruno Andres was a young, pretty widow. Several years before she had been happily married to an outstanding young man. He was successful in his profession and so popular in the community that many of his friends were encouraging him to run for vice-mayor. Then, Bruno heard the call of God to enter the ministry. He left his job and attended the Pastors School at the Methodist Rural Center. His wonderful wife backed him up in that decision, in spite of the fact that there were six children in the family, and she knew they would get very little support from the village churches which he would serve.

Then tragedy struck. This courageous young man became ill with a disease for which there was no cure. He died of internal hemorrhage, and his wife was left without a farm, without land, without a salary—and with six children to support. There were no jobs available for her. The only way she could earn food for her family was to be up by 4 A.M. to cook, wash, iron, pack lunches for her children, and then to walk out to a distant field to help her neighbors harvest in order to earn a small share of rice and corn for her own family's needs. She worked hard, with desperate urgency, for seven months after her husband died. Late at night, by the light of a flickering oily-rag lamp, she would still be mending, ironing, or cooking for the next day.

And then the pastor began asking for contributions for the new church. He reminded the members of their obligation to give God at least one tenth of their income, more if they could. Oh! the struggle that raged in her breast! Her heart told her that she must obey God's commands. Yet how hard it was to feed and clothe her young brood! Many nights, as the family slept together on the floor under their one large mosquito net, she lay awake long past midnight. She wondered how the little cash that she had could be stretched to pay for a son's school registration fees, for a new dress for her daughter, for all of their other needs. And now the pastor was asking for one tenth for the church. It seemed impossible!

But when the next Sunday came, I happened to be visiting the church in M'lang and I saw that Mrs. Andres was one of the very first to bring her pledge up to the front of the church. It was for $8—for her an amazing amount. The average pledge from other members of the church was for only $3 to $5. The richest man in the church, who owned 100 acres of land, had pledged only $15. I learned a great lesson from this pretty young widow. I learned that it is not the amount of money we have, but the depth of our commitment to Christ that determines how much we give to Christ and His church.

All of these thoughts had been passing through my mind as I sat on the straight-backed benches in the church and watched the organization of the conference get underway. Bishop Valencia led in a very moving prayer, and then he informed the conference of the Disciplinary basis for the organization of the Mindanao Provisional Annual Conference. He read the Enabling Act of the General Conference held at San Francisco, California, in 1952. Every one present was aware of the significance of this forward step in the church. There were fraternal delegates from the three northern conferences, who sent greetings from the churches on Luzon and wished us well in our new annual conference. Telegrams from friends and mission leaders overseas strengthened our feeling that we were a part of a world-wide church, that we were being carried along in a world-wide momentum of advance for Christ and His people.

The town of M'lang where this first conference was being held was just twenty-five miles southwest of Kidapawan in the province of Cotabato. It was at the gateway to the Allah Valley ("Valley of God"), the supposedly rich rice-growing heart of the island. However, first one natural calamity after another had plagued the farmers of the area—drought, rats, and then

211

locusts—and hard times were pressing heavily down upon the people, both the thousands of new settlers and also the many Mohammedans, who had been there a much longer time.

As I drove the jeep southward to reach M'lang on the first day of the conference, I gloried in the beauty of the colorful countryside. Many times I saw the Moros, in their bright robes and turbans, working barefooted harvesting their rice. Some of the people had built bamboo towers twenty feet high, with bamboo floors, where the rice was thrown. Three or four men would be up on top, stamping their feet up and down, threshing the rice. As their feet separated the grain from the stalk, the small grains would fall between the bamboo strips onto a waiting cloth stretched out below. Then the women would put the rice on flat baskets and throw it up into the air, where the wind blew the chaff away, just as in Bible times.

The jeep bounced and bumped along the road in the broiling heat. Our speed varied from around twenty miles per hour to less than ten. No, the bridges were not out. The road was perfectly dry. But it was so rutted and filled with gaping holes and bumps that it took us more than two hours to cover the twenty-five miles to the conference.

Food for the conference was furnished free by the church members to the nearly 100 delegates. The men and women of M'lang cooked it, Boy Scout style, in big pots over open fires on the ground. For breakfast we had pork and white squash, cooked together like a stew. For lunch, we had pork and squash; for supper, the same. This stew, together with rice, was our diet for the whole time we were there. The delegates were lined up at the palm-frond-covered table and given tin plates heaped with rice. Then we all began eating with our fingers. While this fare seemed monotonous to me, it was a rare treat for many of the delegates who came from rat-infested towns where they had been suffering from real hunger. One afternoon we had refreshments—boiled *camotes*, the Philippine sweet potato. The delegates ate them like ice cream cones, and with the same relish!

Our church members here, like most people all over the world, are tenant farmers. Seventy to 80 per cent of the billions of people in the Orient are farmers, and a large percentage of these farmers do not even own their own land. Hence, "Dame Hunger" is an ever-present companion. She sleeps in their homes. She stands in the shadow watching every opportunity to pinch the bellies of the children. She looks at me through dull, pain-filled eyes, as I visit these friendly folk. The extra fat around my waist jabs my conscience, stabs my heart, as I realize that the extra fat on my body would keep a child from the scourge of the Orient—tuberculosis. I wake up in the nights hearing the hacking cough of the mother who again and again has taken the food from her own mouth to keep her growing child well. I can never forget these people, these wonderful, wonderful people who so gladly tighten their own belts and endure hunger in order to take us in and welcome us to their church and feed us!

With what warmhearted generosity the members of the church welcomed us into their homes! In the openhearted ways of Philippine hospitality delegates were accepted, not by the number of beds in a house, but by the number of small sleeping mats that could be accommodated on the floor. The small farmer's home where I slept, while already having eight people in the household, took in three women delegates, a pastor, and a missionary. The pastor and I slept in the tiny living room, 7 by 9 feet. After everybody else had come in, around 10:30 or 11 P.M., we would put down our mats on the split bamboo floor, and sleep fitfully until the early dawn, when the young farmer would wake us up stepping over us in the 4:30 A.M. moonlight, on his way out to feed the pigs and chickens. Then we would listen to the snapping of twigs and rustling of pots as the young mother bent over her open, smoky fire, just outside our window, and began preparing her family's breakfast. I continued to marvel at this dedicated family. Though poor, they opened their home to make it possible to have this conference. How small their house, but how wonderfully big were their hearts!

As I sat in the conference sessions all during those five historic days, I could not help asking myself the question: "How could such an annual conference be organized in such a short time in Mindanao? How could this 'new baby' have been born so soon?" Then I happened to glance across the aisle to the section where the lay delegates were sitting, and I saw a man named Aurelio Cortado. Then I knew the answer! It could never have been done without the hard work and daring of ordinary men and women who believed in Jesus Christ enough to serve Him. Mr. Cortado was one of the first Methodists to come to Mindanao. He claimed a homestead and started farming at a little town called Lambayang. He was a devout man, a real tither, an able Sunday school teacher, and a hard, hard worker. He was one of the most successful farmers in the area, because of his hard work and initiative. As Aurelio read his Bible each day, as he prayed, as he studied his Sunday school lessons each week, he began to be aware of a quiet pressure from God, the gentle leading of the Holy Spirit. He began to realize that he should be visiting his neighbors and sharing with them his faith in Jesus Christ. At first he tried to resist this leading of the Spirit, arguing with himself, "That's the pastor's job. He's supposed to do the visiting." Yet he remembered that they had no pastor in their little congregation. The quiet inner voice was persistent. Day after day, week after week, the words of Jesus kept bothering him. "Go . . . make disciples."

Finally Aurelio prayed, "Yes, Lord, I know I must begin to witness to my neighbors. But please tell me *how*." He seemed to feel that God wanted him to begin at the house of his nearest neighbor, a farmer like himself. He knew his neighbor worked hard in the fields from sunup until sundown, and then went to bed with the chickens. He could not possibly have an evening meeting with him. He must find another time to talk with him. Finally he decided to try visiting very early in the morning, before his neighbor could go out to the fields.

The next day he was up at 4 A.M. He got his Bible, said a short prayer for God's guidance and blessing, and then began hiking over to the next house, across the fields. The stars were still shining brightly, though the eastern sky was beginning to brighten when he reached his neighbor's door. He banged on the door, and called out the traditional Ilocano greeting, "Apo" ("Sir"), "naimbag a bigat yo" ("good morning"). Sleepy, gruff voices finally answered, "Go away. We are still asleep." Aurelio banged again. "Apo, it is I, your neighbor, Aurelio Cortado." Slowly the man arose and came to the door and opened it a few inches. "Apay? Apay? Why? What's the matter, friend?"

Aurelio tried to explain to him that he had come to pray with the family. This news went over like a lead balloon, but for the sake of neighborly friendship, the man opened the door and invited him in. By now the wife was up, the children were awake, and the family-size mat in the middle of the floor was rolled up and standing in the corner of the small room. Since they had slept in their clothes, everyone was dressed. Aurelio explained to the wife and family his reason for coming. Heavy silence greeted his explanation. However, he was undaunted. He opened his Bible, drew the small ink-bottle lamp closer, and began to read the beautiful words of Jesus. After a short selection, he said, "Let's pray," and then he prayed a fervent prayer asking God's guidance and warmest blessings upon this family. He asked that Christ would enter into every heart in the home in a very real way and lead each member of the family on to higher ground. His simplicity of manner and his earnestness touched the hearts of these people. His neighbor

215

who had been gruff and skeptical at first was now appreciative, and the mother shook his hand warmly. They asked him to come back again.

From this simple beginning this good layman began a custom which he has continued to the present time, visiting his neighbors and sharing his faith in Christ. He formed the plan of speaking to them in the late afternoon, so they'd expect him and be ready the next morning. Then at 4:45 or 5 A.M. he would join his neighbors in their own homes for Bible reading and family prayers. He learned that people were genuinely hungry for the Good News, that they appreciated his coming.

This busy farmer witnessed for Christ and preached the gospel once or twice a week, *every* week. Impossible, you say? Maybe. But laymen since the time of Jesus have done the impossible. And it is people like Mr. Cortado, people who have a living, life-changing faith in Jesus Christ and who are filled with the "Holy Go," who have been the cutting edge of the church. Long before there are any organized churches or regular ministers, individual Christians like Aurelio Cortado take the gospel from house to house, and build the church of Christ. On the frontier houses are far apart, and visiting two or three families may mean hiking many miles. Yet these humble farmers like Mr. Cortado, once they have been won to Christ, make wonderful "soldiers of Christ." They understand hard work, sacrifice, and the necessity of sharing. They are the hope of the church.

A year later the second session of the Mindanao Provisional Annual Conference was held in Nabunturan, Davao Province, a tiny little town way, way out on the frontier. It was at the very end of the road that led out of Davao City and ended in a northern valley, nestling between the fingers of the mountains. It began to rain the first day of the conference, as if to greet the arriving delegates. A typhoon was sweeping past the Visayas, and it brought heavy rain and wind. The village church was about 200 yards from the road, and as the downpour deepened into heavy torrents of rain, the path became a quagmire as hundreds of feet splashed to and from the church three times daily. One hundred yards behind the church the lush tropical jungle pushed up its tall green head high into the air, reminding us that if puny man left the place even for two or three months, the green carpet of the jungle would soon cover everything. The frontier church in its tiny clearing was covered with hand-split boards (shades of Abe Lincoln!). Inside the church the dirt floor had been pounded smooth by the trampling of bare feet. There were no pews, only some hand-sawed backless benches.

The first day people wore their best clothes and shoes to church, in spite of the mud. The second day, white clothes disappeared, and khakis and "bakyas," or wooden clogs, appeared. The third day found most of the delegates, including the missionaries, slogging through the mud barefooted in their oldest clothes. Most reports were given on the conference floor by pastors who were barefooted, their pants partially rolled up, and their feet covered with drying mud.

The pouring rain continued. The main road caved in at several different spots, and some of the delegates were not able to reach the place at all. Before the week was over, long stretches of the remaining road were under water, and people were talking about "the worst flood in the history of Davao Province." However, in spite of the rain steadily pounding on the galvanized iron roofing and the cold dampness that settled over everything, the spirits of the delegates were high, for we could sense the tremendous vitality in the church. In spite of hardship, suffering, sickness among some of our pastors and their families, the work of the church had gone forward in a big way. Our conference, the baby just born at M'lang the year before, was growing—slowly, of course, but it *was* growing. In fact, one might say it was beginning to crawl.

One of the inspirational speakers for the conference was the Reverend J. B. Holt, pastor of Knox Church in Manilla. J.B. was young, handsome, dynamic, and always impeccably dressed. His suit was always nicely pressed. He shined his own shoes every day. He knotted his neckties with careful precision, and his hair was always neat. Straight from the plane from the city of Manila he came to the wet, muddy, sloshiness of this wild frontier spot. Nabunturan was a trial for J.B.! But I must admit he was a grade-A sport about it all. Since we have very few members of our church in Nabunturan, there were very few homes where we could sleep. One grand family who owned a small store had taken in Mariam and me, and at least two dozen other people. When J.B. arrived, he was given a corner of our floor. Dressing was a problem. Most men like to change their pants in private, but we soon learned there were only two places where we could change—outside, in the rain; or inside, surrounded by eight or ten people. J.B. soon learned to turn his back, change his pants, tuck in a new shirt, without even a blush.

J.B. had to leave on the third day of the conference, immediately following his third inspirational message, and so I offered to drive him in the jeep as far as the washout, from where he would have to walk a kilometer or two and then catch a bus to Davao. Fortunately, the sun came out and we left in good spirits. J.B. was still dressed in the neat brown suit which he had worn in the pulpit, and was wearing a handsome matching tie and two-tone brown shoes freshly shined for the plane trip back to Manila. When we got to the cave-in on the road where the jeep could no longer pass, J.B. got out, grabbed a suitcase in one hand and his rolled-up blankets in the other and started off down the trail. However, the path was slippery as glass. Even though the sun was now out, the mud was still deep and boards thrown across the deepest of the mudholes were wet and uneven and hard to negotiate. Turning back toward me to say something, J.B. lost his balance and slipped. In a split second he was up to his waist in the gooey, slimy, sticky, clinging mud. He let out a yell that could have been heard all the way back to the conference. I didn't hear all the words, but there was some question in my mind about whether everything he said had come from the Bible! I sat in the jeep and roared. The more I laughed, the madder J.B. got, but I just couldn't help it. The expression of horror and distaste on the face of this good-looking "city slicker" was the funniest thing I have ever seen in all my born days. I laughed until my sides ached. In the meantime, J.B. had scrambled back on his feet and laboriously picked his way through the mudhole. When he reached solid ground again, he stopped and took stock of himself. His trousers were literally covered, impregnated, with the thick, slimy mud. He knew he would not be able to sit down on the bus for the next four hours in such a self-borne "mud puddle," so he nonchalantly bent down and took off his pants, and looking neither to the right nor to the left, started walking down the road, his muddy clothes held out to the right in one stiffly outstretched arm, his mud-covered suitcase held out to his left. What a sight! As long as I live, I shall carry indelibly printed on my mind's eye this picture of young, handsome J.B., spic and span from the waist up in coat and tie, tearing off down the road in the midst of many people . . . without his pants.

I returned to Nabunturan to the conference, heartened not only by the good laugh I had had, but also by the interest and concern which had made J.B. willing to come all the way to Mindanao to help us with this baby conference. His church— Knox Memorial in Manila—had taken on the support of one of our district superintendents to help us get started. His women's and men's groups in the church were sending gifts for the work on Mindanao. We were deeply grateful for the interest and support of this great missionary-minded church. Since the early days when Knox had sent us some of its own young people to hike to Palanan for our first Work Camp, this great church had been in the vanguard of those valiant souls pushing forward the frontiers of the church.

On the next to the last night of the conference, it was a great thrill to me to be invited by the program committee to lead the closing evangelistic service. Though outside the church it was raining again, and a wet, penetrating chill blanketed the small town in gloom, inside the church the old hymns and the glorious story of God—the God who walked down the altar stairs of heaven to lead men out of the mud and mire of sin, to be rejected by us at the very time He was serving us and to be crucified, saying, "This is my Body, which was broken for you" —brought that crowded church full of people to the altar for a new consecration of their lives to Him. Here, as in the early days in the West in America, hearts were bowed and eyes over-flowed with tears. It was a page from the church history on the U.S. frontier, come to life again in this remote, frontier place in Mindanao!

Bit by bit the thrilling news of the growth of the Mindanao Provisional Annual Conference began to come out. Ten new churches had been organized, one as far away as Agusan Province. While the leading evangelical churches in America had shown a net increase during the past year of 3 to 5 per cent, here in this annual conference we had had an increase of 20 to 25 per cent. The membership had risen from 1045 to 1630, an increase of approximately 44 per cent. The number of Sunday schools had almost doubled, from twenty-six reported at the conference at M'lang to forty-two reported this year. Truly, these figures represented a miracle of consecrated effort by our pastors and deaconesses,

To serve in these little frontier churches these loyal workers had to take, in a very real way, the vow of poverty. The members were few in number and desperately poor; they could not adequately support the church workers. And yet, these wonderful Christian leaders never gave up. They never quit. One young man wrote me that he had sold his last good pair of pants in order to buy rice for his children—but he never gave up his charge. Another young man, typical of our consecrated co-workers in Mindanao, was sent by his district superintendent to a new territory which was ten miles from the nearest road, and twenty-five miles from any town. He had no salary pledged for his support, no money in the bank, no source from which he could borrow. He and his wife and his eight children moved to this new assignment on *faith*, walking. The pastor was able to find a farmer who was a Methodist, who allowed them to move into his already crowded home. The farmer shared what little he had with the pastor. That young man began visiting, preaching, praying with people, and doing whatever odd jobs he could find in between times to get food for his family. Though sometimes meals were missed, the amazing thing is that a new place was opened for the Master, and a new little bamboo church was built. In a year this pastor was able to establish this one church, and also to go out to the next barrio and start a second preaching place. For all this labor he received a total of $40 in cash and approximately $60 in kind—rice, vegetables, chickens—for a family of ten.

The high point of the conference for me came when seven more young men and two young women "took the vow of poverty" and volunteered for the full-time ministry. These young men and women knew what they were getting into. They had talked with the other church workers who were attending the conference. They knew full well the sacrifices and hardships that would be demanded of them. And yet, they went forward to volunteer to serve their Lord and Master and to receive appointment from the Bishop to the frontiers of Mindanao. Tears welled up in my eyes as I watched one of our finest young pastors, Amado Pidut, moving his lips in prayer for these new workers. He had been a pastor for two years now, and he knew only too well the hardships that lay ahead of them—and he was urging them forward! He was advising them to become ministers of Christ Jesus in this difficult land.

Pastor Pidut was one of our most gifted young men. He could speak in four dialects, besides his own. When I first met him, he was living in M'lang and had a good job with a government agency, the Malaria Control Unit. His friendly, easy manner, together with his ability to speak with the Moros, made him a valuable asset in the government's program of rural improvement, and he was in line for a promotion. I first met Amado when he came to attend our first Pastors School in Mindanao. He was one of those young men who joined with us in the Work Camp to pour the cement for the floor of the Rural Center building. He had thrown off his shoes and worked with us with a spirit and a verve that impressed us all. He got a month's vacation from his job and came to attend the Pastors School because, as he put it, "I wanted to know more about the Word of God, and I figured this was my chance."

Then a wonderful thing happened. Amado, who came as a simple layman interested to learn more of the Word of God, heard the voice of God speaking personally to him, calling him to become a minister. This would be a difficult decision to make, for he was already a married man with a family of five children. Amado walked down beside the wandering mountain stream, thinking, and praying, and seeking greater certainty of God's will for his life. He spent long hours sitting out under the coconut palms on the beautiful green hillsides, studying the Bible, and meditating. Finally, when the Bishop spoke on the last evening of the one-month's school, asking if there were young men who would like to become "apostles" of Christ, to be *sent out* to preach, Amado Pidut came to the front of the room, knelt before the altar in prayer, and gave his life to his Lord. He resigned from his well-paying government job with its glittering promise of future security and went to work for Christ out on the frontier.

His first assignment was Bulacanon, a small village just about five miles from the Rural Center in Kidapawan. He found there a few Methodist members, but no church. He began to talk with the five or six families there about putting up a church building, but they told him frankly that they were hard up and that they could not afford to support a pastor and at the same time buy the needed materials for the church. They donated a lot, and went to the forest in their spare time and cut logs and sawed lumber. But still they could not put up a church, because they lacked money for cement and nails and roofing. And then Amado did a brave thing. He told them to forget about the salary of the pastor, and use all their money on the church. They built the church at the urging of the pastor! To be able to stay in the ministry and not starve, Amado sold his only work animal, his carabao. He did this gladly, in order that the church of Jesus Christ should be established.

If you should go to visit Pastor Amado Pidut, you would find him, his wife, and his children living in a small bamboo hut. Their total income for a year would be less than $50-worth of gifts in kind and around $10 in cash. He is living close to the ragged edge of starvation in order to serve Christ. And yet, as I sat looking at his radiantly smiling face during that service of consecration of the new supply pastors, I realized that I had never heard him complain or gripe about his lot in Christ's Kingdom. Truly, this man of God fully exemplified before his younger brothers in the ministry the words of Jesus: "Follow me . . . that your *joy* might be full!"

# 14

## Arakan Valley

"WHAT'S ON THE other side of the mountain?" Many, many times, as I sat at my office window looking out at majestic Mt. Apo rising almost 10,000 feet into the sky, I wondered about this question.

It was my custom to spend a few minutes of every morning looking up into the beauty of Mt. Apo, towering above the golden-tinted clouds of the eastern sky, for in the grandeur of this mountain, in its multicolored reflections of the sun's rays, in its varied and rugged neighboring mountain ranges and foot-hills I seemed to feel God's presence and to draw strength from Him for the day's tasks. The pagan Manobo tribes who lived way back in the mountains call the mountain peak "Guino-o," their name for God, for they believed that God lived in the crater at the top of the mountain. They felt the mountain was a holy place, and they were afraid to go to the top of it for fear God would strike them down.

For me too this mountain—while not the *only* abode of God, as the pagans believed—became a place where God could be found. Mt. Apo was for me a constant reminder of God, a source of power and peace as it brought me a strong awareness of His presence. Both in the early mornings when its majestic peak was a tower of gold, and in the late afternoons as it was bathed in the pink and rose and velvet-purple tones of the setting sun, I found in this beautiful mountain assurances from God, the peace and serenity and power that flowed from Him. Daily I experienced the words of the psalmist: "I will lift up mine eyes unto the hills, from whence cometh my help. My help cometh from the Lord, which made heaven and earth."

Always, after spending some time looking at Mt. Apo, I would find my mind returning again to that question, "What's on the other side?" A thousand times that question flitted in and out of my mind and troubled me. On the wall in front of my desk I had pinned a large map of Mindanao, covering several square feet, and I studied it intently. In the very center of that huge map was Mt. Apo. The map showed a number of small mountain ranges, and quite a large number of rivers were drawn in, but some whole sections in this huge map were absolutely blank. I saw the Arakan River lined in, northeast of Mt. Apo, cutting through a huge valley. There were no towns or cities on the map, just a wide, blank area between two mountain ranges. This was the famous "Arakan Valley" I had heard people talking about. For a year or two I had been hearing of people hiking into this area in search of land. Occasionally, settlers had come out for supplies and had told tales of its tremendous size and potential. More and more I was intrigued by the idea of seeing this giant valley for myself. Like the bear in the old nursery song, I wanted to go to "The other side of the mountain, to see what I could see."

First, I decided to fly over the valley in my plane and have a "look-see" from the air. The government was beginning to survey the area with the idea of opening it up to settlers. Long-range plans were being made for townsites and for a government road, and I was anxious to see the area for myself. I had heard it estimated that within a period of five years there would be thousands of families living in the Arakan Valley. I knew that in the future expansion of the church in Mindanao, the Arakan Valley would be a strategic area, and I wanted us to be in on

225

the "ground floor," so to speak. The church must not be caught napping.

I took off in my small plane from our little runway in Kidapawan, under the shadow of Mt. Apo, early one morning while the air was still and smooth. I climbed steadily, and within fifteen minutes I was approaching the giant valley. My first impression was surprise at its size. I was looking down at a vast expanse, mostly green grassy plains, stretching about forty to fifty miles in one direction and about ten to fifteen miles the other way. Then, as I studied the small government map I was holding in my hand, I began to notice wide discrepancies between the map I was holding and the actual terrain as I could see it from the air. The rivers, clearly visible from the air, were not where the map showed them to be. They were many miles at variance. I continued to circle the area for a while, noting sixty or seventy little houses located and built in such a way as to indicate they belonged to the Manobos or the primitive Aetas. Then I returned to the Rural Center.

I invited the mayor and the municipal secretary to accompany me on my next flight, and they were thrilled to have this opportunity to study the Arakan Valley from the air. We circled the valley for the better part of one whole morning, while they very carefully and painstakingly drew maps, marking the rivers and hills and mountains in great detail. They were deeply grateful for the information they got from the air, as they were in the process of working out plans in their Municipal Council, laying out townsites and marking boundaries, and reserving land for schools, markets, and churches.

These flights from the air just served to whet my appetite. I still wanted to go in for myself and really *see* the Arakan Valley. My good friend, Amado Pidut, who could speak the dialect of the Manobos, volunteered to go along as my companion and guide since he had been up there before. Curran and David, our fourteen-year-old and thirteen-year-old sons, decided they wanted to come too and persuaded me to include them in our plans. They were challenged by the adventure of hiking into an unknown area, and I think they also wanted to show their "old man" they could keep up with him. I felt it would be a good experience for them. If they could "earn their letter" the hard way, hiking five to six days through the roughest jungle, carrying a regulation army back-pack up mountains and across rivers for a hundred miles, they would prove their worth, both to themselves and to the "old man."

Finally, after weeks of planning and preparation, we were ready to go. We loaded the jeep with our army packs, canteens, mosquito nets, blankets, and about twenty pounds of dried fish and forty pounds of rice, and we drove as far as the jeep could go over the rough, mountain trail. By 6 A.M. we had left our "jumping-off place," loaded our gear on our backs, and were on the trail, really stretching our legs in the cool of the early morning.

Our level trail soon became a jungle trail, as we left "civilization" and got deeper and deeper into the mountains. We crossed swift mountain streams and labored, panted, sweated our way ever upward toward the forbidding mountain pass. Our shoulder packs got heavier and heavier and heavier, and we fell to the ground many times in utter exhaustion. We reached the top of the 2500-foot plateau about 4 P.M. and then started down into the valley called Basak, meaning "low place" in the language of the primitive tribes who inhabit the area. By late afternoon we reached the house of Datu Embac, the chief of the Manobos of the area. He and his wife graciously invited us to sleep in his little house. While Pastor Pidut and I were getting acquainted with these interesting people, Curran and David went out and rode his fine horses. They were having a wonderful time . . . until a tree loomed up out of the gathering dusk in front of David! He pulled the horse sharply to one side, but lost his balance and fell off and got kicked in the face. The

227

half-inch gash over his eye was bloody, but not serious, and we soon had him on his feet again.

The *datu* is a most unusual fellow. Though the Manobos over whom he rules are still quite primitive and backward, he himself is a teacher and speaks English easily. He was a most interesting conversationalist, and we found ourselves, dead-tired as we were, sitting up long hours learning about this man and his people. In his territory are scattered more than a hundred families, in an area equal to a small county in the United States. His duties include performing marriages, granting divorces, punishing small crimes, settling disputes, and giving help in the people's economic problems. He is looked upon somewhat like a father to his children. He showed us his school for his people, which goes up to the fourth grade. In spite of hand-hewn seats and desks—reminding me of the Pilgrim days in America—dirt floors, lack of books and library, he was doing an amazing job of teaching his people.

The Manobos, who live in much of the wild mountainous jungle that still covers more than half of Mindanao, are sturdy, courageous, hard-working people, in many ways similar to our Indians. However, unlike the Indians they do not live together but prefer to spread out, building their bamboo houses on the highest hills or mountainsides, and farming the steep slopes and plateaus. "Kaingin" farms are everywhere to be seen—cleared places in the jungle where men have felled tall trees on the mountainsides, letting them fall as they will, and then cleared and burned the heavy brush. The older women next took over, punching holes into the ground with two sticks, one in each hand. The younger women and children followed after, dropping a couple of seeds of corn in each hole.

On this trip we learned many interesting beliefs and customs of the Manobo people. A simple animistic people, they worship and greatly fear among other things the "Balete Tree." The balete is a giant vine that grows up alongside and onto a big tree, soon completely covers and kills it no matter how large it is. The chief explained to us that his people (most of whom are still pagan, though the Christian and Missionary Alliance Church numbers about 10 per cent of them among its converts) place food under a tree where a balete vine is growing for the Balete Spirit to eat. Believing in evil spirits as they do, these people also make small rafts and place food, tobacco, and other gifts on them and float them down the river when some loved one gets sick, hoping thus to lure away the evil spirits causing the sickness so the person will recover.

The next day Datu Embac graciously consented to be our guide on the trip from Basak through the uncharted mountain wilderness up into the Arakan Valley proper. We started just at daylight. The trip consisted of more of the same: jungle . . . streams to be forded . . . bugs by the millions . . . up and down the mountains. Walking through the jungle is hard under any circumstances, but with a heavy, bulky pack it is the worst. Our packs kept biting into our shoulders, or sliding to one side and throwing us off balance. Every vine, every thorn seemed to have a personal grudge against each one of us. We stumbled, we fell, we got stuck with thorns, bitten by leeches, stung by insects—and yet through it all we were constantly challenged by the beauty of the land, the vastness of it, its rich promise for the future.

We learned many interesting things from Datu Embac, as we walked. We were impressed by the strong sense of personal honor among even these pagan tribes. The Manobos teach their children to tell the truth, never to steal, and to maintain at all costs both their own honor and the honor and standing of the tribe. One of the men we passed on the trail was carrying a seven-foot spear, made with a beautiful hand-polished hardwood handle, and we learned that he carried it for "aggressive self-protection," as the *datu* put it. He told us that only the previous week one of his men had killed another with just such a spear, because he had run away with his wife. His *honor* had been damaged. Another strong belief of the Manobos in the Arakan Valley is that if a person dies, all the occupants of the house where he died must leave it. In the middle of the second afternoon we came across a beautiful farm location, cleared and cleaned, with a very nice little house on it. Yet it was vacant. On the other side of the house we saw the reason— a new grave, with a little shelter over it to keep out the rain. Under the shelter we saw a plate, heaped high with food.

The second day we reached the Arakan Valley proper and began walking down the length of it. Two whole days were spent covering twenty-five to thirty miles of this area, an area that will be heavily populated in the years to come when the government completes its plans for releasing these fertile lands for settlement. We looked for good landing sites for the plane, near places that might become small towns and villages. It took a lot of imagination! In our two or three days of hiking in the Valley we passed an occasional house, every two or three hours, along the winding trails among the gently rolling hills.

The next night we slept with the chief of the Aetas, an even more primitive mountain tribe. Here I saw something that took me back over 1000 years—a homemade forge for working metal, making knives, bolos, axes, and other tools. The forge was constructed from two large pieces of bamboo tubing, to act as bellows, and the wind was made to go through the tubes by two sticks, the ends covered with small feathers. I finally persuaded the chief to sell me one of his handmade knives for 50 cents, so that I could show people when I came back out.

The next day we started out westward. We had to cross another low mountain range, and it took us until nightfall to reach the small community of Kulaman, meaning in their dialect "place where the rivers meet." There were about twenty houses here. We met with Datu Ombas, a strong, wiry, colorful figure, and some of his local leaders. I found a long, clear, grassy area, and the *datu* and his men agreed to try to construct a landing field within the next sixty days. They were eager to have me bring in our Rural Center doctor and dentist, and I promised to try to do so, if they would clean and mark and carefully prepare the needed strip. In no other place in the Philippines have I ever seen such medical need and such human suffering! Every time we reached a house, the leaders would approach me and ask if I had any medicines for their sick. Sometimes it would be malaria, and then I was grateful that I did have some medicine I could give. But most of the time there were problems which I could not treat. At lunchtime on the fourth day we had been in one man's house only a few minutes when they brought to me a young woman with the most heartbreaking case of tropical ulcers I have ever seen. Her leg was a mass of raw flesh. There was little I could do. After cleaning up the running sores, and gently binding them with gauze, I gave her a test shot of penicillin, and then, after no reaction, the largest dose I had.

The need of the neglected people of this far region is best illustrated by our experience here at the Methodist Rural Center one week not long after we got back. Five families, distant kin of our neighbor, Datu Icdang, hiked out from the Arakan Valley to come to our clinic at the center. They were sixteen people in all. They had heard the news that at our clinic they could have free examination and consultation and pay only minimum costs for medicines. Our doctor and nurse spent hours giving this group of Manobos a careful examination. Findings? All sixteen of them have tuberculosis!

The purpose of our trip, which took five days of the hardest hiking I have ever known and covered approximately 100 miles, was to survey this new, undeveloped territory, to locate possible church sites, find landing strips, and look toward the future when there will be many new settlers coming into the area from other parts of the Philippines.

We were four tired, footsore individuals the afternoon we

finally made it back to the center. There wasn't a toe on my foot that didn't have at least one blister, and some of them were nothing but blisters. And yet, tired as we were, we were happy as we came in. I was proud of Curran and David, who had kept smiling the whole trip. There was never a word of complaint from those two young soldiers of Christ! I was proud, too, of Amado, of his wonderfully friendly, Christlike personality, which had been such a help to us in meeting new people and in preparing the way for the coming of the gospel into this place. Most of all, we were thankful to God, who had opened yet another door of opportunity for service, who had given us the vision to go to this great valley and the strength to endure the hike and to return safely.

A few months after this first Arakan trip we received an urgent call for medical help. Datu Ombas sent out a messenger with the plea: "Many people are sick. Please bring medicines." I took off in the plane and flew over the area to check up on the landing strip, but I could see that it was just well begun. It could not be used. The plane would be out of the question. It meant another 100-mile hike back into the fastness of this giant valley, if . . . and it was a big *if* . . . our clinic doctor and dentist would volunteer to hike. I could not ask them to, or force them to, for the trip was too hard. However, I told them as simply as I could exactly what the needs were like, how hard the hike would be, what they could expect to find in the Arakan Valley. Then we lifted the problem up to God, asking His guidance.

After spending about half a day in prayer and thought, the wonderful young people of our staff came to me and said, "Sir, we would like to go." Dr. Hernan Reyes, the doctor, and Dr. Andrea Agatep, the dentist, were both slight in body. They had spent most of their youth in the city of Manila and had had no experience in "roughing it" out in the open, hiking, or sleeping in the woods, or climbing mountains. They were real "tenderfeet," but they wanted to try. In addition, our local pastor, the Reverend Jose Sanchez, decided he wanted to go along too to help in presenting the Good News to the people in darkness in this faraway area. This trip our middle son, Stephen, aged twelve, wanted to go along. He wanted to win his "jungle letter" too and so it was decided he could accompany us.

We were one heavily laden group of people as we started out this time, for we had not only the food and clothes and bedding for a week, but also all of the medical supplies we could possibly carry. Our guide this time was a Manobo man who lived in a small village near us. He told us he had been to Kulaman before, and that he knew the way, but by 2 P.M. of the first day as we trudged over the mountain slopes, he finally admitted, "I'm not sure of the way." There we were, heavily overloaded, with Dr. Agatep, who had never hiked as much as ten miles in her whole life, near the point of complete exhaustion, and we found out we were lost! It's a good thing I could not express my thoughts in the Manobo dialect!

There was nothing to do but keep going. I knew that if we reached the top of the ridge, we would be more able to see what lay ahead, and I was hoping I would recognize some part of the trail where I had passed before. We huffed and puffed, and puffed and huffed, and kept going. The spirit of those kids was marvelous! There was many a wisecrack that escaped between puffs, but never a complaint. Finally, we reached the top of the 2500-foot ridge and started down on the other side. The tropical rain forest through which we hiked was beautiful, with dense undergrowth and huge trees. There were many singing birds, colorful butterflies, chirping insects of all sorts, but we couldn't enjoy the beauty of our surroundings because of having to watch our every step so carefully. The rocky trail was wet and slippery, and we had to step carefully.

Just about 5 P.M. we reached a tiny village of about fifteen houses and a little bamboo schoolhouse. We went into the schoolhouse and collapsed on its plain dirt floor. We were too tired to care where we lay, as long as we would get off our feet. Our guide started a fire and started cooking some rice to go with our dried fish. By 6 P.M. we managed to sit up again and started stuffing our stomachs with the rice and fish, not because we liked it, but simply because we knew we'd never be able to hike the next day if we didn't eat. In another hour we had tied up our mosquito nets and stretched out on our mats, dead to the world. Oh, blessed sleep!

We were on the trail before 6 A.M. the next day, for more, much more of the same. The going got harder and harder, and by 9 A.M. I realized that, because of blisters, Andrea just could not walk any more. That tiny, courageous girl was game and did not complain, but she was not used to the continuous up-and-down mountain trails, and I could see that without help she would never make it. Fortunately, we were able to find and rent a horse for her, and then after we loaded some of our medical supplies on the horse too we began to make better time. The second night we slept in a settler's cabin, and on the third day we crossed the Arakan River and were now in the heart of the giant Arakan Valley.

We reached our destination, Kulaman, just about noon. We found the house of our young schoolteacher friend, Mr. Dahan, and gratefully threw ourselves down on his floor. We had made it! The young doctor, fresh from Manila, had hiked every step of the way without a word of complaint. Stephen had made it. Jose, our young pastor, had succeeded in making the longest hike of his entire life. And Andrea, our little dentist, had made it too and was smiling large as life!

Datu Ombas, and his son, Mailan, had sent runners out to tell all the people that we were there. After a good night's sleep, we were up early the next morning, but the people were even earlier. Mr. Dahan's house was already full to overflowing with the sick and afflicted. Such horrible sights greeted us—huge tropical ulcers, swollen bellies, listless babies too weak and sick even to cry! Malaria was rampant in the area, and many people had the enlarged spleens, racking chills, and general wasting away of physical strength that went with this chronic crippler. Hernan and Andrea, after a reading from the Scriptures and a fervent prayer for the Lord's guidance and help, opened up their boxes of supplies and began to work. The "clinic" was open. All day long they worked, in the midst of this packed mass of humanity, in heat and humidity that made their clothes stick to their sweat-soaked bodies. I had to take my hat off to these two dedicated young people. They treated more than a hundred people that one day, working all day without stopping.

Since this was the first time a doctor or a dentist had ever been in Kulaman, people crowded in from all sides, for miles around. The sick came for help, the well came from curiosity. As I looked around at all these tribal people packed inside the small house, my first impression was to be almost overcome by the powerful smells emanating from so many bodies perspiring in the heat and from so many unwashed clothes. The average Filipino is very clean, but in some of the pagan tribes in these backward regions people go for weeks without a bath. My second impression was to be amazed to notice that there was not one single fat person in the room. As my eyes wandered around the room, I noted that these people were lean and hard, and some were thin to the point of emaciation. The prominent bones of their rib cages made me think of the term "walking skeletons."

As a father of five active, noisy boys, I was surprised to notice how quiet all the children were. The small babies clung to their mothers' legs in abject fear, too terrified to move, and I could understand their reaction since this was the first time they had seen white faces. But even the older children, who understood who we were and why we had come, stood about so still and apathetically that I asked Dr. Reyes about them. I had never seen children sit still so long or be so well-behaved. He explained that they were too weak from malnutrition and from the effects of dysentery to have enough energy to misbehave. They just sat—or stood—and nearly broke my heart.

The clothing of these people was motley, ranging from the complete nakedness of the small children to the short, colorful pants of the men, topped by ragged, colored undershirts, torn shirts of one kind or another, and dirty rags tied around their heads, turban-style. The younger, unmarried women wore short blouses or boleros, as well as the wrap-around skirts which were the only garments of the older women. Whatever the color of the original garments, most of them were so dingy and dirty and patched now that they looked gray and nondescript.

The necks and arms of the women were usually covered with beads and metal bracelets. Both the men and the women had large holes in their ear lobes, where they had placed bone ornaments. The women had colorful tattoos on their waists and arms, and the men, too, had colorful tattooed designs on their chests and arms. They were infinitely patient as they squatted in the little room, entertaining themselves with conversation and watching the work of the doctor and the dentist, who was also filling in as a nurse. Their chief recreation, as far as I could tell, was chewing "buyo," or betel nut. This is a curious combination of eating and relaxing, and must be done in a carefully detailed manner. Betel nut and a small amount of powdered lime are first wrapped in a small piece of tobacco leaf, and then this mixture is wrapped in a second and larger green leaf. I have been told, although I have no way of being sure, that chewing betel nut has a mildly narcotic effect. After watching one day a woman being tattooed I thought, "I hope that betel nut she is chewing has come pain-killing properties." It was a very simple process, but it gave me the shivers. A man just took his knife and cut a line across the abdomen of the woman to be tattooed until the blood ran. Then he took some lampblack from the roof of the hut over the stove and rubbed it into the wound.

All of the intricate designs on their bodies are made in just this way, merely cutting with a knife and then rubbing in lampblack.

There is a certain "wild wisdom" involved in their betel-nut chewing. These primitive people know nothing of nutrition and and have no instruction in the value of calcium for building bones and strengthening their bodies. Yet, their bodies long for lime, and generation after generation they have been chewing lime together with their betel nuts. A thousand miles north of Mindanao among another tribe, the Negritos, I discovered the same custom. Both use lime. Where do they get the lime? They pound up snails, crabs, even the soft bones of some animals in order to get this needed body nutrient. In even the most primitive cultures there is found this God-given "wild wisdom."

Toward the end of the morning Datu Ombas brought in one of the most gruesome medical cases I have ever seen. A grown man had fallen down a cliff and broken his leg, making a terrible compound fracture. Both bones of the leg were protruding through the muscle and flesh. He was picked up and carried to his house, and a local "herboleria" was called. This native "doctor" brushed off the dirt, washed off the blood, using an ordinary rag and river water, and then had four men hold down the injured man while he jerked the leg straight. After this Himalayan experience of pain, which he endured without even an aspirin tablet to ease his agony, the man was too exhausted to even cry out. The "doctor" then wrapped his leg tightly in wet bark and left him. Within a week's time the leg became a putrefying mass of infection.

His family made a raft and floated him down the river, and then carried him by stretcher to the small hospital in the nearest town. Here the doctor took an X ray which revealed that the leg was set wrong and would be horribly out of shape unless broken again and reset. He filled the man with antibiotics, and waited for the wound to heal enough to make the

237

second operation possible. However, after two months there was little improvement in the infection. The man was growing weaker. At last he decided that if he was going to die anyway, he wanted to die at home, and so he made arrangements for his friends to carry him back up into the Arakan Valley.

There was little we could do. Hernan cleansed the leg, which was a huge open wound thickly encrusted with dried pus and dirt. It smelled to high heaven. Where the two bones had punctured the skin and muscles there were now oozing holes. After cleaning the leg and giving him the most massive doses of medicines that he could, the young doctor gave him instructions for daily care and left him a supply of sterile gauze, adhesive tape, and more medicines. Then we left him there in that faraway valley, not knowing whether he would live or die.

That night we held a service in Mr. Dahan's house, which was filled to capacity, and beyond. We told these people of a great invisible God who rules the universe, who flings the stars into their places in the heavens, who controls the sun and the moon, who sends the rain on the waiting plants of earth, and who made each one of us, His children, and who loves us as His children. We told them that He loved us so much that He entered our lives on this earth as a Babe in Bethlehem, in order that we might have life, radiant life, abundant life, joyful life. We told them how He died at the hands of cruel men in order to redeem us from our fears, our selves, and most of all, our *sins*. The people were much interested and listened attentively when we spoke of a God who was powerful enough to cast out "evil spirits," for they believe in evil spirits. We tried to break through all the barriers of language and custom and distance that separate these simple people from their Christian brothers, and to witness as strongly as we knew how to the love of the Great Spirit whom they could trust and serve with confidence.

Early the next morning we hiked over to the suggested site

238

for our landing strip. If only we could get a landing strip here in Kulaman, the very geographical heart of the Arakan Valley, we could fly in in twenty minutes, instead of hiking three days or more over the roughest possible terrain. The site still seemed fine, in an almost level cogonal plain, but very little work had been done. These people are very sincere, and they really meant it when they promised to prepare the field, but the hard physical labor of digging out stumps, cutting tall grass, and cleaning the long length needed will be a big job. I got a pledge from twenty men who said they would go right to work on it. However, these people will promise anything—even the moon with a fence built around it—but I knew I would have to come back again to get the job really finished.

Datu Ombas then suggested that in going home we take rafts down the river, thus shortening the amount of hiking the medical staff would have to do. He and his son took charge personally of the work, and things began to hum. They decided to make two rafts, since the river was very swift and full of whirlpools and sunken logs. They figured that if one raft overturned, there was still a chance that the other would get through, and only part of our supplies and clothes would be lost. If we had only one big raft, we might lose everything. They cut thick bamboos and made each raft four feet wide and twenty feet long, two layers thick. It was decided that Datu Ombas would go along on one raft, and Mailan on the other, to steer us through the rapids. This was their way of showing us their appreciation for our coming.

By the middle of the morning we were all loaded on the two rafts and pushed off, to the shouts and good-byes of our newly made friends. We thanked them for their help and then headed off down the Kulaman River, excited about reaching the giant Rio Grande for a two-day trip that we knew would be full of thrills. All that first day the river cut through a deep canyon. We floated along the river at the bottom of the chasm, with the walls on either side of us sloping upward 100 to 150 feet. Consequently, there was no breeze, and it was a blisteringly hot ride. We had been told to be sure we stayed aboard and did not fall out, as there were crocodiles in the river. Once or twice Stephen shouted, "There's one!" but I never saw any. However, the knowledge that there *might* be crocodiles kept us on our toes and we were all careful to sit tight.

We stopped about two in the afternoon to go ashore and cook some rice. I wanted to keep going and try to reach the mouth of the Arakan River so that we could sleep at the house of the Muslims there. The *datu* was skeptical, since we would have to negotiate some of the worst part of the river after dusk, and perhaps even in the dark. He wanted to just sleep on the river bank, but I persuaded him to keep going. "Visions of home" were dancing through my head, and I was determined to get home as soon as possible.

As we continued our journey downstream, we enjoyed the chatter and playfulness of the monkeys in the overhanging trees. It is always interesting to see an absolutely untouched virgin land in all its lush, bountiful, unspoiled beauty, before man begins to "improve" it. We marveled at the giant height of the trees along the shore. From almost every tree long rattan "ropes" were hanging, so that we could almost imagine Tarzan himself swinging out from tree to tree. We passed through thick jungle undergrowth, revealing all sorts of beautiful flowers and shrubs I had never seen before. Without thinking, we all began singing,

> This is my Father's world,
>     And to my listening ears,
> All nature sings, and round me rings,
>     The music of the spheres.

By late afternoon it was obvious that we would not be able to reach the Muslim's house by dark. However, I urged that we go on. After all, did we not have three good flashlights? We could watch out for logs and rocks and whirlpools. Datu Ombas was very unconvinced, but he just grunted, and moved to the front of the lead raft. The dusk descended quickly about us, and the darkness deepened. The river channel was becoming narrower, so that we began to be swept along more and more swiftly. The big job of the *datu* was to use his big pole to push the raft away from rocks or logs, but in the growing darkness it became increasingly difficult. Then Andrea dropped one of the flashlights overboard! We still had two, one for each raft, but their feeble light hardly cut through the inky darkness. We could not see the shore line at all.

About 7:30 P.M., in the midst of the eerie darkness, we heard yells and screams and gurgles, as the second raft hit a rock. My heart sank! Andrea, who could not swim a stroke, was on that raft, as were Stephen and Hernan and Mailan. We were going so fast on our raft we couldn't stop. I could just see a slight blur back where their raft had overturned. The *datu* headed our raft for the bank, while I raked the darkness of the river with the flashlight, looking for heads. We saw none. An eternity went by, an eternity of anguished prayer, before we saw their flashlight pointing toward us. They were all safe, though wet and scared stiff. Their raft had crashed into a huge log and been knocked over at a very high angle. However, as they fell into the water, they had been able to grab hold of the raft's sides as it righted itself, and had pulled themselves back on. The raft drifted into a large whirlpool, but by some miracle of heroic strength Mailan had been able to hold on to his giant pole. He was able to push the raft out of that vortex of roaring, twisting, sickening waters. He couldn't explain *how* he did it, and we didn't argue. We just thanked our Father, "whose eye is on the sparrow," that He had been watching over us and had kept us safe in the midst of this harrowing experience.

By moving slowly along the shore we were able to pole our

way cautiously down the river without any further mishap. We arrived at the place of the Muslim a few hours later, and he graciously took us in and allowed us to sleep on the floor of his house. As we unrolled our mats and lay down in the little room to stretch our cramped muscles and try to get some sleep, I could not help wonder whether I would have welcomed so freely a group of wet, dirty, scraggly-looking people if they had come pounding on my door long after I had gone to sleep. I thought, "How much, how terribly much we Americans have to learn from the kind, gracious Orientals!"

We were up the next day by 5 A.M., preparing for the last day of our journey homeward. It was a long, hot, exhausting day of floating down the river under the broiling sun. The river was wider now, and we no longer had the protection of the overhanging trees. We were all burned a crisp, burning red before we finally reached Carmen about 4 P.M. There we were able to flag a bus to Kabacan, and by 8 P.M. we were back at the Rural Center. Home, sweet, *sweet* home! Nothing in all God's green, green, wonderful world is as satisfying as getting home again after a trip like that!

A few weeks later I made several survey flights in the plane over the valley. At first I could see they had done very little work on the landing strip. However, the sight of my plane seemed to inspire the men, for the work speeded up a little. I was terribly anxious to try out the landing strip there, to open up this vast Arakan Valley for future trips in. I could see great possibilities for evangelism as soon as I could fly in our student pastors for week ends, and for youth rallies, and the like. I was anxious to keep faith with Datu Ombas and our good brothers there, whom I had promised to help in case of medical emergencies. I knew that if I could fly regularly into the Arakan Valley, I could take our doctor and nurse back for a week or two at a time throughout the year. I could see great possibilities for the future, if only we could solve the problem of transportation to this remote place.

On the other hand, I realized full well the dangers involved in flying into a new area and trying out an untested strip. If anything happened to the plane, I would be months getting any new parts brought in for repairs. It was a hazardous undertaking, at best. I continued to fly over Kulaman ever so often, trying to see from the air just what the condition of the landing strip actually was. Then, Dave Williams, a young agricultural missionary who was also a pilot and understood what was involved, volunteered to hike in to supervise the final work on the strip and to be there for my first test-run, "just in case." Pastor Pidut, that wonderfully selfless young pastor, agreed to go along as guide, and Emiliano Berganio, one of our neighbors, also decided to go along to help. They had a very difficult hike for the rains had started and had made a mess of the trails, but they made it. Dave got a team of the local men working, leveling out the worst spots, and preparing for my attempted landing.

Three days later I flew over Kulaman and buzzed the strip. Immediately I could see people start running toward the landing strip. This would be the first time a plane had ever come to the Arakan Valley. They had never seen a plane up close. Nobody wanted to miss this chance! As I slowly circled the strip, I could see that Dave and his men had done a good job of cutting the grass and hauling away the rocks and boulders. There was still one big problem. There was a dip of four feet right in the center of the 450-yard strip. I knew that when the plane touched down at 60 m.p.h., there would be a very real question about whether the nose gear and landing gear would hold together when I hit that deep bump. I knew the landing would be tricky. I had never landed on a rougher strip. I checked the wind for the umpteenth time, and went over every possible emergency procedure, repeating all the while the words of one of my early instructors, "When in doubt, *go around again!*"

"Gas on full tank . . . check; half flaps . . . check; carburetor heat . . . check." A last glance at the instrument panel showed everything in the green. I was ready if I ever would be ready. With a last, silent prayer dedicating this plane and this airstrip to God's use, I turned from the cross-wind leg into the final approach and began to inch back on the throttle and at the same time raise the nose. "Three hundred yards . . . full flaps . . . it's now or never!" The plane was dropping too fast, and I gave her a last burst of the throttle. She was on the ground. Now the brakes . . . easy . . . again. . . . She slowed . . . hit the dip . . . more brakes and ah-h-h-h-h . . . she slowed to a stop. Dave came up smiling, saying, "Not bad! Not bad!" I smiled back, and started getting out of the plane.

Seconds later the plane was surrounded by yelling, excited, jumping, jabbering people. I thanked all the men who had been helping on the strip, and then I got Mailan to get some of his strong followers to help me in keeping the pushing mob of happy people from picking the "giant bird" apart. Right there on the open field, standing beside the plane, we held a short, impromptu service. I told the people again of the all-powerful God who held the plane in the sky and who controlled all that was in the universe, and yet who loved each one of us, individually, as His own dear children. The Spirit of God descended upon that unruly mob in a most miraculous, moving way. We bowed our heads in prayer, and dedicated the plane to God's use and to the service of His children in need.

I spent an hour or so going over the strip with the men, making a few suggestions for some minor changes, some improvements here and there. It had to be widened a little, and it would have to be filled in where it dipped in the middle. It was a rough strip, but I knew we could use it. Dave came up then and told me that one of the men was sick. He wanted to know if I could fly him out. Already the plane could be a means of blessing to someone in need!

# ARAKAN VALLEY

I put the sick man aboard, and one other, and prepared to take off. On such a rough strip I knew I did not dare to take the plane's full load of four persons, including the pilot. I headed down the runway, not knowing what to expect, but . . . the plane was off in a flash, and in sixteen minutes we were landing back at the Rural Center. The next flight back to Arakan took me only fifteen minutes, and this time I took out Dave and Pastor Pidut. By 1 P.M. we had flown out everybody, including Datu Ombas. Fifteen minutes a flight, compared with three hard days' hiking! It was incredible! Only a person who had hiked the rugged, mountainous, jungle trail could appreciate the miracle of this fifteen-minute flight. It had taken three hard hikes to this place, and three weeks of hard work in preparing the strip, but at last we had a door opened to the Arakan Valley. The Preface had been written; now we were ready to go to work.

My heart was full of thanksgiving to God as I landed the plane on the last flight back from the Arakan. I was thanking Him for His help and protection, and praying for His guidance for our future work in that great valley, when I noticed Pedro, our next-door neighbor, coming racing down the runway, full speed, riding bareback on his horse. He drew up alongside the plane and jumped off. Pedro was just fourteen years old. He came over to stand beside me as I was closing the plane and preparing to push it into the hanger. He pointed to the plane and to me, and then to his horse, self-confident and smiling. I understood —he had been flying, too. We were both pilots. He flew on the ground, and I flew on the air.

Pedro was an orphan. He had been born in the Arakan Valley, in a family of the Aeta tribe. Some of these Aeta people wear clothes, and go to school, but most of them are still very savage and primitive. They are not Christians. They have never met the courageous Christ, nor learned of His loving and helpful ways. Pedro's father was beheaded by a member of his own tribe. He was mistakenly killed because they thought he had stolen something. So his own people beheaded him! His mother was also killed, and the children became slaves, servants of the man who killed their parents.

For years Pedro was only a little boy around his master's house. He hauled water from the river, planted corn on the hillside, or pulled weeds. If he made his owner angry, he was beaten or kicked. Pedro could take the beatings. They hurt only on the outside. But Pedro had a deeper hurt, on the inside. The other children of his place all laughed at him and taunted him. They were very cruel because he had a split upper lip, a harelip.

One day Datu Icdang was visiting relatives on the outskirts of the Arakan Valley, and happened to be in the home where Pedro worked. Feeling pity for this small boy, Datu Icdang paid his master a small amount and took Pedro home with him. Even though his own home was already full of people, eleven living in a three-room house, Datu Icdang was a Christian, and God led him to rescue Pedro. Pedro was happy in his new home. The food was better. They didn't kick him or beat him, and best of all, the other children did not tease him about the hole in his face that made him so ugly. But though his body was well fed, though he was able to go to school for a few years, Pedro still had a longing deep down inside of him. He was ashamed to go out in public because his three front teeth always stuck out. He wanted a face like other people's.

Several years after he had come to the Icdangs to live, a wonderful thing happened. The Methodist Rural Center started a small clinic next door to his house, and Pedro gathered together his courage and went over and stood timidly in the clinic door. The kindly Dr. Hernan Reyes examined Pedro's face. A mild hope, a dream, leaped alive in his heart. "Oh, if only my face can be made like other children's faces," he thought.

One day the doctor took him into the clinic and put him up on the wooden table, put a local anesthetic in several places on his face and lip, and began to operate. How Pedro prayed! How hard he prayed that that ugly hole could be closed! For a week his face was covered with bandages. On Saturday, Pedro reported back to the clinic, his heart pounding with hope, and yet he was afraid, too. Then the doctor took off the bandages, and handed him a mirror. There was no more ugly hole, only a small scar. How happy Pedro was! He smiled a great deal after that! To pay for his operation, Pedro began carrying water for the Rural Center, at 5 cents per five-gallon can. His happy, smiling face became a regular sight around the center, as he worked faithfully every day to pay every penny of the cost of his operation.

Pedro walked with a new pride in his step, a new joy in his heart. His smile was contagious. As I watched him ride off on his horse with his reckless, grinning braggadocio, I could not help thinking of all the other boys from the Arakan Valley, boys just like Pedro, whom we hoped to save from poverty and despair. I thought of all the men and women of the Arakan Valley who needed to be saved from sickness and sin. As I rolled the plane into the hangar, I thanked God for the change that had come into Pedro's life, and then I prayed that He would help us in all our plans and dreams for bringing that kind of change to the other hundreds and thousands of people who needed our help. I asked Him to help us to be faithful in bringing the Good News to all the Pedros of this world—the Good News of health, of salvation in Christ.

About a year later, tragedy struck. Pedro won't be smiling by my side any more. One day as he was galloping down the runway, full speed, he fell off his horse, and sustained internal injuries. Pedro died almost instantly of an internal hemorrhage. Almost his last words were, "Help me, Lord Jesus."

Pedro was my next-door neighbor, and I miss him now. And yet, somehow I have a feeling that up there now, somewhere in the beautiful land of heaven, Pedro is riding his horse full speed across the skies, smiling broadly at the angels.

# 15

## The Big Job

AFTER NEARLY 2000 years of work and the expenditure of the lives of hundreds of thousands of dedicated Christian missionaries, only one third of the world's population is Christian. Today's high birth rates are almost everywhere outpacing the rate of conversions. *We are losing the fight to win the world for Christ!*

Specifically, Christianity accounts for less than 1 per cent of China's vast 600 million population, for about 2 per cent of India's 400 million people, less than 1 per cent of Japan's 90 million people. Because of the tremendous birth rate in the countries of Asia, even the percentage we have is slipping away from us. For example, in China alone the population increases 12 million yearly. Bluntly, our situation is this: nearly two billion of the people of the world are either non-Christian or anti-Christian.

I copied the following sobering figures from the "Map of the World" published by the Friendship Press:

Estimated population
of the world      2,800,000,000
Population of Asia     1,500,000,000

### WORLD'S RELIGIONS
(in round figures):

| | |
|---|---|
| Christians | 835,000,000 |
| Buddhists | 350,000,000 |

248

| Muslims | 350,000,000 |
|---|---|
| Hindus | 300,000,000 |
| Confucianists | 300,000,000 |
| Taoists | 50,000,000 |
| Shintoists | 25,000,000 |
| Jews | 10,000,000 |

*Christians:*

| Roman Catholics | 425,000,000 |
|---|---|
| Protestants | 225,000,000 |
| Eastern Orthodox | 175,000,000 |
| Copts | 10,000,000 |
| Total | 835,000,000—or 29.8 per cent of world's population |

*Protestants and Evangelicals:*

| Lutherans | 68,000,000 |
|---|---|
| Presbyterian and Reformed | 41,000,000 |
| Baptists | 40,000,000 |
| Methodists | 30,000,000 |
| Anglicans | 30,000,000 |

The situation is actually more depressing than even these figures would indicate, for there are still many great states or provinces in China and Central Asia where there is not a single Christian church. Among the great Islamic countries there are few or almost no churches among 200 million people.

The Christian Church has sent out thousands upon multiplied thousands of the most dedicated men and women into the far corners of the world, and yet still one half of the people of the world live in darkness, unable to read or write. Even in this so-called enlightened twentieth century, most of the babies of the world are born and die without ever having the services of a doctor. Poverty is still the scourge of millions of the underprivileged people of the world. Even in the Philippines, one of the "better-off" nations of Asia, hunger is an ever-present spectre. *The Free Press,* of September 12, 1959, stated: "Here are the latest facts on the Filipino people: Three out of ten barrio (village) people have a cash earning of less than $50 a year. This means that one third of the rural people make $4.20 per month, or 12 cents a day. The average income of the rest ranges from $100 to $150 per year. *But 16 per cent of all those interviewed reported no cash income at all for the previous year.*"

In the face of the world's need, what is the Christian Church doing about it? Not enough! For example, one of the great denominations in America had a membership of 4 million members and was sending out 2500 missionaries in 1932. Today, in 1960, that same church, with a membership now of 9 million is sending out only 1500 missionaries. Why? In the face of the greatest spiritual need in the world's history, why are we doing so little?

There are many reasons, but the most important one is that young people are just not volunteering for the mission field. The culture of big cars, movie extravaganzas, modern comforts has taken its toll in spiritual values. Soft mattresses, the life of ease, the extra layer of fat around the mid-sections of the American people have weakened our devotion and watered down our willingness to sacrifice. The world is screaming, "God, send us men!" —and too many of our young people turn a deaf ear and pass by on the other side.

Another factor in the losing fight of the church to save the world is the high cost of missions. Costs for missions, like costs of weapons, have gone up enormously. Giving to missions in our churches has failed to keep up with the 50 to 100 per cent increase in costs since 1945. One mission board has recently estimated that it costs $10,000 to recruit one missionary, give him minimum training, and send him and his family and equipment to an overseas mission station.

Having said all this, let me also state that there are some encouraging factors in this world picture. In some places there are greater opportunities before the Christian Church than at any other time in the history of missions. Dr. Donald McGavran, in the March, 1958 issue of *The Christian Herald*, said:

We live in a ripening world. This is perhaps the most revolutionary and encouraging fact in missions. More populations today are responsive to the gospel than ever before. Movements which multiply churches are possible in land after land, not only among backward tribal people, but also in advanced culture populations.

Consider the encouraging growth of evangelical churches in Chile, where one in ten of the population is now said to be a Biblical Christian. Look at the trebled membership of some denominations in Brazil. Ponder the fivefold growth of the Disciples of Christ Church in only twenty years in Puerto Rico .... And we have not yet mentioned ripe tribal populations. In Africa alone, 100 million Animists are going somewhere in our lifetime—to Islam, Communism, Roman Catholicism, or the Evangelical faith.

Dr. McGavran believes that some churches and many people have lost their way in missions. He goes on to say,

There are many ways of getting lost; indeed, the difficulty is not in losing our way, but in keeping our sense of direction. . . . The first deviation is the imagining that in some vague way *other* religions confer salvation, and hence their followers do not need the Saviour. Any person who believes this weakens his own will to propogate the Christian faith. The Christian faith becomes to him something like UNICEF. Christians get off on this trail while looking for that excellent commodity—a genuine respect for other men's opinion and a humble, Christian way of commending Christ. But *do* other religions confer salvation? Can we correctly say, "You follow your way, I'll follow mine, and we'll both get to God"? Must not all of us follow God's way? Religion is a matter of truth. The world's religions teach important doctrines directly opposed to those of Christianity. All cannot be equally true.

Our Lord said, "No man comes to the Father but by me." He made many similar statements. If what He said about Himself and what the church has always claimed about Him is true, then all

251

without Him—whether they be our own children or men in far-off lands—are *really lost*. Missions then becomes a matter of winning lost men to belief in the Saviour and to the abundant eternal life resulting from such belief.

The second deviation substitutes good deeds done to men for the winning of lost men to Christ. The Christian mission then becomes charity on the other side of the world. . . . There is a greater need than lack of food, clothes, or education. It is a lack of salvation. No famine is as devastating as the famine of the Word of God. No destitution is as weakening as that of people destitute of churches, Bibles, or Christ. Consequently, while we should continue to do many good works, *bringing winnable men to Christ should have priority*. If, busy in various charities, we have little time, strength, or inclination to win the winnable, we have lost our way.

I am grateful to Dr. McGavran for these strong words which express so well my own personal convictions. *The world needs Christ*. It needs Him as it has never needed Him before, and it is the purpose of my life to bring Him to as many people of the world as I can. I am sure I have made many mistakes, and I shall make many, many more—but at least I shall make them in *trying*, in trying to give my best in the most exciting, challenging, satisfying job in all the world, the job of being a missionary of Christ Jesus. And it is my hope and prayer that other young men and women who read this book will also find their minds captured and their wills caught by the enormity of this challenge that is before us, this task that waits for men and women of daring—*Winning the world to Christ!*

> Rise up, O men of God!
>   Have done with lesser things;
> Give heart and mind and soul and strength
>   To serve the King of kings.
>
> Rise up, O men of God!
>   The Church for you doth wait,
> Her strength unequal to her task;
>   Rise up, and make her great!

# THE BIG JOB

For there is no hope of winning this world to Christ through the efforts of professional missionaries and ministers only. It is far too big a job. The only hope in a day when the forces of darkness threaten to overwhelm us is to mobilize the total manpower of the church—every pastor, every missionary, and also every lay man and woman must be Christ's ambassador, if we are even to begin to measure up to the fateful hour in which we live.

The church has always moved forward because of the witnessing and working of ordinary men and women. There is a strong probability that the great church at Rome was first started by laymen returning to their homes or going to the great city on business, after having met the Master, the Risen Lord, through the preaching of the apostles. Some histories affirm that the story of Christ was first carried to England by traders and by soldiers.

Christ needs missionaries in every office, every factory, every classroom, every basketball court. The Record says clearly that every individual Christian must be a missionary. "And he said to them all, If any man will come after me, let him deny himself, and take up his cross daily, and follow me" (Luke 9:23). Here is the piercing call to every man to enter the fray. We are *all* called to be soldiers of Christ. We are all called to enter into the fellowship of suffering. We are all called to witness through work, word, service, and sacrifice, that Jesus Christ is Lord. If we name the name of Christ with our lips, then our lives must show forth His praise. Hard . . . yes; difficult . . . extremely so; . . . impossible . . . *no*. We can use our desks as pulpits, our drill press as a lectern, our stove as an altar for prayer. Wherever we are, we can be ambassadors for Christ. But such a life requires of each one of us real dedication and devotion.

Ordinary men and women of all the Christian churches of the world hold in their hands the answer to godless atheism and insidious, overpowering materialism. However, it will be necessary for all church members to go deeper than ever before, to love more, and to give of themselves much more sacrificially. Air-conditioning our sanctuaries, or re-doing our central heating plants, or buying new choir robes will not save the world for Christ. At a time when revolution stalks the face of the earth, when the four horsemen of the Apocalypse storm across every continent leaving the dead and dying on every hand, we must rise above preoccupation with buildings and material things, and get down to the heart of Christianity. Jesus stated very bluntly to a high church official, "You must be born again!" Not until our church men and women are wholly and completely brought under the control of Jesus Christ will there be missionaries, ambassadors, men and women of courage and daring who will "carry the cross" into all the dark places of the earth.

Someone said, "Christianity has been tried and found wanting." But a wiser, more humble Christian replied, "No, Christianity has not been tried and found wanting. It has been found to be so difficult that it has not been tried at all." Where are the men and women who would *dare* to follow Christ? Where are the men and women who would dare to place their lives in His hands, to let Him use them as His witnesses, as His ambassadors, His missionaries?

I have been privileged to know one such young man here in the Philippines. He was a young man. He was not interested in missions. No, he was young—about twenty-five years old—and he had his mind on other things. There was a pretty girl in the picture, and there were dreams of a rosy pink future. Then, one day his district superintendent challenged him to become a lay pastor, an active worker in the church. He called him in and told him about a young, struggling church, very weak, with a few active members. They could give very little pastoral support. The church was in a distant place, so far away he knew almost nothing about the area, except that he did remember that he had heard the river flukes were in that area and that many people were sick with the dread disease which they carried, schistosomiasis. He did not want to go there. Actually, he did not want to go anywhere, but he did listen carefully as the superintendent told him about the need.

As he listened to the older man, part of his mind wandered. The cold, clammy hand of fear gripped the pit of his stomach as he thought of that horrible sickness. Why should *he* be a missionary to that difficult place? He wouldn't mind becoming an accepted supply pastor, but he wanted a nice little church nearby, with a decent salary so he could get married! But the voice of the superintendent urged on, "There are many children in that place . . . ten or twelve young people. . . . They need a pastor." In closing the conversation, he lifted up the picture of the suffering Saviour, who was wounded for our transgressions. He suffered for our sins. He give of Himself that we might have life. The young man promised to pray about his decision, to try to find the mind of Christ for his life.

He prayed. He thought of Jesus' words, "Go ye therefore, and teach all nations. . . ." And then this young man *went*. The first year he nearly starved to death. The crops were poor. Many days he ate only one or two meals a day. He felt like quitting, but the picture of Christ on the cross kept him steady. Day after day he walked in the midst of suffering. He saw the bloated bellies, listless faces, hopeless eyes of people sick with schistosomiasis. Many died. Finally a government specialist came. The only hope was to drain off all the low swampy places, and get rid of all standing water in the fields and near the houses. In private, the young pastor asked the government doctor, "What can be done for the people already infected with the disease?" He said nothing . . . just looked at the ground, and shook his head.

Only a month later, the young pastor himself began to be sick. From the first time he went to the doctor in a nearby town, and saw the look in the doctor's eyes, he knew. The doctor said many words . . . too many . . . but the young man wasn't listening. He was thinking about a young girl . . . some cherished dreams. Months later we took him to a hospital. He lived on for several months. Whenever I visited him, we laughed and talked about the future, and his lips smiled. But in his eyes there was sadness. Pastor Herminio Buron died.

He wasn't particularly interested in missions, either. But when Jesus said, "Go," he went. His example in obedience, even unto death, stabs my easy complacency, and keeps me awake. Why should this young man go out—and die—and I not share in the sickness and suffering of the world? Was it any more his responsibility than mine? Or *yours*?

Away in the distance I seem to hear the voice of a man in agony, as if from a cross. He whispers, "If you are serious about my mission, if you are really in earnest about this thing. . . ." He pauses. I hear Him gasp for breath, in pain, and then begin again, "Whosoever will come after me, let him deny himself, and take up his cross, and follow me."

These are the words of my Master. He is speaking to *me*. He is raising questions which I must answer, even if it takes my lifetime —or my death. How can I enter redemptively with Christ into the sufferings of the world? How can I get *me* into the cross?

> God—let me be aware.
> Stab my soul fiercely with others' pain,
> Let me walk seeing horror and stain.
> Let my hands, groping, find other hands.
> Give me the heart that divines, understands.
> Give me the courage, wounded, to fight.
> Flood me with knowledge, drench me in light.
> Please—keep me eager just to do my share.
> God—let me be aware.

CURRAN L. SPOTTSWOOD, Methodist missionary to the Philippines since 1946, is credited with developing the work of the Methodist Church on Mindanao Island, his station since 1953. A native of Mobile, Alabama, Rev. Spottswood became known early in his missionary career as flying evangelist and work camp director in the Philippines, logging more than 1,000 hours in the air on missionary business. Prior to becoming a missionary, he served churches of New Mexico and Florida and was director of the University of Florida's Wesley Foundation. Married and the father of six sons, he is a former instructor of Manila's Union Theological Seminary.

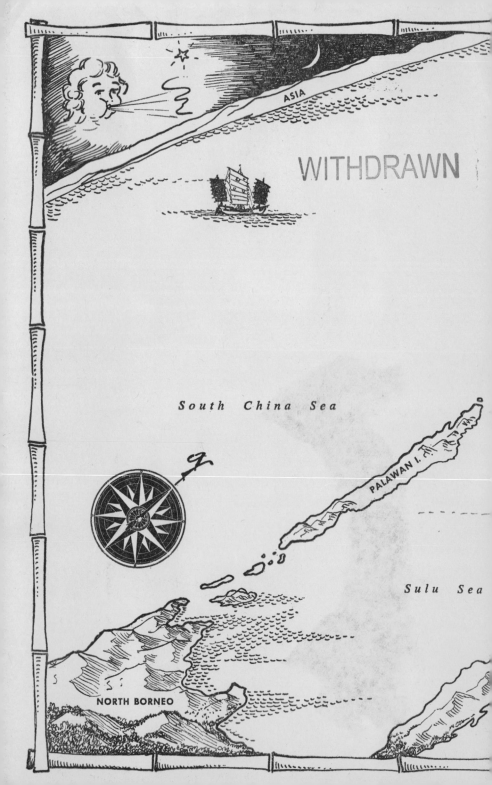

ASIA

WITHDRAWN

South China Sea

PALAWAN I.

Sulu Sea

NORTH BORNEO